厦门及其周边地区

Amoy and the Surrounding Districts

来自一位厦门海关税务司的观察

Compiled from Chinese and Other Records

[英]乔治·休士（George Hughes） 编著

张跃军 袁永丹 译

厦门大学出版社 XIAMEN UNIVERSITY PRESS
国家一级出版社
全国百佳图书出版单位

图书在版编目（CIP）数据

厦门及其周边地区：来自一位厦门海关税务司的观察 /（英）乔治·休士（George Hughes）编著；张跃军，袁永丹译. -- 厦门：厦门大学出版社，2023.5

（厦门社科丛书）

ISBN 978-7-5615-8840-6

Ⅰ. ①厦… Ⅱ. ①乔… ②张… ③袁… Ⅲ. ①厦门—地方史—史料 Ⅳ. ①K295.73

中国版本图书馆CIP数据核字(2022)第220456号

出版人　郄文礼
责任编辑　章木良
封面设计　蒋卓群
技术编辑　朱　楷

出版发行　厦门大学出版社
社　　址　厦门市软件园二期望海路39号
邮政编码　361008
总　　机　0592-2181111　0592-2181406(传真)
营销中心　0592-2184458　0592-2181365
网　　址　http://www.xmupress.com
邮　　箱　xmup@xmupress.com
印　　刷　厦门集大印刷有限公司

开本　720 mm×1 000 mm　1/16
印张　11.75
插页　2
字数　200千字
版次　2023年5月第1版
印次　2023年5月第1次印刷
定价　52.00元

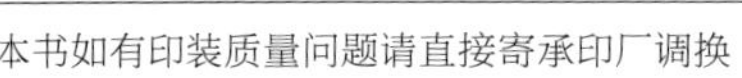
本书如有印装质量问题请直接寄承印厂调换

厦门大学出版社
微信二维码

厦门大学出版社
微博二维码

厦门社科丛书

编委会

编辑部

目 录

CONTENTS

第一部分

PART I

早期与日本的交往

关于厦门及其周边地区的早期中文记载由于明显失实而显得模糊晦涩，以至最多只能算作令人不甚满意的史料，可供描摹出该地区的历史概况。可用的史料展示出了一幅阴郁的图景，其中既有诡计、侵犯和杀戮的一面，也有偏执狭隘、剥削榨取和独裁暴政而导致骚乱和野蛮的一面。中国的历史学家认为，日本原称“倭”，是一个藩属国；在公元670年，即唐代咸亨元年，才改称日本，意为最接近日出东海的地方。

在宋代（950—1280[①]）之前，中日在各个朝代均有来往，日本一直向中国朝

Early Intercourse with Japan

The early Chinese records of Amoy, and its vicinity, are so obscured by statements obviously untruthful, as, at best, to be but very unsatisfactory data, from which to extract a précis of its history. The information available, presents a dreary picture of craft, aggression, and bloodshed, on the one hand, and of haughty intolerance, exactions, and misrule, ending in rebellion, and savagery, on the other. Chinese historians claim that Japan was the dependent state named Wō, 倭; and that in the period of Han-chêng, 亨咸, of the Tang dynasty, A.D. 670, its name was changed to Jeh pên, 日本, or the day spring, from its proximity to the rising sun, in the Eastern Ocean.

That up to the date of the Sung 950-1280, there had been intercourse, under every dynasty, between China and Japan, and that the latter country had paid tribute uninterruptedly; but that after this period, it was discontinued; whereupon the warrior founder of the Yuen, Kublai Khan, dispatched several envoys to demand this proof of allegiance. The proud and warlike Japanese, resenting with disdain the Mongols' attempts to induce them to pay homage, and smarting under slights and injuries, slew a tribute seeking envoy, and his entire suite. To exact vengeance for this massacre, and to subjugate Japan, Kublai Khan, sent a large fleet bearing a hundred thousand men, under the command of Fan Wan-h'u. It reached Wu-lung-shan, where it was wrecked in a storm, and most of the illfated troops, who escaped the fury of the sea, perished by the swords of the Japanese. Few, if any, ever returned to China. After this disaster intercourse between the two countries, was suspended until the close of the Yuen dynasty, 1366.

During the Ming dynasty, in retaliation for this attempt at invasion and conquest, the Japanese made frequent raids, carrying fire and sword along the coast of China from Che-kiang to Kwang-tung. In 1368 an envoy bearing an Imperial letter, was sent to ascertain the cause of these incursions; but he was contemptuously entreated, by the Japanese, though, curiously enough, it is stated, that, about this time tribute was frequently tendered, but as it was unaccompanied by the proper forms of vassalage, it was always rejected.

In the 20th year of Hung-w'u, 1386, means were taken to put the coasts of Chê-kiang, Fuhkien, and Kwang-tung, in a state of defence, the former province was directed to furnish one hundred war junks, and the two latter, double that

贡。但宋代之后，日本便不再朝贡；元世祖忽必烈派遣使臣要求日本归顺。高傲好战的日本人对于试图索贡的蒙古人不屑一顾，认为受到了蔑视和欺侮，便杀害了索贡的使臣及其所有随从。为了报复并使日本臣服，忽必烈派遣范文虎率十万水兵前去征讨。舰队抵达五龙山时不幸遭遇风暴，很多从海难中逃生的不幸的士兵又丧命于日本人的剑下。极少有人回到了中国。此次灾难过后，一直到元朝末年，中日间再无往来。

明朝时，为了报复这次入侵和征服的企图，日本人经常明火执仗地袭扰从浙江到广东的沿海地区。1368年，明朝派遣使节携带国书，去日本调查这些袭扰的原因，却遭到了日本人的轻慢对待。同时蹊跷的是，据说这个时期日本频繁进贡，却由于没有采用恰当的臣服形式而被明朝拒绝。

洪武二十年，即1386年②，浙江、福建和广东采取了一些措施，加强海防。浙江打造了一百艘战舰，福建和广东各两百艘。这时，朝中能干但狡猾的丞相胡惟庸正预谋着一场叛变，并寻求日本的支持。

日本派遣僧人如瑶带领四百人，乔装成朝贡的使团，准备帮助胡惟庸。所谓的贡品是一个巨烛，内藏武器和火药。但胡惟庸因谋反失败而被问斩，这场预谋的叛乱公之于众，假冒的朝贡者被抓并受惩处，对日交往再次中断。嗣后，在明朝开国皇帝下令编纂的《皇明祖训》中，日本被列入十五个不征之国的名单。③

明朝永乐年间的1401年④，日本前来朝贡，这次携带了得体的国书，以及二十个对马岛和壹岐岛的首领，这些人曾袭扰劫掠中国的海岸。从此以后，日本朝贡时总是进献这些被抓获的海盗。贡品上覆盖的国书称："海寇旁午，故贡使不能上达。其无赖鼠窃者，实非臣所知。愿贷罪，容其朝贡。"然而，对海岸的袭扰依然猖獗，直到1418年，刘荣将军在望海埚击溃了劫匪，类似的搅扰才暂告一段落。⑤此时，日本进贡也似乎再次中断。

明正统四到八年（1459—1463⑥），日本人在两个叛贼周来保和钟普福的的挑唆下，几次袭击了台州的府衙和海宁地区。⑦

number. At this period an able but crafty minister of the Throne, named H'u-wei-yung, was projecting a rebellion, and sought the aid of the Japanese, who sent one Jü-yao, a Budhist priest, at the head of four hundred men, disguised as tribute bearers, to his assistance; the supposed tribute consisted of a large mass of wax, in which were concealed arms and gunpowder, but in the meantime H'u-wei-yung, had been overthrown, and beheaded, and the contemplated treachery becoming known, the pseudo tribute bearers were seized and punished, and intercourse with Japan, was again discontinued. Subsequently, when the chronicles of the founder of the Ming were drawn up, Japan was added to the list of unconquered states, fifteen in all.

In the reign of Yunglö, 1401, the Japanese sent tribute accompanied by the proper address, together with twenty of the chiefs of Tui-ma, and Tai-chi, who had been piratically harrying the coast of China. From this time, tribute was always accompanied by such pirates, as had been captured. The address to the Tahwang-té, which covered the tribute, was couched in these terms: "If on the Islands of your majesty's servant, there be persons without regular calling, who engage in piracy, it is in truth without the knowledge of your servant, and he prays your indulgence (or that their fault be not laid to his charge.") Attacks on the Coast, were, however still rife, until 1418, when General Lui-chiang, inflicted a very severe defeat on the marauders at Wang-hai-wõ, after which there was a temporary cessation of these raids. At this time, the payment of tribute appears to have been again discontinued.

From the fourth to the eighth

years of Ching tung, (1459-63) the Japanese, at the instigation of two renegades, named Huan-yeu, and Lung-yeu, made several descents upon the departments of Tai-chou, and the district of Tai-ming.

There is little doubt that many of these raids were in retaliation for injustice the Japanese had received at the hands of the Chinese, for while the Government jealously sought to exclude them from their coast, the people of Chê Kiang, and Fuhkien, welcomed them for the trade they bought, but at the same time evaded, where practicable, paying them their just dues. When the Eunuchs, who held the posts of Superintendents of Trade, at Ning-po, and at the ports in this province, whose duties were to collect the Revenue, and fix the price of cargoes, were dismissed, and their offices abolished, the control they had exercised, passed into the hands of merchants, until communication with foreigners was strictly prohibited; it then passed into those of persons, who though of birth and station, repudiated their debts to the Japanese, to a more disgraceful extent than the others had done.

In 1547, intercourse was strictly prohibited by a Hsüne-fu, or Governor, named Chü Hwang, who mercilessly beheaded those who broke the prohibition. His action entailed upon him the hate of the people of Chê Kiang, and Fuh-kien, and he was impeached by a Fuhkien man, named Chao Liang, a censor, for putting to death some ninety people as pirates, who had been made prisoners, and forced to aid their captors. He was stripped of office, and he destroyed himself; and the prohibition fell into desuetude. In 1552 the Japanese, aided by a rebellious Chinaman, one Wang Chih 汪直 and his followers, with a fleet of some hundreds of junks, made a descent on the coast. The alarm was given simultaneously east and

毫无疑问，多数的劫掠是为了报复日本人认为的明朝对其不公正的对待。虽然政府尽力将日本人赶出沿海地区，浙江和福建的居民却乐于与他们开展贸易，同时在可行的情况下，规避付给他们应得的钱款。执掌宁波和浙江其他口岸市舶司的是些宦官，主要职责是收税和给货物定价，当他们被罢免，衙门也被撤销后，操控权落到了商人手里。后来实施海禁，权力又到了有身份和地位的人手中，但这些人赖起日本人的账来更加不管不顾了。

1547年，一个名为朱纨的巡抚严禁通番，并残忍地处死那些违反禁令的人。他的行为引起了浙江和福建两地人的怨恨。后来，朱纨被一个名叫周亮的闽籍御史弹劾，因为他把大约九十人当作海盗处死，这些人先前被关入监牢，并被迫帮助关押他们的人。朱纨后被罢官，并自杀身亡，他的禁令于是被废止。1552年⑧，日本人在一个名叫汪直的中国叛贼及其同伙的协助下，带领几百艘船只组成的舰队袭击了沿海一带。钱塘江⑨的东西两岸、长江的南北岸，方圆数千里同时告警。

倭寇炮轰昌国卫，入侵太仓州，破上海县，洗劫江阴，袭击乍浦。他们劫掠金山卫，进犯崇明、常熟和嘉定。次年从太仓到苏州一路劫掠，攻打松江，之后再次渡过长江，向北迅速迫近通州和泰州。攻陷嘉善、崇明，再度洗劫苏州。崇德、吴江和嘉兴相继不保。他们继而占据柘林，随兴致所至往还无碍，如入无人之境。1554年[10]，倭寇截获一些船只，进犯乍浦、海宁，攻陷崇德，沿途劫掠塘栖、新市、横塘和双林。与新到的倭寇汇合后，他们突犯嘉兴，但在王江泾，被兵部尚书张经所部痛击，据说约两千倭寇被歼，残部退回柘林。苏州再遭劫难，并殃及江阴、无锡，血流成河。倭寇中十分之三是日本人，其余七成则为中国人。他们出入太湖，没有对手。

倭寇来去无踪。尽管有时吃了败仗，所经之地也都被他们劫掠一空。1556年，他们挥师南下，其恐怖的身影出现在了浯屿。不久同安、惠安、南安沦为废墟；福宁府被攻陷；福安、宁德陷落之后，倭寇在1557年围攻福州长达一个月；福清、永

west of the Chê river, and North and South of the Yang-tse-kiang, for several thousand li.

They stormed the fort of Chang Kwo, invaded Tai-tsang-chou, stormed the city of Shang-hae, sacked Kiang-yin, and attacked Chá-pú. They plundered the station at Kin-shan, and invaded the districts of Tsung-ming, Chang-shu and Kia-ting. In the following year they marched from Tai-tsang, upon Suchow, which city they pillaged; attacked Sung-kiang, and repassing the river, rapidly, made a stand at the North of it, at Tung-chau, and Tai-chau; Kia-shen was razed to the ground, Tsung-ming stormed, and Suchow again ravaged; Tsung-teh, Wukiang, and Kia-hing, were captured. They then took up a position at Cheh-lin, (the wood of Cheh) whence they moved through the country at their pleasure, as if it were uninhabited. In 1554, they seized some vessels, and made an onslaught on Chá-pú, and Haining, destroying Tsung-teh, and ravaging Tang-tseh, Sin-shè, Hung-tang, and Shwang-lin. Uniting themselves with some newly arrived Japanese, they made a sudden descent on Kia-hing; but at the river Wang-king, they met with a severe defeat from the troops of Chang-king, president of the Board of war, who had taken the field, and who beheaded, or said he had done so, some 2 000 of them; the remainder fell back upon Cheh-lin. Again was devastation carried into the region around Suchow, and the land from thence to Kiang-yin, and Wú-sih, was stained with blood. They were on an average only three Japanese in every ten, the remaining seven being Chinese. They crossed and landed from the Ta-Hu, or great lake, without opposition.

It is bootless to follow them; although at times suffering defeat, they appear to have ravaged and destroyed, almost where they listed. In 1556, they directed their course Southward, and made their dreaded appearance at Wu-yü in this prefecture. Desolation was soon carried through the districts of Tung an, Hwui an, and Nan an; Fuh-ning-chou was assaulted, and after storming and carrying Fuh an, and Ning teh, they, in 1557, beseiged and blockaded Foochow, for a month. The towns of Fuh-ch'ing, and Yung-fuh, fell before them and were destroyed, the wave of conquest rolled down to Hing-wei, whence a sudden irruption into the Changchou prefecture was made, and dire alarm was felt at Chao-chao-fu, and even at the distant city of Canton.

The accounts, which should be the fullest, of these sanguinary invasions here, are, in the Hsia mén-chih, and Chúan-chou-chih, or Chinese histories of Amoy, and Chin-chew, lamentably bald and meagre. Little else than date, place, and event being recorded.

According to these books, the first attack by Japanese, was in 1369, on Chin-chew; the result, as in most of the accounts of subsequent attacks, is not clearly stated, but it may be gathered, without difficulty, from the context. From this date, they do not appear to have again visited this region, until 1552, when they swept down upon Sien-yü-hsien and An-chi-hsien. In 1556-7, they committed the depredations already recorded; and in 1559, they again captured and plundered the cities, and towns, of Chin-chew, Tung-an-hsien, Wei-an-hsien, and Nan-an-hsien. In the following year, Chin-chew was again assaulted, and Wei-an-hsien fell, with the loss of the district magistrate, and many soldiers and inhabitants. In 1561, another onslaught was made upon Chin-chew, which city, from its situation, and apparent helplessness, seems to have been constantly selected for attack. Thence they fell upon Tung-an, where, this time,

福的村镇被攻陷并摧毁。他们席卷兴化，又突入漳州辖县，潮州府甚至广州城都能听到刺耳的警报声。⑪

这些血腥侵略的翔实记录，本该出现于《厦门志》《泉州府志》，或关于厦门、泉州的中文史料中。遗憾的是记载非常简单、贫乏，在日期、地名和事件之外鲜有其他记录。

根据这些史书的记载，倭寇的第一次来袭为1369年进犯泉州。其结果如同之后的多数进犯一样，缺乏详细记载，但可以从前后历史来加以推测，这并非难事。从彼时起，他们似乎未再进犯该地区，直到1552年横扫仙游县和安溪县。1556—1557年，史记记载倭寇再次进犯。1559年，他们再次攻陷并劫掠泉州、同安、惠安和南安等地的村镇。翌年，泉州再遭袭击，惠安县失陷，知县身亡，士兵与民众伤亡众多。1561年，泉州再受攻击，可能是其地理位置，以及明显的孤立无援的境地，使其经常成为攻击目标。之后，倭寇攻打同安，遭到顽强抵抗，据称该城被围困长达四个月。1562年，同安终被攻陷，同时陷落的还有南安，两城均惨遭屠戮，被洗劫一空。倭寇占领四十天后，将两座城池付之一炬，随后弃城而去。大约在此时，倭寇攻占了南澳，也许是为了方便对内陆发动出其不意的袭击。据称，倭寇在那里兴建房屋，并盘踞一年之久；然而，他们占据的时间很可能更久。1563年，倭寇似乎攻占了富庶的重要城市漳州府；他们再次劫掠同安县，并烧毁了晋江县的大量房屋。1564年，他们在泉州杀害了很多官吏、士兵和百姓；1567年，再袭泉州，连续三天屠杀劫掠。在对这些沿海地区长达两百年的滋扰劫掠之后，他们被戚继光将军赶了出去。戚将军有勇有谋，他1569年在泉州击退并重创了倭寇，1572年全歼前来滋扰的两百名倭寇。从此以后，倭寇就从这个地区的方志中消失了；然而万历年间（1571—1619）[12]，日本人强占了台湾部分地区，直到万历末年才被驱逐。

they seem to have met with a stout resistance, as it is stated they besieged it four months. It was taken, however, in 1562, as was Nan-an, and both cities were given to the sword, and completely pillaged. After an occupation of forty days, they were set fire to, and abandoned. About this time, the Japanese moved to, and occupied, Namoa, 南澳, probably for the convenience of making unexpected irruptions on the mainland. It is stated that they built themselves houses, and remained for a year there; but most likely they occupied the Islands for a much longer period. In 1563, they appear to have captured the wealthy and important city of Chang-chou-fu; again plundered Tung-an-hsien, and to have burnt a great number of houses at Chin-kiang-hsien. In 1564, they killed many mandarins, soldiers, and other people at Chin-chew, which place they again assaulted in 1567, slaughtering and looting for three days. After having harried the coast for 200 years, they were expelled from this region, by General Chi-chi-kuang, 戚继光. This general seems to have been a man of ability and valour, he repulsed, with heavy loss to the Japanese, an attack on Chin-chew in 1569; and, again, in 1572, slaying the entire assaulting party of 200 men. After this date, the Japanese do not appear in the annals of the district; but in the reign of Wan-li, （1571 to 1619） they possessed themselves of part of "Formosa" （present-day Taiwan, China, the same below）, which they held until near the end of this reign, when they were driven out…

倭寇之狡诈

倭寇在狡诈算计方面无人能及：他们粗野而狡猾，用诡计迷惑和误导对手。他

The Japanese Craft

The Japanese seem to have excelled their foes even in craft; rude, yet cunning, artifices, were resorted to bewilder and mislead them. They carried in their armed ships, articles, which, should no opportunity occur for a savage descent upon some unprotected part of the coast, enabled them to seek the shelter of a port, as the peaceful bearers of tribute. Skirmishers bobbed up and down, a tempting shot, to draw their foes fire, and when their arrows and ammunition, were exhausted, the enemy dashed upon them; baits of seemingly abandoned spoils, and wine, and women, were left to draw them into ambush. The beleaguered town, saw the scaling ladders prepared under its walls, and the next morning found the besiegers had effected an unmolested retreat, and were committing depredations miles away. Chinese prisoners were dressed in Japanese attire, and forced to fight in the van, their tongues were so tied that they could not articulate the sounds of their own language, thus, in the event of escape, or wound, their death, by the hands of their own countrymen, was tolerably certain. The traditions of these fierce and sanguinary descents by the Japanese, and native pirates and cut-throats, who joined them, yet live in the minds of the people here; and the Amoy matron, coerces her fractious urchin with the black bogey of Woo-jin-lai-liao, or "the Japanese have come," up to the present hour.

Troubles with the Dutch

About 1622, another fruitful source of trouble sprang up, caused by the Dutch having taken possession of the Panghu, 彭湖 islands, ("Pescadores") and commencing to build forts thereon. This step pleased no one; it

们在战舰上装载普通货物，如果没有合适的机会洗劫毫无防范的沿海地区，便以运送贡品的和平使者的身份寻求庇护。打前哨的倭寇到处佯攻，引诱对手开火，而当对手的弓箭、弹药耗尽之时，他们便开始冲锋；他们假装丢下战利品、酒和女人，引诱对手进入埋伏。被围困在城墙内的人发现倭寇架了云梯准备攻城，次日清晨，倭寇却早已悄无声息地撤退，在数里外发动袭击。中国战俘被穿上倭寇的服装，被迫去打头阵。他们的舌头给打了结，话都说不清楚，一旦想要逃跑或受了伤，他们注定会被自己的同胞杀死。倭寇以及投靠他们的当地海盗和暴徒发动的残忍血腥的袭击，老百姓是不会忘记的。直到今天，厦门的主妇们吓唬顽皮的孩童，还会说"倭人来了"。

与荷兰人的摩擦

大约在1622年，荷兰人侵占了澎湖，并着手修建堡垒，这为以后的一系列麻烦埋下了伏笔。这一行为谁都不讨好：它威胁到了马尼拉和中国间的贸易往来，干涉了西班牙人的利益，也对澳门和日本间的葡萄牙人的贸易构成了威胁；对于中国人，这是“一种无法忍受的无尽伤害”。明朝皇帝断然命令荷兰人撤出澎湖，后者却称所求“不过是与中国之间的自由贸易，同时禁止中国人与马尼拉的西班牙人进行贸易”。双方进行了多次谈判，但都告失败。荷兰人于是派遣八艘船只到中国海域，在所到之处大肆劫掠，企图迫使中国人与之贸易；“滋生了很多暴行，沿海的几个村子被毁，有辱基督圣名”。⑬谈判重启后，荷兰舰队指挥官雷尔生（Cornelis Reijersz）⑭派遣使者到厦门。使者受到了高规格的款待，被待之以礼，但却被告知要跪地磕头，“以让旁边的人可以听到他脑袋撞击地面的声音”。他拒绝了这一古老习俗，谈判再度破裂。于是，荷兰人封锁了泉州，阻止商船进入马尼拉，这真是拜错菩萨进错了庙吧。荷兰指挥官希望与福州方面修好，却被告知只要荷兰军队占据澎湖，通商便是不可能的；但他们可以在台湾修筑防御工事，条件是撤离澎湖。荷兰人接受提议。1624年，荷兰人与明朝官员达成协议，获得了全面的经商特权，同时拥有了一个对

threatened the commerce between Manila and China, and in this interfered with the Spanish; and it was a menace to the Portuguese trade, between Macao and Japan; and to the Chinese it was "an incessant and intolerable grievance." The Emperor peremptorily required the withdrawal of the Dutch from the island. They, on their part, required "nothing more than liberty of commerce with China, and the prohibition of it between the Chinese, and the Spaniards, in Manila." The negotiations hereon entered into, fell through, and the Dutch dispatched eight ships to scour the sea and to seize, or destroy, whatever they could along the Chinese coast, in order to compel the Chinese to trade; "many cruelties were thus committed, and several villages on the coast ravaged, to the disgrace of the Christian name." Negotiations were resumed, and the Dutch Admiral, Keizerroon, sent an envoy to Amoy, who was received with great pageantry, and some politeness, but being required to knock his head against the ground "so that the bystanders might hear the cracking of his skull," he declined this fine old custom, and the discussion was again broken off, whereupon Chinchew was blockaded to prevent junks going to Manila, and as *argumentum ad hominem*; and the Admiral repaired to Foochow, where he was told that so long as the Dutch retained possession of the "Pescadores", no trade would be permitted; but permission for them to fortify themselves upon the island of "Formosa",... was offered as the price of the evacuation of Panghu. This offer was accepted, and in 1624, the Dutch conclude a peace, obtaining full commercial privileges, as then existed, and, at the same time, an entrepot for their

Chinese, and Japanese, trade.

From 1624, to 1644, China was convulsed with civil war, and foreign invasion. In the latter year, Peking has fallen, and a Tartar was on the throne, and in the following, twelve of the fifteen provinces had acknowledged his sway. The province of Fohkien, however held out; and it was not until some years afterwards that it was subdued. This district bore fully its share of the miseries entailed by this long epoch of bloodshed, when according to Chinese records, "the blood of the people flowed in sounding torrents," and of 25 000 families, which fled to "Formosa", it contributed more than its full quota. These bitter years produced a host of daring, and desperate men,...on pain of death, to shave off the long and thick tresses they had worn from time immemorial as a cherished ornament, and adopt the Tartar fashion of a long plaited queue, or tail, as well as the Tartar costume; but piratical also, from the necessity of paying, and feeding, the forces they gathered round them, or from having put themselves outside the law, by some act against the officials, who were sometimes their colleagues, and sometimes their accusers and judges.

Chêng Chih Lung, Chêng Cheng Kung (Koxinga)

Amongst these men one of the most celebrated is Chêng Chih Lung, 鄭芝龍, who was born of obscure parents, at a village on the seashore at the entrance of the Anhai creek, in the district of Nan-an. There are many accounts of his life, and much of the following is abridged from Nienhoff, in the sec-

中国和日本贸易的中转港⑮。

从1624年到1644年，中国战乱频仍。1644年，清军入关，定都北京。次年，十五个省中的十二个承认了清朝的统治。福建省不在此列，它直到几年后才臣服。该地区长久以来饱受流血时代带来的苦难，据中文史料记载，“血满沟渠”，有两万五千户人逃往台湾，超过台湾原有的人口数量。严峻的岁月造就了一批勇猛无畏、铤而走险的人。朝廷以他们的性命相威胁，强迫汉人剪掉自古以来就备受珍视、作为装饰的又长又厚的头发，代之以满人样式的长辫子，穿满人的衣服，以示臣服。但这里也孕育了海盗，他们为了养家糊口，只好啸聚为盗；或者由于一些抗拒官员的行为，而亡命海上。官员们有时就是他们的同伙，有时却控告、审判他们。

郑芝龙与郑成功（国姓爷）

这些人中名气最大的是郑芝龙，他出生寒微，生于南安县安海的一个海边小村子⑯。关于他生平的说法不少，以下多摘自纽荷夫⑰在《中国丛报》第二卷里的说法。

据称，郑芝龙早年就以坚韧无畏、长相英俊、性格谦和而与众不同。据杜赫德⑱所言，郑芝龙年轻时去了澳门，并成为一名基督徒，取名尼古拉斯·加斯巴德。随后，他受雇于在台湾的荷兰人，可能出于充分的理由，更名为“一官”。据记载，他后来去了日本平户的荷兰商馆做事，并娶了一个日本商人的女儿为妻。他们的儿子名叫郑成功，后来受封国姓，当地人称“郑国姓”，他以国姓爷的名号成为闻名遐迩的商人、成就卓著的将军，并进行统治。⑲

郑芝龙受日本人委派，指挥船队前往中国海岸的港口进行贸易。他得到指令，必要时可用武力。很难说他是否随船队一起返回。无论如何，郑芝龙的能力不逊于各国同龄的杰出海军指挥官，一旦情势于他有利，他就从商船首领的角色摇身一变，成为私掠者或者海盗。他联合了一位同道中人颜思齐，后者占据着邻近的一个岛屿。此后，他们常年掠夺过往船只。颜思齐死后，郑芝龙毫无异议地当选为海盗首领，成为中国东南海域令人生畏的人物。他屡战屡胜，名声大振，引来了诸多船只加盟。

ond volume of the Chinese Repository. He is described as having been early distinguished by a resolute and fearless disposition, good looks, and agreeable manners. According to Du Halde, when quite young he found his way to Macao, and became a christian under the name of Nicholas Gaspard. Subsequently he was employed by the Dutch at "Formosa", where, probably for good reasons, he had changed his named to Kwan. Thence he is stated to have gone to the Dutch factory of, Firando, at Japan, where he married a daughter of a Japanese merchant; amongst the issue of that marriage, was Chêng-cheng-kung 鄭成功, who received the title of Kwŏ-hsing-ah 國姓仔, called in the Amoy dialect Te-kok-seng, which gave rise to the names Kosenga, Coshinga, and Koxinga, by which latter name, he became celebrated as a ... trader, general of no mean ability, and self created sovereign.

Chêng Chih Lung (the father) was entrusted by the Japanese with a command of vessels trading to ports on the Coast of China, with instructions, probably, should occasion serve, to employ them in a less peaceful manner. It is questionable whether he ever returned with this fleet. At all events with a facility not uncommon amongst distinguished naval commanders of other nations, of the same age, he changed his role of merchant captain to that of privateer, or rover, as circumstances arose, advantageous to himself. He combined forces with another worthy of the same stamp, named Yen Chin, who possessed one of the adjacent islands, whence, for years, they plundered passing vessels. On the death of Yen, Chêng Chih Lung, was unanimously elected Pirate-in-chief, and in that capacity became the terror of these seas.

The fame of his successes attracted to him a number of vessels ... with the prizes he took, he gradually acquired a fleet so formidable, as to bid defiance to the Imperial junks, and to give him the command of the sea coast of Cheh-kiang, Fohkien, and Kwang Tung. The policy of the authorities was then as now, and finding that they could not defeat nor entrap, this crafty and powerful chief, they recommended their Imperial master, Tsung Ching, the last of the Ming dynasty, to purchase his allegiance by bestowing on him high rank and office. The irresistable bait, of course, took, and Chêng replied that he was ready to submit if assured of rank, security to himself and followers, the enjoyment of their wealth, and such employment in the Imperial service, as would enable them to show their devotion and valour. The Court readily acceded to these demands, and about 1636, conferred on him the office of Admiral. For the next ten years, he took a most distinguished share in the naval operations of the Chinese ... He devised a source of wealth and power, by assuming a monopoly, to some extent, of the lucrative trade with the Dutch at "Formosa", the Spaniards at Manila, the Portuguese at Macao, and with the Japanese, by compelling all trading vessels to supply themselves with his permit to trade, at a heavy cost. His retirement from the piratical command, caused great consternation, and dissatisfaction, amongst his quondam associates, who had not followed him in giving in their allegiance, and who well knew the virtuous zeal with which an official just created from out of a band of desperadoes, would root out and punish evil doers. Their

他逐渐建立了一个令人畏惧的舰队，足以向明朝的舰队发起挑战，他得到了浙江、福建、广东沿海的控制权。那时朝廷的政策与现在一样，人们发现无法打败或捕获这个狡猾且强大的首领，便向明朝的最后一位帝王崇祯皇帝谏言，以高官厚禄使郑芝龙归顺朝廷。郑芝龙难以拒绝这些诱惑，他回应称，只要确保他本人及其部下的安全，让他们享受荣华富贵，他们便接受招安，为朝廷尽忠。朝廷即刻答应了这些要求，约在1636年，授予他福州都督之职。在接下来的十年中，他控制了所在水域的经营大权。为了谋取财富和权力，他迫使所有贸易船只以高昂的代价获取贸易许可证，因此一定程度上垄断了与在台湾的荷兰人、在马尼拉的西班牙人、在澳门的葡萄牙人，以及与日本人之间的贸易，他从中获利颇丰。郑芝龙以海盗首领的身份被招安，引起没有和他一起归顺的昔日同伙的极大恐慌和不满，他们很清楚，由暴徒摇身一变成为官员，其热切效忠的意愿将驱使他铲除并惩罚作恶之人。他们的预料很对，郑芝龙的第一个任务就是消灭他的继任者，一个在泉州一带干着他的老本行的老伙伴。他欣然而忠诚地执行了这个任务。不久后，他又被派去歼灭另一个海盗首领刘香。经过一整天的殊死战斗，刘香点燃了弹药库，炸毁了自己的船只，但与对手同归于尽的企图失败了。余下的很多船只都被缴获，郑芝龙得胜而归。海上一时很清静，就如中国人所说的那样，“海氛平息”。

此时，郑芝龙的名望达到了巅峰，他的权力几乎不输皇帝，富可敌国，并拥有一支强大的舰队，而舰队完全效忠于他，并深信他是不可战胜的。当时所有的竞争派系都希望得到他的好感和支持。据说，在南京登基的福王将一位宗室女许配给了郑芝龙的儿子。当清军攻入福建、逼近泉州之时，郑芝龙在朋友的劝说下，听信清廷对他的承诺，宣告臣服。清军将领对他颇为尊敬。之后他上岸时为表示对这位即将赴京的官员的尊敬，不像平常那样有所戒备，于是他被强求同官员一同入京，领受因其功绩而许诺给他的近乎至高无上的封赏。由于无法拒绝，他只好被迫入京。

convictions were quite correct. His first commission was to destroy the pirate who had succeeded him, an old comrade, who was following his profession in the neighbourhood of Chinchew. He cheerfully and faithfully executed this commission. Shortly, after, he was despatched against another chief, named Liao Yang; after a desperate battle, which lasted all day, Liao Yang fired his magazine and blew his vessel up, in an unsuccessful attempt to destroy his enemy; many of the remaining ships were taken, and Chêng returned triumphant, and for a time there was peace upon the seas, or as the Chinese express it "the seas were free from foam."

Chêng was now at the zenith of his fame; he had attained a power little short of imperial; his wealth was enormous, and he possessed a large and powerful fleet, entirely devoted to his will, and implicitly believing in his invincibility. His favor and his aid, were intrigued for, by all the rival and contending factions of the day, and it is said that the Prince of Fuh, on ascending the imperial throne at Nanking, bestowed a princess of the blood, in marriage, on his son. On the invasion of Fohkien by the Manchus, and their advance on Chinchew, Chêng, at the advice of his friends, and relying on the promises made him, tendered his submission. He was treated by the Tartar General, with profound respect. Subsequently on his landing, without his usual guard, to do honor to the approaching departure of that officer, for Peking, he was pressingly invited to accompany him to the Court, to receive the almost regal rewards, promised, as due to his merit. Objections were unavailing, and his attendance was compelled.

From this moment he recedes into shadow, and gradually disappears. He is no more heard of as a power; and, by and by, vague rumours from the capital, reach his son, that he is in captivity, and then that he has died, but how no one can tell. He has passed away. Koxinga, now took command of his father's fleet, and followers, and proceeded to exact from the Manchus, a bloody retribution for the treachery shewn his sire. ... All attempts to restrain him were ineffectual, and of the wars of the conquest, his are said to have been the most terrible. In 1650, the scattered remnants of the Chinese armies, had been gathered together in the city of Canton, to make a last stand against the Tartars. On the approach of the enemy, the assistance of Koxinga was sought by the Governor; it was willingly accorded, and his well practised fleet, inflicted heavy loss on the Tartars unaccustomed to naval warfare. The siege of the city was protracted for eight months, and thrice it was on the eve of being abandoned; and it was only when the city had fallen, through the treachery of those in charge of the north gate, that Koxinga withdrew his fleet; maintaining his supremacy upon the sea, long after all the provinces of the kingdom, had submitted to the Tartar rule. In 1653, he made a descent on Amoy, with the design of capturing Hai-têng, its then port. The Tartars went to its relief, and in a naval engagement which ensued, were worsted, with a loss, it is stated, of seven or eight thousand men. The town was then carried by assault, and all bearing arms were slain, but injury to the peaceful inhabitants was prohibited. It was at once occupied, heavy guns mounted, and its walls repaired; and it formed

从此以后，他逐渐隐没，杳无音信。再也没人听闻过他的权势，渐渐地，京城一些流言传到他儿子的耳朵里，说他被囚禁，之后又说他已经死了，但无人知晓真相。他已经消失不见。国姓爷现在执掌父亲的舰队和部下，向清军进行血腥的报复，认为这是他们背叛他父亲应得的报应。他所向披靡，战力极强。1650年，南明军队的残部在广州集结，与清军最后一战。当清军逼近时，两广总督向国姓爷求救，他欣然同意。他的舰队训练有素，给不熟悉海战的清军造成重创。清军围城长达八个月，有三次濒临失守；后来，镇守北门的士兵变节，城门被攻陷，国姓爷这才撤退了自己的舰队。当所有的省份都臣服于清廷的统治很久以后，国姓爷还维持着海上霸权。1653年，国姓爷进攻厦门，目的是为夺取当时这一地区的港口海澄[20]。清军前去救援，在随后的一场海战中，清军大败，据说损失达七八千人。攻城之战中，只针对士兵，未伤及平民。海澄港被占领后，郑军立刻架设重炮，并修复城墙；这样便形成了一个基地，以便攻击曾被清军占据、但他们撤走后无人防守的地带。漳州和泉州以及一些小城镇被搜刮一空，郑军截获了数不清的战利品。随后，当他们搜刮泉州一带时，清军援兵赶到，郑军被迫撤回船上，并损失了大量战利品。1655年，他再度进攻泉州和兴化，搜刮这些地方。清军增派了援兵，海防得以强化，郑军继续袭击这里的话已讨不到好处。于是国姓爷谋划夺取江南㉑，攻占了长江入口处的几个地方后，他率领一支八百艘船的舰队沿江逆流而上，企图围攻省会南京。他初期的努力取得了一些小胜利，但清军发动了一次坚决而猛烈的夜袭，郑军大败，只得逃回船上，损失了超过三千的兵力，以及大批武器、帐篷和战利品。1659年，朝廷决定组建一支舰队，以便消灭这个穷途末路的人。国姓爷逮到这支舰队，并在随后的战斗中彻底将其消灭，缴获或摧毁大量船只，还俘虏四千战俘。割下这些战俘的鼻子、耳朵之后，他就放他们离开了。

这些可怜的家伙返京后，因为被俘而被全部处死。国姓爷虽然取得了战场上的胜利，但由于种种原因，他在大陆建立一

a base whence to attack the open country, left unguarded by the flight of the Imperialists. Chang Chou, and Chinchew, were heavily mulcted, and smaller cities, and towns, sacked, immense booty accruing to the conquerors. Subsequently, whilst pillaging the department of Chinchew, reinforcements of Tartar troops arrived, and compelled Koxinga's forces to retreat to their ships, with the loss of much of their plunder. In 1655, he again made a descent on Chinchew, and Hsing-hua despoiling these places. The Tartars now applied for additional forces; they were granted, and the coast so strongly garrisoned, that further raids here, were unprofitable. Koxinga now conceived the project of making himself master of the province of Kiang-nan, and after seizing certain places at the entrance of the Yang-tze-kiang, proceeded up that river, with a fleet of 800 sail, and attempted the siege of Nanking, the provincial city. Some slight success attended his early efforts, but the Manchus made so fierce and determined a night attack on his forces, that they had to fly to their ships, routed, and with the loss of over 3 000 men, arms, tents, and spoils. In 1659, the Imperial Court, resolved to equip such a fleet, as would effectually destroy this desperate man. He sought it, and in the action that ensued, utterly defeated it, capturing or destroying the greater number of the ships, and making 4 000 prisoners, whom, after cutting off their noses and ears, he sat at liberty.

These miserable wretches were all put to death on their return to Peking, for permitting themselves to be captured. Finding, notwithstanding his successes, that his hopes of establishing a kingdom on the mainland, were frustrated, owing to a combination of circumstances, he turned his attention to "Formosa", as a suitable asylum and dominion.

This beautiful island, called by the Chinese Taiwan, or Terraced Bay, includes in length from North to South, over three degrees of latitude, its greatest breadth is about eighty miles, and it is separated from the Chinese coast, by a channel varying from seventy-five, to one hundred and twenty, miles, in width. It is distant from Amoy, only a day and a half, or two days sail. The Dutch, on obtaining possession of the island in 1624, had built a strong fort named Zelandia, and a second, less strong, named Province, at the principal harbour on its southwest face, now known as Tai-wan-foo; and, in course of time, had formed settlements at Tamsui, and Kelung, and in the interior, in the neighbourhood of their principal fort. ... and the long continued anarchy on the mainland of China, arising from the invasion of the Manchus, had peopled the island with thousands of fugitives, whose industry soon brought it under cultivation; and rich crops of rice and sugar, were waving over heretofore unproductive land. At first the Hollanders encouraged this immigration, and then, becoming alarmed, tried to prevent it. How far the measures taken by the Dutch, in this endeavour tended to their own downfall, by alienating the goodwill of the Chinese, it is difficult now to conjecture, but it is certain that the Chinese entered into correspondence with Koxinga, and, on his attack on the island, assisted him with hearty good will.

The Dutch Governor Coyet,

个王国的希望破灭了，于是他转向台湾，视之为一个理想的避难所和领地。

台湾这个美丽的岛屿，自北向南跨越3个纬度，最宽处约80英里[22]；与大陆隔开，中间是一条宽为75～120英里的海峡。它距离厦门仅一天半或者两天的航程。荷兰人1624年侵占台湾岛后，在此修建了十分坚固的堡垒，名为热兰遮城；第二座堡垒坚固程度稍弱，名为赤崁城，位于岛的西南面的主港口，今称台湾府。随着时间的推移，荷兰人逐渐在淡水、基隆，以及远离海岸的岛内主要城堡附近，开辟了新的居民点。明末清初的战乱使大陆陷入混乱状态，成千上万的难民涌入台湾岛，他们一上岛便辛勤地垦荒；不毛之地很快变成盛产水稻和甘蔗的农田。起初，荷兰人鼓励移民，可后来变得恐慌起来，试图加以阻止。荷兰人无视中国人的善意而采取的措施，在多大程度上导致他们自己的垮台，如今很难推测。但可以确信的是，这些中国人与国姓爷建立了联系，并在他攻打台湾岛时，诚心诚意地协助他。

荷兰总督揆一留意到国姓爷在厦门的

备战，于是在1650年尽可能增加在热兰遮城和赤崁城的驻军。几年来，虽然双方产生了很多猜疑和不满，却并无敌意。然而，在南京战败之后，国姓爷很显然只能进攻台湾岛，否则由于给养不足，他的舰队及部属就会解散。这时荷兰人意识到了岛上的中国居民与国姓爷有所往来，他们提高警觉，扣押了一些重要的移民作为人质，逮捕可疑之人并严刑拷打。揆一早有准备，他急切地向巴达维亚[23]求援，后者随即派了十二艘船携带大量援军前来相助。巴达维亚方面还发布指令，一旦证实台湾无警讯，舰队则开往澳门。当时台湾府的兵力已达一千五百人，指挥官认为这些足以对付中国军队。国姓爷被问及要战还是要和时表示，根本没想过与荷兰开战，并派了一些商船前往台湾，但他仍然在厦门和金门备战，所以荷兰总督不敢掉以轻心。

然而，大多数评议会成员认为当下尚无危险，于是增援船被遣往各自的目的地。指挥官回到巴达维亚，指责总督揆一无故猜疑，导致揆一被革职，并被勒令返回巴达维亚为自己辩护。他的继任者克伦克于

marking the warlike preparations of Koxinga at Amoy, increased as far as possible, in 1650, the garrison of his forts, Zelandia, and Province. But for several years, although there was great mutual distrust and dissatisfaction, there was no hostility between the parties. However after Koxinga's defeat at Nanking, it was evident that, unless he attacked the island, his fleet and followers would be dispersed, for want of the means of subsistence; and the Dutch, aware of the correspondence between the resident Chinese and the chieftain, increased their vigilance, seized some of the most important emigrants as hostages, and arrested and tortured others on suspicion. The wise prevision of Coyet, induced him earnestly to request assistance from Batavia, and twelve ships, and large reinforcements, were despatched thence, with orders that, if the alarm at "Formosa" proved groundless, the fleet should proceed against Macao. The force at Taiwanfoo, was now augmented to 1 500 men, sufficient, the Admiral thought, to oppose any number of Chinese troops. Koxinga was asked "whether he was for peace, or war." He replied that, "he had not the least thought of war against the company," and sent some trading junks to Taiwan, but as he still continued his preparations at Amoy, and Quemoy, the Govemor's suspicions were not removed.

The majority of his council, however, were of opinion that there was no present danger, and the ships were ordered to their respective destinations. The Admiral returned to Batavia, and accused the Governor of unreasonable apprehensions, and he was suspended from office, and ordered to Batavia, to defend himself. M. Clenk, his successor, sailed for "Formosa", in June 1661.

Shortly after the departure of the ships, Koxinga with a large fleet, and 25 000 of his best troops, appeared off forts Zelandia, and Province; and, assisted by thousands of his countrymen, on shore, began to land. He was first attacked by 240 Dutch soldiers, and by four ships. He met the attack of the former, with skill and bravery, and succeeded in turning their flank, on which they gave way, became panic striken, and were so routed, that only half the division regained the fort, one captain, and nineteen men, being abandoned to the enemy. The ships fared no better, they sank a few junks, but one was destroyed by a fire ship, another escaped to Batavia, and the fate of the other two is not stated.

No further opposition was offered, and in four hours the Chinese landed, cut off all communication between forts Province and Zelandia, and between the latter fort, and the open country. The instant surrender of the forts, was now demanded, under the menace that if not complied with, all would be put to the sword. A deputation from the Dutch waited on the chief, to offer, rather than lose all, the surrender of fort Province. It was received with some state, but was told that, "Formosa' had always belonged to China, and now the Chinese wanted it, the foreigners must quit the island immediately. If not, let them only hoist the red flag." Next morning the red flag was flying on fort

1661年6月启航前往台湾。

增援船离开不久，国姓爷便率领一支大型舰队和两万五千名精兵，出现在热兰遮城和赤崁城两个要塞的不远处，并在成千上万名当地同胞的帮助下登陆。郑军首先遭到二百四十名荷兰士兵和四艘船的袭击，国姓爷以精湛的战术和无畏的精神迎敌，成功地从侧面袭击。荷军败退，惊慌失措，溃不成军，只有半数官兵退回要塞，失去一名上尉和十九个士兵。荷兰舰队的情况不比这个好，几艘沉没了，一艘被火攻船烧毁了，另一艘逃往巴达维亚，另外两艘未被提及。

郑军没遇到什么抵抗，在之后的四小时里顺利登陆，切断了热兰遮城与赤崁城两个要塞之间、热兰遮城与居民区之间的所有联系。要塞里的人被要求即刻弃城投降，如若不从，所有人都将死于非命。荷兰人派一名代表拜见国姓爷，表示愿意弃守要塞，以换取所有人的性命。荷兰人的请求被接受，并被告知："台湾历来属于中国，现在中国人想要收回，外国人必须立即撤离这座岛屿。若不服从，便升起红旗决战。”次日早上，红旗飘扬在热兰遮城上方，而赤崁城的守军则缴械投降。所有能操作武器的荷兰人都集中到了热兰遮城，他们到处放火，但也不能有效地阻止中国人抢救供其栖身的房屋。郑军调集二十八门大炮攻打要塞，但荷军火力持久，准头又好，导致郑军大量伤亡。围城者只得设法突击，躲过枪炮。国姓爷进攻不利，将策略改为更严密地围困，将怒火发泄到没有防守的广阔地带。他不放过任何一个荷兰人，把他们全都抓来当俘虏，尤其是牧师和教师，他认为他们暗中怂恿教区的居民杀害住在一起的汉人。有些人在各自的村子里被钉十字架而死，其他人则以较为仁慈的方式被处死。囚犯里有位名叫范堡㉔的牧师，被国姓爷派去向总督提弃守要塞的条件，如不弃守，国姓爷就将对荷兰俘虏进行报复。他的妻子和两个孩子被扣为人质，如果谈判失败他只能等死。但最终，他带着总督拒绝投降的消息回来了。范堡㉔、温世缪㉕以及其他几位牧师和教师都丧命了。在巴达维亚评议会才谴责揆一的多疑，并派遣其继任者克伦克前往台湾的两天后，

Zelandia, but fort Province, with its garrison and cannon, was surrendered. All the Dutch capable of bearing arms, were now taken into fort Zelandia, and the city fired, but not so effectually, as to prevent the Chinese from saving many buildings, which afforded them shelter. They brought up twenty-eight cannon, to bear against the fort. Its fire was, however, so sustained and well directed, that numbers were killed and wounded in this attempt, and the besiegers, making a sally spiked the guns. Koxinga, baffled in all his attacks on the fort, began a close blockade, and vented his rage on the open country. He made prisoners of all the Dutch he could lay hands on, especially clergymen, and schoolmasters, alleging that they secretly encouraged their parishioners, to kill the Chinese residing among them; some were crucified, their crosses being erected in their respective villages, while others were put to death in a more merciful manner. One of the prisoners taken, Mr. Hambrocock, a clergyman, was sent by Koxinga, to the Governor, to propose terms for the surrender of the fort, the alternative being vengeance on the Dutch prisoners. His wife and two children were detained as hostages; and he had no hope but that death would be his portion, if he failed in his negotiations. ... Eventually he left with the Governor's refusal to surrender. Messrs Hambrocock Mus, and Winshaim, clergymen, and several schoolmasters, perished in this massacre. Two days after the council at Batavia had censured Coyet for his fears, and despatched his successor Clenk, to "Formosa", the ship which had escaped, arrived with the news of the attack on that place. They revoked the censure and suspension, and fitted out ten ships, with 700 soldiers, for the island, but Clenk arrived first off fort Zelandia, where he saw, instead of the rich and peaceful Governorship he had flattered himself with obtaining, the red flag flying, and hundred of Chinese war junks anchored in the north roads. Thereupon he sent his despatches, on shore, and, without landing, sailed for Japan. When the succours from Batavia arrived, the besieged, began to act on the defensive, and an unsuccessful attempt was made to dislodge the enemy from the town, in which two ships, and many men, were lost. The garrisons of Kelung, and Tamsui, were ordered to reinforce the besieged, and the women and children, and other helpless persons, were sent to Batavia. These preparations checked the approaches of Koxinga; but the inexplicable imprudence of the Dutch, lost them their advantage. The Governor, received letters from the Tartar Viceroy of Fohkien, requesting his cooperation in expelling the remains of Koxinga's forces from the coast, and promising his aid, afterwards, to the Dutch in "Formosa". Five ships were accordingly sent away for this service, but of these, three were lost in a storm, and the other two returned to Batavia. These circumstances were such, as Koxinga, in his wildest dreams, could scarcely have hoped for, while to the besieged, they brought utter despair. Desertion commenced, and a deserter

战争中败逃的那艘船就带来台湾被袭的消息。他们撤销了对揆一的谴责和停职决议，并配备十艘船和七百名士兵前往台湾进行增援。当克伦克快到热兰遮城的时候，他看到的不是自以为要接管的太平富庶之地，而是成百艘飘扬着红旗的中国战舰停泊在北部航道。克伦克在岸边送上快信，没有登陆，而是直接驶往日本。当来自巴达维亚的增援部队到达的时候，被围困的荷军开始反抗，试图将郑军驱逐出去，但失败了，还损失了两艘船和大量兵力。基隆和淡水的守军奉命增援被围困的荷兰人，妇女、儿童和其他弱者被送往巴达维亚。这些工作牵制了国姓爷的进攻，但荷兰人莫名其妙的轻率却让他们失去了优势。总督揆一收到福建总督[26]的来信，信中请求荷兰人帮忙将国姓爷残余势力驱逐出大陆沿海地带，并许诺事成之后会向在台湾的荷兰人提供援助。于是，荷兰人派遣了五艘船出发前去执行任务，结果三艘葬身于风暴中，另外两艘折回了巴达维亚。这是国姓爷做梦都想不到的情况，也给被围困者带来了彻底的绝望。一些荷兰人开始弃城而逃，一个逃兵向郑军透露了荷军防御最薄弱的环节，这使荷军遭到三面夹击，突破口被打开，防线被占领，显然荷军就要失败了。为此，荷兰人召开了一次战时评议会，大多数人认为热兰遮城守不住。在被围攻九个月、损失一千六百人之后，他们决定投降。荷兰人登船驶往爪哇岛，总督揆一和评议员都被监禁于此，其财产被没收，而总督本人被判处终身监禁在班达群岛的一个岛上。㉗于是，1662年，荷兰人结束了在台湾和附近海域长达三十余年的盘踞。㉘

国姓爷如今在台湾岛实行君王般的统治，在热兰遮城㉙兴建宫殿，并将驻军精心部署在台湾的西部地区。岛上呈现出新的社会面貌，大陆的法律制度、行政系统、风俗习惯以及产业都被引入台湾。同时，他派遣部队向大陆沿海地区的居民强制征税，为台湾提供必要的补给。清政府无力制止这种无休止的、无法忍受的强取豪夺和掠杀，因为曾为国姓爷俘虏、后被清政府所杀的那四千个可怜人的悲惨命运仍历历在目，所以很难指望能招募到新兵。

pointed out to Koxinga's forces, the weakest spots; they were assailed from three batteries, a breach was made, and a redoubt gained, and the assault was evidently about to be given. On this the Dutch held a council of war, and the majority having decided that the fort was untenable, it was surrendered, after a siege of nine months, and a loss of sixteen hundered men. The Dutch embarked for Java, where the Governor, and his council, were imprisoned, their goods confiscated, and the Governor, himself, condemned to perpetual imprisonment on one of the Banda isles. In such wise, after thirty years duration, ended in 1662, the Dutch territorial possessions in "Formosa", and the seas.

Koxinga now constituted himself king of the island, assumed sovereign style, fixed his palace and court, at Zelandia; and distributed his garrisons, with skill, over the western region of Taiwan. The island assumed a new social aspect, Chinese laws, forms of government, customs, and industry, were introduced; and at the same time, expeditions were fitted out, to lay the inhabitants of the sea coast on the mainland, under contribution for whatever supplies were necessary. The Imperial government, was utterly powerless to check these incessant, and intolerable, acts of spoliation and murder; and as the fate of the wretched 4 000, was too fresh to hope anything from the employment of military force, recourse was had to a measure peculiarly Chinese, which could not, perhaps, have been put in force in any other country in the world. In 1662, an Imperial edict came forth, commanding "all the people upon the coast of the maritime provinces, to remove themselves and their effects, into the Interior, to a distance of thirty li (10 miles) from the shore, on penalty of death; also, that the islands be abandoned, and commerce utterly cease." This remarkable edict, was actually carried into effect; and for seven years, all the rich, and populous cities upon the coast, were deserted; and whole villages crumbled into ruin, and disappeared. Meanwhile Koxinga was devising plans for the extension of his power and dominion, he cast his eyes towards the rich Philippine islands, and an expedition was in course of preparation against the Spaniards there, when it was cut short, by the death of this redoubtable chieftain. His possessions passed to his son, who did not inherit his father's great military ability. Ten years later, when the provinces of Kwangtung, and Foh-kien, revolted against the Emperor Kanghi, this son resolved to join the king of Foh-kien; but the latter refusing to acknowledge him as a sovereign prince, he declared war against him, defeated him in several battles, and so destroyed his power that he was compelled to tender his submission to the Emperor. The Emperor Kanghi, abolished the title of king, and appointed a Governor over Chekiang, and Foh-kien. This officer seized the "Pescadores", a group of islands about twenty five miles from "Formosa", and proclaimed an amnesty, to all who submitted to the Imperial rule. His pol-

清政府只能采取一种中国特有的方式，也许这在世界上任何其他国家都无法实施。1662年，清朝颁布诏书，命令沿海各省居民及其财产均需内撤三十里，违者处死；同时隔离岛屿，严禁通商。这非比寻常的诏书得以实施；执行七年后，沿海富裕繁华、人丁兴旺的城镇一片荒凉；所有的村子沦为废墟，甚至消失。与此同时，国姓爷计划扩大其势力和统治版图，他的目光投向了富饶的菲律宾群岛，并准备派遣一支远征军对付那里的西班牙人，但计划却因这位令人敬畏的首领的过世而终止。国姓爷所有的遗产都传给了儿子郑经[30]，但后者却没能继承他杰出的军事才能。十年后，广东和福建两省联手反抗康熙皇帝，郑经决定联合福建的靖南王。但后者拒绝承认郑经作为继承者的身份，于是郑经向靖南王宣战，几次战斗后打败了靖南王，摧毁了他的势力，靖南王被迫归顺康熙皇帝。康熙皇帝罢黜了靖南王的头衔，任命了一位总督[31]治理闽浙两省。这位官员还管控澎湖，一个距离台湾大约二十五英里的群岛。他宣布对所有归顺大清者实行特赦，这一政策达到了预期效果，成千上万到台湾的移民被吸引回大陆，从而削弱了台湾的郑军力量，使之难以维持下去。1683年，国姓爷的孙子只好归顺康熙皇帝。在石井的郑氏宗祠里供奉着一尊国姓爷的塑像，据说除了大年初一之外，祠堂的正门一律不准打开，以免令人敬畏的国姓爷重生，给统治王朝带来麻烦和灾难。

失去台湾后，荷兰人在巴达维亚组建了一支由十二艘船组成的舰队，这支舰队被派往福州，和清朝谈判，希望签订条约，恢复对台湾的管控。他们占据了一个海港，又得到另外十六艘船的增援，其中大部分是商船。他们与清政府联合进攻并拿下了厦门、金门，但清政府不允许他们占有两地。多次谈判都没占到便宜后，这支舰队最终回到了巴达维亚，一无所获。

英国人侵占厦门

经过一段动荡凄苦的岁月，福建似乎出现了多年的和平局面，渐渐恢复活力，重现往日的繁华。很值得记上一笔的下一次灾难，是厦门被英国人攻占。这起事件

icy had its desired effect, thousands of "Formosan" emigrants, being induced to return to China, thereby weakening the enemy on the island, until, finally, it could no longer be held; and "Formosa" was surrendered to Kanghi, by the grandson of Koxinga, in 1683. In their ancestral hall at Shih Ching 石井, there is a figure of Koxinga; and it is said, that the front door of the hall, is not allowed to be opened, except on New Year's Day, lest the dreaded chief should go forth, and be born again, to bring trouble and disaster on the ruling dynasty.

After the loss of "Formosa", the Dutch equipped a fleet of twelve vessels at Batavia; which they despatched to Foochow, to enter into a treaty for the recovery of the island. They possessed themselves of a sea port, and being reinforced by sixteen other ships, most of them East Indiamen, attacked, in conjunction with the Manchus, Amoy, and Quemoy, both of which places they captured, but they were not permitted by the Manchus, to retain possession of them, and after much profitless negociation, their fleet returned to Batavia, having achieved nothing.

Capture of Amoy by British

After the period of internecion, and misery, narrated, the province appears to have enjoyed many years of peace, in which it recuperated itself, and regained its prosperity. The next calamity which befell it, of sufficient importance to call for note, is the capture of Amoy, by the British. This was brought about by a series of irritating grievances, under which Great Britain has been smarting for years, terminating in the troubles and complications, arising out of the Opium trade at Canton, in 1837-40, which led, as had been foreseen, to war, and on the 23rd June 1840, the van of the British naval and military forces, arrived off Macao, and a notice of the blockade of Canton, was published. Commander Sir Gordon Bremner, in the Wellesley, 74, his fleet consisting of three steamers, four ships, and twenty-one transports, sailed northwards; on the 5th July, Ting-hai, was taken and occupied, and on the 6th, the joint Plenipotentiaries, Admiral Sir G. Elliot, and Captain Elliot, R.N., arrived at Chusan, in the *Melville*, 74. They sent a copy of Lord Palmerston's letter to the Emperor, setting forth the grounds of complaint, to the authorities at Amoy, and Ningpo, for them to forward to Peking, both of whom declined taking the responsibility. The visit to these two cities, shewed that the Chinese were preparing for defence, by arming the forts, making rafts, and posting troops. Amoy, was forthwith blockaded. This act on the part of the British, induced an unsuccessful attack on one of the blockading ships. Strenuous endeavours on the part of the Chinese were now made to bring their forts, and defences, into the most efficient state possible, and a large reward was offered for the heads of "rebellious barbarians," and the capture of their ships. Fourteen months later, all negociations with the Governor General of Chihli, and Imperial Commissioner, Kishên, at Taku, and Canton, having proved

的起因是：1837—1840年间，英国在广州的鸦片生意遭遇了一系列的麻烦和纠葛，英国为此怨恨多年，并最终引起了一场战争。1840年6月23日，英国的海、陆军先头部队抵达澳门，并发布了封锁广州的公告。英军司令伯麦乘坐装载七十四门炮的"威里士厘"号驶向北方，他的舰队由三艘汽船、四艘帆船和二十一艘运输船组成。7月5日，定海被占；6日，舰队司令懿律和上校义律作为全权代表，乘坐装载七十四门炮的"麦尔威厘"号抵达舟山。他们把《巴麦尊致中国皇帝钦命宰相书》递送给厦门、宁波当局，请他们转呈北京朝廷，但遭到拒绝。他们到访这两个城市，发现中国人在构筑工事，制作木筏，调配军力备战。[32]厦门即刻被封锁，英国的这个行动导致一艘封锁船被开火击中，但损失不大。中方不遗余力地加强要塞，使之尽可能坚固；他们还设下重赏，悬赏民众取"逆夷"头颅、俘获英军船只。十四个月之后，总督耆英、钦差大臣琦善与英方在大沽口和广州的所有谈判均告失败，皇帝又决意与英国作战。第一道防线上的穿鼻、大角山和虎门等地的炮台，连同沿海到广州沿线的所有要塞、木筏、大炮、兵营以及防栅都被英国人摧毁或占领。1841年5月26日或27日，英军控制下的广州被要求以六百万元赎回。双方刚签下休战协议，30日，一千五百名村民和散兵袭击了英军。村民们士气高涨，郭富㉝爵士要知府即刻解散民众，否则将纵火烧城。鉴于此，一位钦差和知府在一个英国军官的陪同下出城，哄骗村民们解散。皇侄奕山作为统帅，宣告取得了大捷，并以驱除英军出广州城为名，奖励部属。事实却是清军受制于英军，被赶着向内地撤退了六十英里，并驱散了民众。战争期间，英国在广州的鸦片贸易依然进行，没有受到太大干扰，税费照常征收，好像两个国家相安无事。1841年8月21日，英军离开香港，开始了远征，目的是攻占厦门，并在浙江开展军事活动。这是蓄谋已久的，因为一年前英方“布朗底”号曾经携带着《巴麦尊致中国皇帝钦命宰相书》到访过厦门，表明这些“鼠窜”的蛮夷知道战争的不可避免。防御工事被加强，每座岛屿和俯视港口、护卫海岛的

fruitless, and hostilities having been resumed by the Emperor, the forts of Chuenpi, Taekotan, the Bogue, and those at the First Bar, together with all the forts, rafts, batteries, camps, and stockades, between the ocean and Canton, were destroyed, or taken by the British. The city of Canton, which lay at the mercy of the invaders, was ransomed for $6 000 000, on the 26th or 27th, May, 1841. The terms of abstention from aggressive acts on both sides, which had just been agreed to, was followed, on the 30th, by an attack from 1 500 villagers, and dispersed troops. The villagers having assumed a still more menacing attitude, Sir Hugh Gough, told the Prefect that if they were not instantly dispersed, he would fire on the city. On this, one of the Commissioners, and the Prefect, accompanied by an English Officer, went out and coaxed them to retire. Yih-shan, a nephew of the Emperor, and chief generalissimo, at the same time proclaimed a victory, and rewarded his troops with decorations for driving the English out of Canton; the fact being, that he was compelled by the victors, to march these same troops sixty miles into the interior, and disband them. During the war, trade at Canton continued without any serious interruption, the usual duties and charges being paid, as if the two nations were at peace. The expedition for the capture of Amoy, and for military operations in Cheh-kiang, left Hongkong on the 21st August 1841. The attack had been anticipated here, from the visit of the *Blonde*, the year before, with the letter for Peking, which showed that the barbarians, "sneaking in and out like rats," were aware of its existence; and the fortifications had been increased, and every island and protecting headland, overlooking the harbour, had been occupied and armed. The measures taken were useless, and its capture on the 26th August 1841, is thus described in the *Chinese Repository* Vol. X. p. 621: "The capture of Amoy, was chiefly a naval operation, and the little that was left for the troops to do, was done by the 18th Royal Irish. Scarcely had the fleet taken up their position opposite the batteries of Amoy, when a boat bearing a white flag was seen to approach the Wellesley. An officer of low rank, was the bearer of a paper demanding to know what our ships wanted, and directing us to make sail for the outer waters, ere the Celestial wrath should be kindled against us, and the guns from the batteries annihilate us. The line of works, certainly, presented a most formidable appearance, and the batteries were admirably constructed. Manned by Europeans, no force could have stood before them. For four hours did the ships pepper at them without cessation. The *Wellesley*, and *Blenheim*, each, fired upwards of 12 000 rounds, to say nothing of the frigates, steamers, and small craft. Yet the works were as perfect when they left off, as when they began, the utmost penetration of the shot being 16 inches. From 20, to 30, people, were all that were killed by this enormous expenditure of powder and shot. It was nearly 3 P.M. before the 18th landed, accompanied by Sir Hugh Gough, and staff. They landed close to a high wall, which flanked the mainline of batteries, covered by the *Queen*, and *Phlegethon*, steamers. The flank companies soon got over the wall, driving the enemy before them. They opened a gate, through which the rest of our men

陆岬，都有军人驻守。然而，这些措施全都没用，1841年8月26日厦门被攻占，《中国丛报》第十卷第六百二十一页中如此描述：“攻占厦门主要是海军完成的，陆军付出很少，具体是由爱尔兰皇家第十八团承担的。舰队刚开到厦门炮台的正对面，就有一艘插着白旗的船靠近‘威里士厘’号。守军中的一位下级军官举着一份文件，询问我们的目的，并要我们驶向外海，否则天怒将惩罚我们，炮台里的炮火会毁灭我们。一整排的工事看起来很有威慑力，炮台也造得极好。可在欧洲人的军舰面前，敌军将灰飞烟灭。炮战连续不断地进行了四个小时，‘威里士厘’号和‘伯兰汉’号各发射了一万两千多枚炮弹，还不算护卫舰、轮船和小木筏。然而，防御工事禁得起十六英寸[34]的穿透力，所以在这一波炮弹面前安然无恙。二三十个人葬身于这强大的火力。下午近三点，与郭富爵士及其部下一起，第十八团登陆。他们在‘皇后’号和‘弗莱吉森’号两条轮船的掩护下，靠近炮台主工事侧面的一堵高墙处登陆。侧翼的英军迅速越过那堵墙，将面前的敌人驱散。

他们打开一个缺口，其他人一拥而入，沿着炮台前进，迅速清除对手，两分钟内杀的人多于该阵地上士兵一整天的战绩。我方三位士兵被打倒，还有人受了伤。一个中国军官在石壁炮台前自刎，另一个异常冷静地投海自尽。我方部队一到，敌人就四散开了。我们晚上尽量露营，次日早上毫无阻力地占领了整座城市。财宝被劫掠一空，只留下装财宝的盒子。军械库里发现了大量的军械物资，铸件设备还能使用。一两艘仿制我们的装载三十门炮的双层甲板船正准备下海，其他的还在船坞。但是，这里却很少有战船，中国部队的司令此时未和战舰在一起。战斗中，'弗莱吉森'号遇到了大麻烦，它突然靠近清军一座隐蔽的炮台对面，恰在对方射程之内，对方立刻开了火。幸好海水足够深，这艘轮船才得以靠岸。麦克里夫蒂船长命令部下立刻上岸，直取炮台，杀死了大量守军。"

老将士郭富爵士认为，中国人的抵抗比他想象中"弱得多"。但是，也有人说"中国人英勇抵抗炮火的轰击"，坚守阵地，直到他们被背后的步枪射杀。英军参与进攻

entered, and advancing along the batteries, they quickly cleared them, killing more men, in two minutes, than the men of war did during the whole day; three of our fellows were knocked over, besides others injured. One officer (Chinese) cut his throat in the long battery, another walked into the sea and drowned himself, in the coolest manner possible. The enemy fled on all sides, so soon as our troops approached. We bivouacked, as best we could, during the night, and next morning, took possession of the city without hindrance. Much treasure had been carried away, the mob leaving only the boxes which had contained it. Immense quantities of military stores, were found in the arsenals, and the foundaries were in active operation. One two decker, modeled from ours, and carrying 30 guns, was ready for sea, and others were on the stocks. But few war junks were stationed here, the Chinese admiral being, at this time, absent with his fleet. During the engagement the *Phlegethon*, steamer, was very severely handled. She came suddenly opposite, and close to, a masked battery, the guns from which, having the exact range, opened on her. Fortunately for the steamer, the water was sufficiently deep to come close to land. Captain McCleaverty immediately landed his men, advanced directly on the battery, and took possession of it, killing a great portion of the garrison."

That gallant old fire-eater, Sir Hugh Gough, considered the resistance of the Chinese, "more feeble," than he had anticipated, yet it is stated, by others, that "the Chinese did endure the fire right manfully," standing to their guns, until they were shot down by musketry in their rear. The attacking force consisted of H. B. M, S. *Queen*, *Sesostris*, *Blonde*, *Druid*, *Modeste*, *Bentinck*, *Wellesley*, and *Blenheim*, supported by seven more ships of war, and fifteen transports, bearing the 18th, and 55th, regiments, and detachments of the 49th, and 26th, regiments, with engineers, and artillery. The Chinese officer, who walked into the sea, and drowned himself, "in the coolest manner possible," was the Tsung-ping, or General, then commanding, in the absence, of Admiral Tao-chin-pin, windbound to the northward; he is described in a memorial to the Emperor, as having fallen into the water, and died, in endeavouring to drive back the British troops, as they were landing. Four other officers, Colonel Sing-chi, and lieutenants Hwa-kwo-ching, Yang-shan-chi, and Li-chi-ming, are reported killed, and two lieutenant colonels, and one major, wounded; while amongst the soldiers, "very many," are reported to be killed and wounded; and 3 000 000 taels of silver, （£1 000 000） are craved, for immediate use.

Yen-pih-t'ou, the then Governor General of Fuhkien, and Chekiang, who was at Amoy at the time of the attack, gives, in a memorial to the throne, dated the 28th August 1841, a version of the affair, that is highly creditable to his imagination. This mighty man of valour, relates how, at the head of his invincible braves, he attacked and sunk, one steamer and five ships of war, killing an innumerable number of the rebellious

的舰只包括"皇后"号、"西索斯梯斯"号、"布朗底"号、"都鲁壹"号、"摩底士"号、"班廷克"号、"威里士厘"号和"伯兰汉"号，外加驰援的七艘战船、十五艘运输船。这些船载着第十八团、第五十五团，以及第四十九团、第二十六团的特遣分队，外加工程兵和炮兵。

那位"异常冷静"地投海自尽的中国军官是一名总兵㉟，他是代替去北方公干的水师提督窦振彪坐镇指挥。呈交皇帝的奏折称他奋力击退登陆的英军，不幸落水而亡。另外四位军官，副将凌志，把总纪国庆、杨肇基、李启明，全都阵亡，还有两位副将和一名守备受伤。据说"死伤众多"，还需三百万两银子（相当于一百万英镑）救急。

当时，闽浙总督颜伯焘正在厦门。在1841年8月28日给皇帝的奏折中，充满想象力地给出他自己关于该事件的版本。这位勇敢的大人物宣称，他如何富有谋略地击沉一艘轮船和五艘战船，杀死敌兵无数。但是（就像他的故事中的纸上勇士一样），他杀得越多，越多的敌兵前赴后继，因此他不得不策略性地以退为进。事后大家都知道他狼狈逃窜了，这保住了他的官印，但衙门却被英军付之一炬。他小心翼翼地隐瞒损失了五百人，外加兵工厂和船只的事实，还宣称情况很快会好转，他从厦门撤离是为了联合一百个村子、召集一万多名士兵，准备再战英军。有鉴于此，有些需求是免不了的，他提出要三百万两银子。由于厦门已经收复，皇帝下旨革去他的官阶和职位，免他一死。厦门已被英军搬空，这很能说明问题。

这些石壁炮台因其坚固而受赞誉，其目的是防御蛮夷（可能指日本人、荷兰人）和中国海上势力首领国姓爷。炮台坚固的美名，来自一位叫林懋时的人在天启三年即1622年[36]3月的一条记录，这是由中左所千户李逢华刻在贝尔拉米船坞的一块岩石上的。炮台要求长50丈，英勇的千户将收到19两银子，即约6.68英镑修筑炮台。我们简单想来，他不得不从自己的腰包里多掏100两银子才能完成这项工程。这条记录刻在石头上的原因已无法得知；这些防御工事是花岗石构筑的，很大也很坚固，花的银子肯定更接近119 000两而不是119两。

此前，双方已经采取了敌对的措施。

barbarians. But, (as with the paper braves in his native fables) the more he slew, the more came on, so a strategic advance, in a direction contrary to the enemy, was necessary. This evolution, known in later days as the skedaddle, was executed with promptitude and despatch, and his seals of office saved, but only when the office had been set on fire by the rebels. He is discreetly silent about the loss of 500 guns, stores, and shipping; and adds that, matters were not to be left long in this state, as more than 100 villages had combined, and over 10 000 warriors were mustered, ready for the battle. On this is founded the inevitable demand, springing forth from every occurrence in China, Taels 3 000 000, are asked for. His Imperial Master replies, and strips him of his rank and office, but spares his head, because Amoy had been recaptured. So its evacuation by the British forces, appears to have been represented.

The long batteries, of whose capacity for hard usage such honourable mention is made, were, according to an inscription of one Lin-mao-shih, cut into a rock at Bellamy's Dock, erected in the first moon, of the third year of the Emperor Tien-chi, or about March 1622, by Colonel Li-kung-hwa, as a defence against foreign barbarians (meaning, probably, the Japanese, Dutch, and the Chinese pirate Chief Koxinga.) They are ordered to be fifty chang long; and the gallant Colonel is to receive nineteen taels, or about £6.6.8, for executing the work; it is naively added that, he was compelled to spend 100 taels more, out of his own pocket, to complete the battery. Why such a statement should be cut into the rock, it is impossible to say; the works being of granite, and of great extent and thickness, must have cost nearer Tls. 119 000 than Tls. 119.

Previous to this, hostile measures had been resorted to. On the 2nd July 1840, one of the boats of H. M S. *Blonde*, under a flag of truce, and bearing the letter from Lord Palmerston to the Emperor, before referred to, was warned off the beach, with haughty threats and insults, by the military authorities, and as she obeyed, was fired into. This treacherous and wanton act, was promptly responded to, by a couple of 32 pr. round shot, from the frigate into the crowd, which caused a general flight.

The *Blonde*, then opened fire on the fort, and on some mandarin junks. This was kept up for nearly two hours, until the fort was unroofed and riddled. An attempt was made to set on fire a large junk, this proving unsuccessful, the *Blonde* did not take further trouble, but, thinking the lesson given sufficient, quietly departed without doing further injury. In August of the same year, the *Alligator*, and *Bræmar*, sunk 16 or 17 junks in the outer harbour, with, supposed, considerable loss of life to the Chinese; but being themselves struck several times from the batteries, and one vessel having her mainyard arm shot away, and a shot lodged in her hull, they retired out of range.

Small Knife Rebels

These operations were followed by the opening of the port to foreign trade, by the

1840年7月2日，“布朗底”号上的一艘小船，插着休战旗，带着《巴麦尊致中国皇帝钦命宰相书》（上文已提及），遭到中国军队傲慢的威胁和羞辱，不得靠近海滩。小船虽照办，却还是被炮击了。这种欺诈且蛮横的行为迅速得到了反击，两枚三十二磅的炮弹击中岸上的人群，人们四下奔逃。㊲

“布朗底”号接着便向岸上的防御工事和清军船只开炮。战斗持续了两个小时，直到工事被开了天窗，打成筛子状。有人试图放火烧船，但没有成功。“布朗底”号没有再找麻烦，觉得给对方的教训已经足够，于是悄悄撤离，不再制造更多伤害。同年8月，“鳄鱼”号和“布里玛”号在厦门外港击沉了十六七艘清军船只，给清军造成了不小的伤亡；但是英军舰只也几次被炮台攻击，一艘舰的主桅上的武器被打掉，还有一发炮弹打进舰壳，于是这些舰就撤退到了射程之外。

小刀会

根据1842年签订的《南京条约》，厦门口岸对外通商，1843年11月2日纪里布任英国驻厦门领事。在之后的11年中，口岸贸易逐渐发展，没发生值得特别记载之事。直到1853年5月4日，这天是个星期六，中国官员得悉，22英里之外的海澄县有三四千名武装分子正准备进攻厦门。18日早上8点，一伙人冲向城门，向城楼上的士兵开火。后者还击，双方间断交火，直到下午1点，官员和士兵都逃跑了；到了下午4点，约4 000名装备很差的人，和差不多数量的厦门暴民一起，轻取了这座几乎不设防的城市。起义军遵守秩序、行为节制，不损害私人财产，只掠夺官方弹药库和军械库。全城巡逻，防止发生抢劫事件；夜里，还驻扎了一队人马保护洋行，同时向外国人表达出极大的善意。厦门口岸没有外国军舰，外国居民的安全有赖于怡和洋行、宝顺洋行的收货船只，它们收到危险通知的第一时间便回到内港。蹊跷的是，文翰爵士[38]却不赞成这样做。很快，在19日这天，起义军就被派去攻占泉州和台湾。厦门人被强征以支持起义军，此举引起了很大的不满，一家富有的商号竟被“征收”4万元。现在应该要看看，如此迅速攻占厦

treaty of Nanking, signed in 1842, and by the establishment of Mr. Henry Gribble, as British Consul at Amoy, on the 2nd November 1843. During the succeeding eleven years the trade of the port was gradually developed, and little occurred worthy of special record, until Saturday the 14th May, 1853, when it became known to the Mandarins, that there was an armed band of 3 000 or 4 000 men, at Hai Ching hsien, about 22 miles distant, who were on their way to attack this city. At 8 o'clock on the morning of the 18th, a party of men advanced in front of the city gates, and opened fire on the soldiers on the walls. This was returned, and the firing continued, at intervals, until one o'clock, when the Mandarins and soldiers fled, and by four o'clock in the afternoon, some four thousand ill-armed men, who had been joined by about the same number of the roughs of Amoy, had taken almost unopposed possession of city. The insurgents behaved with order and moderation, doing no injury to private property, and plundering only powder magazines, and arsenals. Patrols were distributed throughout the city, to prevent pillage, and, at night, they stationed a guard for the protection of the foreign Hongs, expressing, at the same time, towards foreigners, the most pacific intentions. No vessel of war being at the port, the safety of the foreign residents, devolved on the receiving ships of Messrs. Jardine, Matheson & Co. and Dent & Co. which had, on the first note of danger, moved into the inner harbour. This step, curiously enough, was afterwards disapproved of by Sir George Bonham. No time was lost; on the 19th rebel bands were despatched for the capture of Chin-chew, and of "Formosa": and contributions for the support of the rebel troops, were levied on the citizens of Amoy, to their great disgust; one wealthy firm being "requisitioned," to the tune of $40 000. A glance should now be taken at the nature of the force, that had so rapidly obtained possession of the city. It was the Hsiao-tao-hui, 小刀會, or Dagger Society. There had existed for many years amongst the Chinese at Java, Singapore, Malacca, and Penang; a secret society, the ostensible object of which, was mutual assistance and protection. It contained men of all classes, and its rules were so strictly observed, that, it is said, piratical members, meeting on the high seas the vessels of trading members, were content to accept the sign of the society, and to allow the vessels to pass on unmolested. This society was originally called San-ho-hui, 三合會, or the society of the three (persons) united, or as it has been aptly translated, the Triad Society. The three referred to, are 天地人 t'ien, ti, jên, heaven, earth, and man, the three great powers of nature, according to the Chinese doctrine of the universe. It became the T'ien-ti-hui, 天地會 or Society of Heaven and Earth, during the reign of Chien-lung, (about 1795) when it was distinctly political, and had attained such magnitude and power, as to serious endanger that monarch's government. And it was not until eight years after, that the snake was scotched, but not killed, by the seizure and execution, of many of its members.

This society, or an offshoot of it, was introduced into Amoy, during the years 1848-9, by a Singapore Chinaman, named Tan-kêng-chin 陳慶真, a compradore in the employ of Messrs. Jardine, Matheson & Co. The society rapidly took root, and in 1857, numbered some thousands of members; when the suspicions of the provincial government at Foochow, being excited, the Viceroy despatched to Amoy to investigate its character, and to suppress it, a resolute old anti-foreign Taotai, named Chang, 張, the same who served as Wei-yuan to the Governor General Lin, when 20 291 chests of Opium were

门的这股力量到底是什么。他们是小刀会，之前已在爪哇、新加坡、马六甲和槟榔屿活动多年，是一个秘密会社，表面上是互助互保的组织。其成员来自社会各个阶层，纪律严明，据说海盗在碰到公海上的贸易船队时，会对持有小刀会标志的商船放行，不找他们的麻烦。这个社团最初称为三合会，即3种力量联合起来的会党。根据中国人的宇宙观，三指的是天、地、人，大自然中的三大元素。大约在乾隆年间的1795年，天地会成立，其政治性很强，势力庞大，对统治者造成严重威胁。不到8年时间，天地会被镇压，很多帮众被抓捕和处置，但仍有一些漏网者。

1848—1849年，一位在怡和洋行做买办的名叫陈庆真的新加坡华人，将小刀会或它的一个分支带入厦门。它在当地很快扎下根，到1857年，帮众已达数千人，引起了在福州的省府的警惕。总督派了年老的仇视洋人的张道台[39]前往调查并镇压，林则徐总督于1839年在广州焚毁英国人的20 291箱鸦片时，这位道台曾在其手下任职。张道台做的第一件事就是以谋反的名义抓捕陈庆真，唯一的证据是在陈家发现的一本簿册，上面记录着小刀会帮众的名字和地址。这份证据确证了陈的罪行，于是陈被施以酷刑，以便招供更多细节。与此同时，因为陈庆真是在殖民地出生的英国公民，英国领事听说他被捕之后，和另外3位先生一起来到道台衙门，要求引渡陈庆真。领事被告知犯人关押在海防厅（地方官的府衙），尽管据说犯人此时正在衙门后面受刑。到了海防厅，又被告知犯人在道台衙门。领事未能将陈解救出来，陈被折磨致死。第二天早上，怡和洋行开门时便看到了他的尸体，穿戴如常，坐在正对着掌柜门口的一台轿子里。于是，小刀会的领导权落到了一个出生低微，但精力充沛且颇具人格魅力的人的手里，此人名叫黄位。这时候，厦门有一个名叫黄德美的富商，此人乐善好施，很受穷苦人的爱戴。他被迫担任漳州和泉州二府的盐商，该职务在当时人人避之唯恐不及，因为每年必须向盐运使缴纳费用，其金额远高于所能赚取的利润。（盐运使的地位相当于户部，他通常逼迫某位富商接受盐商的职务。）据

surrendered by the British, and burnt at Canton in 1839. Chang's first act was to arrest Tan-kêng-chin, on a charge of conspiring against the government, the only evidence against him, was a book, found in his house, containing the names and residences of the members of the society; but this was deemed sufficient, and Tan was subjected to horrible tortures, to make him confess further particulars. Meanwhile Tan-kêng-chin, being a British born subject, the English Consul, on hearing of his arrest, went, accompanied by three other gentlemen, to the Taotai's Yamen, to demand his rendition. He was told that the prisoner was at the Hai-fang-ting's （the Magistrate's）, although it is said that he was then under torture at the back of the Yamên. At the Hai-fang-ting's he was told that the man was at the Taotai's. The Consul was not successful in obtaining possession of Tan, who was tortured to death. His body was found on the following morning, on opening Jardine, Matheson's hong, dressed as usual, and seated in a sedan chair, opposite his master's door. The leadership of the society, now appears to have fallen on a man of low extraction, but of great energy and force of character, named Hwang Wei, or in the local dialect Ng-wee 黄位. At this time there dwell at Amoy, one Hwang-tê-mei, or locally Ng-teck-be 黄德美, a merchant, once possessed of great wealth. This man bore a high character for charity and benevolence, and was exceedingly popular amongst the poor classes. He had been compelled to accept the post of salt monopolist of the prefectures of Chang-chou-fu, and Chin-chew-fu, an office then greatly dreaded, on account of its holder having to return annually to the Salt Commissioner, a certain fixed sum, far above what he could collect, （the Salt Commissioner, being, himself, in precisely the same position vis-a-vis the Board of Revenue, usually compelled one of the richest merchants to accept the post.) This office resulted in losses to the amount of $800 000, it is said. Smarting under these, and at a second attempt to force the post of monopolist upon him, he probably, although this is not admitted by my informants, joined the society. At all events it is certain that he advanced money to it, and was on terms of intimacy with Hwang, otherwise Ng-wee. The second attempt to impose the detested office upon Ng-teck-be, was seized upon by Ng-wee, as a means of securely enmeshing this wealthy and influential man in the society; about 2 000 of its members, now styled the Hsiao-tao-hui 小刀會 or Dagger society, rose under Ng-wee, at his native village, Gin-tai 沈宅, and proclaiming that they sought to right Ng-teck-be (without his authority and against his wishes, he always declared) marched on and captured Hai-téng-hsien, 海澄縣, Chioh-bei, 石碼, Chang-chou fu, 漳州府 (which they only held for three days), and finally Amoy, where, soon after arrival, the society was found to consist of about 8 000 men, controlled by a Council of six persons, three of whom were Singapore Chinamen, and at whose head was Ng-wee. Many of the subordinate positions, such as centurions, and leaders of ten, were also held by Singapore Chinese. The pay of private soldiers was 100 cash, or about five pence per diem. This was the force that captured Amoy, and retained possession of it, until the 11th November following. On the 29th May, a fleet of Imperial junks entered the port, and landed some 500 or 600 soldiers, who marched on the city. They were met by the rebels, and after a brief skirmish, driven back to their boats, which immediately left. This defeat, considered by the rebels as an auspicious omen, greatly elated

说，该职务可带来80万元的亏空。受此困扰，当盐商的职务再度强加于他之时，黄德美很可能加入帮会，虽然我的消息来源不能肯定这一点。无论如何，可以肯定的是，他向帮会提供经费，而且与黄位关系密切。黄位利用这个令人厌恶的职务再次强加到黄德美头上的机会，确保让这位具有广泛影响力的富商入会。于是，拥有2 000名帮众的小刀会，在黄位的率领下，在他的老家沈宅起义，宣称要为黄德美讨回公道（黄德美一直宣称，此举未得到他本人的同意，且违背其意愿）。他们继续挺进，攻占了海澄县、石码、漳州府（只占领了3天），最后攻占了厦门。到厦门不久，小刀会的成员就增加到了8 000人，由6人组成的议事会领导，其中3人是新加坡华人，首领是黄位。许多下级职位，如百人队、十人队队长，也由新加坡华人担任。普通底层士兵每天的津贴是100文铜钱，相当于5便士。正是这支队伍攻占了厦门，占据该城直到11月11日。5月29日，官军的船队进入厦门港，五六百名官兵上岸，开进城内。他们遇到起义军的阻击，一阵小规模冲突之后，被赶回自己的船上，随后很快撤离。起义军把这次胜仗当作吉兆，士气高涨，还扩充了队伍。他们为扩张做准备，就弹药和军需品等发出征购单，并承诺向占领厦门期间盗用的军械的所有者进行赔偿。起义军首领黄位自称“汉大明皇帝敕授平闽大元帅”，他发布公告，声称将镇压骚乱、施行正义，违者处斩。一个名“振健”（音译）的读书人最先违反规定，四处散布谣言。为严明法纪，他被拿来祭刀。7月4日，清军四五千人在距离厦门东北面约10英里的地方登陆。起义军则在距离他们营地6英里处设置了路障。7日，官军逼近，双方发生混战，后官军被击退，损失18人。同一天，大约42艘官兵的船只挺进厦门港，袭击了大约25艘起义军的船只。交战两小时之后，双方分开，官兵退到六岛之外，起义军的船则回到港口，据目击者估计，大约只有千分之一的子弹命中。第二天早上，起义军的船开往六岛，与官军交战。双方只是远远地攻击，避免造成伤亡，次日官兵撤回。

them, and strengthened their numbers. Preparations for extending their conquest were made, and requisitions issued for the stores, ammunition, &c., stolen from the arsenals, at the capture of the city, for which compensation was promised to the holders. Proclamations for the repression of disorder, and the administration of justice, in which nearly all breaches of regulations were punishable by death, were put forth by the rebel T'ou or head, Hwang or Ng-wee, who now styled himself, Appointed by Imperial Decree, of the Emperor of the Han (Chinese) Ta Ming dynasty, commander-in-chief of the forces for the conquest of the Fuhkien province. As an earnest of his intention to carry out the proclamations, one Chin-kien, an educated man, the first offender, whose tongue was longer than his discretion, was promptly decapitated. On the 4th July, the Imperialists landed between 4 000 and 5 000 men, some 10 miles to the north east of Amoy; the rebels responded by erecting a barricade at their advanced station, 6 miles from them, and on the 7th, the Imperialists having approached, a melée took place, when the Imperialists were driven back with a loss of eighteen heads. On the same day about forty two Imperial junks, appeared off the harbour, and attacked some twenty five rebel junks. After two hours fighting, in which it has been computed, by eye-witnesses, that about one shot in a thousand took effect, the fleets parted, the mandarins standing out to the six Islands, and the rebels returning into harbour. On the following morning the rebel junks went out to the six Islands, and engaged the Imperialists. The action was fought at a sufficient distance to avoid injury to each other, and the Imperialists left next day.

Scale of Duties and Charges Published by Rebel Chief

About this period the contributions to the rebel coffers falling short, an attempt was made to raise funds by the levy of port charges. As the proclamation, and tariff, are curiosities in their way, I shall perhaps be pardoned for inserting a translation of them here: —

"By Kwang, appointed by Imperial decree of the Emperor of the Han, (Chinese) Ta-ming, Dynasty, Commander-in-chief of the forces for the conquest Of Fuhkien province.

"An order for the guidance of the Merchant Shipping, I, the Commander-in-chief, received an Imperial order to come to Amoy to relieve the people, not to harm them, to put down, not to commit, oppression, for by means of their strength, and by a display of power, these Tartar miscreants, have embittered the whole living population; people of all classes asserted their innocence to the Gods both above and below, and merchants, too, had long been suffering their cruel injuries.

"In the absence of a new code of port regulations, which weightier military duties, at this pressing moment, leaves no time for framing in your behalf, I have, for present use, drawn up an abstract of the rules heretofore in force here, for the merchant shipping, which, in comparison with the port charges, levied by the Tartar brigands, will be found considerably reduced. My chief aim being to procure for the people, those benefits which are to their advantage. Accordingly I beg hereby to notify to the merchant shipping of Amoy, that all such ships as are engaged in Import, or Export, trade, are to be duly provided with passes or papers, which will enable them to leave, or enter, the port, on their voyages to and fro, without danger of obstruction.

小刀会颁布的收费标准

大约这一段时期，向起义军缴纳的捐输少了，于是他们尝试通过征收港口税来筹措经费。他们的公告和收税事宜十分奇怪，记录如下：

汉大明皇帝敕授平闽大元帅黄示：[40]

尔商船知悉：照得本帅奉旨临厦，安民非以贱民，御暴非以为暴。清逆倚势作威，荼毒生灵，故并告无辜于上下神祀。尔商民罹其凶害久矣。兹因军中急务，仓卒之际，未暇详议条目，姑就向来旧例，定其大略。较清贼出入关口，倍觉省约，务要因民之所利而利之。合行出示晓谕，为此示仰厦岛商船，凡有通商出入关口，任尔来往，准给牌票，毋得拦阻。酌定条规，胪列于左，各宜凛遵毋违。特示！

（天德）癸酉年六月[41]二十七日

厦门口岸收费标准

一、龙溪、同安、海澄、马巷、晋江、南安及惠安船只，离厦往台属鹿港、淡水及五条港载运豆饼、油、米等货，以及返程载相同货品抵厦，出入口岸：二千担以上四千担以下，收六十元；一千担以上二千担以下，收三十元。

二、龙溪、同安、海澄、马巷、晋江、惠安及南安船只，在厦门装载糖等货，开往天津[42]锦州与盖州，及山东胶州，出入口岸每船收五十元；

三、龙溪、同安、海澄及马巷船只，从厦门往乐清、温州、台州、宁波、上海，复返厦，出入口岸每船收十四元；

四、龙溪、同安、海澄及马巷船只，由厦往台属任何口岸，继而转由天津锦州、盖州及山东胶州，复返厦，出入口岸每船收一百元；

五、晋江、南安、惠安船只，由厦往台，转由天津锦州、盖州及山东胶州，复返厦，出入口岸每船收一百元；

六、云霄、漳浦、诏安船只，往台复返厦，装载豆饼、油与米，出入口岸每船收五十元；

七、云霄、漳浦、诏安船只，由

"Annexed is a scale of charges temporarily fixed upon, to which every one is called upon to obey.

"Dated 癸酉年 Kwei-chow, Cycle year, 5th moon, 27th day, (1st August 1853.)"

Scale of Amoy Port Charges

1.—Vessels belonging to Lung-kee, Tung-an, Hai-Ching, Ma-siang-ting, Tsiu-kiang, Nan-an, Hui-an, leaving Amoy and loading beancake, oil, rice, &c., at Luk-chow, Tamsui, and Woo-tiaou-kiang, in "Formosa", and returning with that cargo to Amoy, for entering and leaving the port

To pay, if of 2 000 piculs and under 4 000 piculs, $60.

··· 1 000 ··· 2 000 ··· $30.

2.—Vessels from Lung-kee, Tung-an, Hai-ching, Ma-siang-ting, Tsin-kiang, Hui-an, Nan-an, taking in sugar and like produce, at Amoy, and going with it to Kin-chow and Kai-chow, in Tientsin, or to Keiou-chow, in Shantung, for every such voyage and back

To pay each such vessel $ 50.

3.—Vessels belonging to Lung-kee, Tung-an, Hai-ching, or Ma-siang-ting bound from Amoy to Taetsing, Wen-chow, Tai-chow, Ningpo, Shanghai, and returning to Amoy, for each such voyage, per ship $14.

4. —Vessels belonging to Lung-kee, Tung-an, Hai-ching, or Ma-siang-ting, bound from Amoy to any port of "Formosa", and thence trading to Kui-chow, Kai-chow, and Keaou-chow in Tientsin and Shantung, and returning to Amoy, for every such voyage, per ship $100.

5.—Ships from Tsin-keang, Nan-an, Hui-an and sailing from Amoy to "Formosa", and thence proceeding to Kin-chow, Kai-chow and Kiaou-chow, in Tientsin, and Shantung, and returning to Amoy, for every such voyage (inwards and outwards), $100.

6.—Ships from Yüne-siao, Chang-poo, and Shao-an, sailing out of port to "Formosa", and returning to Amoy with a cargo of beancake, oil and rice, for each such voyage (inwards and outwards), each ship $50.

7.—Ships from Yüne-siao, Changpoo, and Shao-an, sailing out of Amoy harbour, and returning to Amoy, with a cargo of foreign goods and sundries, from Shanghai, Cha-poo, Wan-chow, Tai-chow, or Chan-tou, Chang-lin, for each such voyage (outwards, and inwards) each ship $20.

8.—Vessels from Yüne-siao, Chang-poo, and Shao-an, with cargoes consisting of groceries, spices, salt and dried fish, salt pomfrets, sprats, &c., for entering and leaving the port, each vessel $10.

9.—Native Amoy boats, and those of neighbouring districts, trading to Fuchow, and returning hither by way of Ning-an, or Ning-teh, for each voyage or every boat, $10.

10.—Ships, such as the Fühwan, and Sanpwan vessels, from neighbouring provinces, or the Woo-tsaou junks, from Cha-poo, or the Teen-tsaou boats from Pang-hoo, in "Formosa", and all like out province vessels, for entering and leaving the harbour, each $20.

11.—Boats from Ho-koo, of the island Tung-shih, Pang-hoo, Tsen-kiang,

For entering and leaving the port, each boat $20.

12.—Coasting junks from Canton, and Chang-lin, laden with foreign cargo and miscellaneous goods, on every junk,

For entering and leaving the port $20.

13.—Junks engaged in Foreign commerce belonging to this port, as well as the Hung-t'ow-ling vessels (with red bows) by the old tariff taxed $1 000, afterwards reduced after the barbarian (夷) disturbances to the following scale, viz.:—

For vessels of 5 000 piculs and upwards $500.

less than 5 000 piculs $ 250.

14.—Natives of Amoy, engaging square rigged ships from Singapore, or other foreign places, to pay for entering and leaving the harbour, port dues on every ship, according to the following rate, viz.:—

For every 3 masted vessel (ship) $300.

...$2\frac{1}{2}$... (barque) $200.

厦出，由上海、乍浦、温州、台州、汕头、樟林载洋货返厦，出入口岸每船收二十元；

八、云霄、漳浦、诏安船只，载南货、香料、盐、咸鱼、咸鲳鱼、鲱鱼等货，出入口岸每船收十元；

九、厦门本地及周边船只，往福州，返程经闽安、宁德，出入口岸每船收十元；

十、邻省玉环、三盘等县船只，或乍浦乌艚、台澎尖艚，及所有外省船只，出入口岸每船收二十元；

十一、何厝、东石、澎湖、漳江出发船只，出入口岸每船收二十元；

十二、广州、樟林驳船载洋货及什货，出入口岸每船收二十元；

十三、厦门本港从事外贸船及红头艇船，旧税收一千元，后经番夷干涉调整如下：五千担及以上收五百元，以下则收二百五十元；

十四、厦门人租用新加坡或他国来船，出入口岸，以船级收费：三桅船三百元，二桅半二百元，二桅船一百五十元。

... 2... (brig or schooner) $150.

官军夺回厦门

厦门已被小刀会占领四个月，虽然外国人习惯一天到晚骑马、散步，但未受到骚扰或冒犯。9月9日，听闻官军较大规模的水陆部队将临，外国船只驶离港口，停留于鼓浪屿后中立且安全的某处。水陆官兵来得比原计划晚约三周，随即便是一连串骚扰性进攻。起义军主要在数百步距离处使用火绳枪，他们藏在路堤和岩石后，伤亡不多。官兵有舰上炮火的支援，白天的战斗优势在他们一方。到了晚上，双方例行退回营房睡大觉，都颇有风度，不搞夜袭、突袭等蛮夷一般的行为来占对方的便宜。9月12日，官军舰队起锚，陆军也向厦门进逼。风停潮退，船只只得抛锚，陆军惨败，部分营房落入小刀会之手。15日，官军水师提督率领七十艘船组成的船队，袭击十五至二十只船组成的起义军船队。这次袭击本应是很成功的，但当提督发起冲击时，只有三四艘船支援，其余的船罔顾他的行动信号，一炮未发。第二天，情况类似，后果也一样。战斗在陆

Recapture of Amoy by Imperialists

The rebels had now been in possession of the city for four months, and although foreigners were in the habit of riding, and walking, through it at all hours of the day, no case of molestation or insult had occurred. On the 9th September an intimation of the approach of a large squadron of Imperial junks, and of troops, was given, and foreign shipping moved out of the harbour, and took up a neutral and safe position, at the back of the island of Kulangsoo. After some three weeks' delay, the junks and troops arrived, and a series of harrassing attacks were commenced; the opposing forces chiefly using the matchlock, at some hundred paces, and being concealed behind embankments, rocks, &c., the casualties were few; but the Imperialists being assisted by the guns of their fleet, the balance of advantage of their daily fights, was theirs. At night each side retired with regularity to its quarter to enjoy the reasonable indulgence of a night's undisturbed repose, for there was an honorable abstention from night attacks, surprises, and such barbarian-like attempts to take a mean advantage of each other. On the 12th September, the fleet of the Imperialists got under weigh, and the army advanced on the city. The wind failing, and the tide receding, the junks had to drop anchor, and the troops met with a signal defeat, a portion of their camp falling into the hands of the Siau-tao-hui. On the 15th, the Imperialist Admiral got his whole fleet of some 70 sail, under weigh, to attack the rebel fleet of 15 or 20 vessels. The attack would no doubt have been successful, but on his bearing down on his enemy, he was only supported by three or four junks, the remainder, disregarding his signals to come into action, did not fire a single gun. A precisely similar attempt on the following day, was attended with a precisely similar result. Thus the combat continued on land, and water, with varied fortune, apparently, but in reality steady success to the Imperialists, who were persistently carrying out their favourite ponderous stratagem of wearying out, and disheartening, their enemy, by incessant menaces and petty attacks, until their confidence in themselves failed, and obedience to their leaders was lost, when, panic, disorganisation, and flight, being the result, the Imperialists would march on to, to themselves, a bloodless victory. On the 11th November, this end was gained. The previous night the fire on either side was heavier than usual, and at daybreak, the rebel junks were found warped out into the stream, and a cloud of small vessels, crowded with people, already underweigh. The large junks soon joined them, and stood up the river, the Imperial junks standing down to the anchorage off the town, passed them, and a few shots were exchanged. It appears that the rebel chiefs had, the previous evening, made preparations for abandoning the place, of which the Imperialists were aware, so the troops at daybreak marched on the city, when finding no opposition, they scaled the walls, and Amoy was once more in Imperial possession. The panic was terrible, hundreds were endeavouring to escape in all kinds of boats, some on rafts, some on boards, some even on doors, and numbers were attempting, and drowning in the attempt, to swim to the opposite island of Kulangsu. Hwang escaped in the fleet, and is, it is said, living at Saigon at the present time; his Admirals, Ma E and Wen-kuan, also effected their retreat, with the greater portion of the fighting men in the junks, abandoning the rest of their miserable dupes to merciless slaughter. And merciless it was. Men and boys, were

地和水上持续，表面上看似变幻莫测，实际上官军正取得稳步胜利。他们坚持运用己方所长的疲劳战术，通过不断的恐吓和零星袭击来激怒敌人，使对方对自己失去信心，不再听从长官，直至惊慌失措，毫无章法，最终仓皇出逃，官军则兵不血刃地取得胜利。11月11日，这个目标实现了。前一天晚上，双方的炮火异常猛烈，破晓时分，起义军的大船在江上互相拖曳着，一大片小船上全是人，已经起航。大船很快赶上它们，逆流而上。官军的船顺流而下到城外的锚地，超过了它们，双方开了几枪。看起来，起义军首领头天晚上已准备放弃这个地方，官军也知道，所以天亮开进城时，没遇到抵抗，便登上城墙，重新占据了厦门。城里的人惊恐万分，成百上千的人试图乘各式各样的船逃跑，有的乘小筏子，有的用木板，甚至是门板，有的试图游到对面的鼓浪屿，却不幸溺水。黄位乘坐快艇逃走，据说他目前住在西贡；他的将领马义、文观（音译）和船上的多数战士都撤离了，剩下的人只好任人宰割。何其残忍！男人和男孩，二十多人一批，被带到洋行对面的码头上斩首，有的斩到一半便被丢到泥泞中，任其徒劳地挣扎。官军觉得这样太乏味，于是用剑、砍刀、长矛和棍棒，像杀死老鼠一样成批地解决这些人。船上也发生着同样可怕的事情，港口满是被砍的、依然在挣扎的人，其中不少是只有十二岁的男孩。（这是一个目击者告诉我的。）这种穷凶极恶、毫无人性的行为从早上一直持续到下午三点。时任驻厦门领事、现为爵士的巴夏礼㊸不顾与海防厅的摩擦而进行干预，告诉官员，正如他先前曾乞求停止一样，他绝不允许大屠杀再继续下去了。他言辞激烈，加上“赫米斯”号和“比滕”号的撑腰，杀戮行为得到制止，肯定挽救了几百条性命；尽管第二天，血腥的杀戮仍在继续，只是地点选在了远离欧洲人房子和船舶的厦门西北部。

至于黄德美，原本他试图逃跑，但是他的亲属却把他扣留下来并交给了官府。可以想象得到，他只有死路一条。

太平军残部攻占漳州府

小刀会起义被镇压之后的第十一个年头，闽南又发生了第二次动乱，像一场疫

brought in batches of twenties, to the jetties next those opposite the foreign hongs, and decapitated, or half decapitated, and tumbled over into the mud; this process proving too tedious, they were attacked with swords, billhooks, spears and clubs, and destroyed like rats by the dozen. The same grisly work was going on in the junks, and the harbour was covered with chopped, slashed, and struggling human creatures, many of them boys of 12 years of age. (I have quoted from an eye witness.) This monstrous inhumanity had been going on from morning until three in the afternoon, when Mr., now Sir Harry, Parkes, Her Britannic Majesty's Consul, throwing to the winds the chafing fetters of that official Fêng-shuey, the responsibility of interference, told the officials, he had previously *begged* to desist, that he would not permit the carnage to go further. The stout words of the Christian gentleman, backed by the presence of H. M. S. *Hermes*, and *Bittern*, stopped the slaughter then, and must have saved the lives of hundreds, though on the following day the bloody work went briskly on, at the Northwest side of the city, away from European houses and shipping.

Regarding Ng-teck-be, he tried to escape, but his own relations detained, and delivered him over to the mandarins, to meet with such a death as may be imagined.

Capture of Chang-chou-fu by a Remnant of the T'ai-ping Rebels

Eleven years only, had elapsed since the suppression of the Dagger Society, when a second insurrection came, like a blight, upon this region. On the night of the 13th October, 1864, no one thought of disaster, on the morning of the 14th the passage boats from Chioh-bei (Shih-ma 石碼) brought in many wounded, men, women, and children, and the news that Chang-chou-fu 漳州府, a large walled city, distant 24 miles from Amoy, of 700 000 inhabitants, had been swept down upon, and captured, by a band of rebels, called indiscriminately Hung-t'ou-hui, and Chang-maos, (the Red headed, or Long haired rebels) who, came, no one knew whence, and of whose existence, in or about the province, no one had an idea. The rich city had fallen to a few men armed with gingalls, swords, pistols, and spears, only; little or no resistance had been offered, and the only casualty on the Imperialist side, was that of the Chên-tai, who had been shot in his chair; the Taotai, Sub-prefect, and Colonel commandant, escaped to the adjacent villages. The inhabitants, who were either unable, or unwilling, to quit their property, suffered severely, being slain by thousands, irrespective of sex or age, the city was fired in several places, and the atrocities of the Northern insurrection, re-enacted.

Day after day, came boatloads of wounded, mostly by the sword, many of whom had deep gaping wounds on the back of the neck (which, strange to say, even then, in spite of exposure and dirt, looked healthy, and were subsequently, in most instances, rapidly cured by Dr. Jones, in his Chinese hospital.) These men said they had been led to execution, but the executioners being boys, they had escaped with a wound, on receiving which, they had fainted, or simulated death, until in the darkness they had found an opportunity to creep away. Many of the wounded were Roman Catholic converts, and the Spanish priests,

病一样席卷了这个地区。1864年10月13日晚，没人料到会发生这场灾难，14日早上，从石码驶来的船上载满了受伤的男女和小孩。随即传来消息，漳州府，一座拥有高墙、距离厦门二十四英里、常住居民七十万人的城市，被一支起义军突袭并占领。这伙人被不加区分地称为“红头会”和“长毛”。他们来自何处，是省内的还是省外的，没有人知道。这座富庶的城市就这样落入了这一小撮装备着抬枪、剑、短枪和长矛的武装分子手中。官府几乎没有什么反抗，唯一的伤亡人员就是一名镇台，他被杀死在办公的府衙；而道台、知府和总兵都逃到邻近的村子里去了。无法或不愿放弃自己财产的百姓饱尝苦难，成千上万男女老少被杀害了。城里好几处地方被放了火，在厦门发生的残暴行径再次上演。

每天，都有载满伤者的船驶来，他们多是后颈处被剑所伤，伤口很深（奇怪的是，尽管伤口暴露而且肮脏，但看起来还不算太坏，而且这些人一般会很快被华人医院的琼斯医生给治好）。他们说自己曾被拉去处决，但刽子手是些孩子，刀砍下来时他们疼到昏倒，或是倒下装死，尽管受伤了，终归是躲过了一死。等天黑后，他们找机会爬出去。受伤的人多是天主教徒，西班牙神父即他们的牧师为了解决他们的燃眉之急，四处奔走，进行募捐；之后，带着一种单纯的奉献精神，他们急忙赶往漳州府附近去救助人，也可能与教众一同被杀，该行为将永远受到生活在此处的外国人的尊重。这个时候，一些吓人的谣言传了过来：漳州府南面六十英里的云霄县城被攻陷；一些人口众多的大村子被攻占；起义军逼近长泰，打算攻打泉州、厦门和福州；还说十六英里外的长泰的百姓，性情暴烈，一向出海为盗，这时收到漳州起义军的好处（据称是两千万元），愿意与对方结盟。这些谣言在当地人的心里引起了恐慌，没人谈论抵抗，倒是讨论起了逃跑；富人雇了船，准备随时跑路。可以确信的是，如果此时有两三百勇士突然攻城，这座城就会被攻破，因为城里三十五万居民几乎不会出手防卫的。面对紧急情况，统治者的孤立无援和摇摆不定，以及政府的名存实亡显而易见。官府的防御措施，是

their pastors, went round and raised a subscription for their immediate necessities, and then, with a simple devotion, for which they will always be honoured by foreigners here, hurried up to the vicinity of Chang-chou-fu, to succour and save, or perhaps perish with, their flocks. Meantime alarming rumours of the fall of the city of Yune-siaou, 60 miles to the south of Chang-chou-fu, of the capture of many large and populous villages, and of the intention of the rebels to march on Têng-hwa, and to attack, Chin-chew, Amoy, and Foochow, were received; and the people of Têng-hwa, 16 miles from here, always a turbulent piratical set, fired with the reported gains of the rebels at Chang-chou（$20 000 000 according to the rumours）, were said to be desirous of allying themselves with them. These rumours created amongst the Chinese population here, an utter panic, no one spoke of resistance, only how to get away, vessels were chartered by the wealthy, and arrangements made for instant flight. It is tolerably certain that, if at this time two or three hundred resolute men had made a dash at this city, it would have been carried, without scarcely a single blow being struck by its 350 000 inhabitants, in its defence. The helplessness, and infirmity of purpose of the rulers, and the utter worthlessness of their system, in face of an emergency, was painfully apparent. The defensive measures adopted, were the mustering of a few hundreds of militiamen, armed with rusty bills, tridents, matchlocks, flags, and other obsolete weapons; the subsidising of two or three neighbouring villages, with Taels 600, and the distribution of a mace a day, to each of the ruffians in the city, to keep quiet, who were then, as now, numerous and greatly feared.

Connection of Foreigners with Them

Their real reliance for the protection of the city, was on H. B. M. Surveying vessels *Swallow*, and *Dove*, which, happened to be in harbour. Foreigners had not been idle. Kulangsoo, and the settlement, were patrolled nightly, by volunteers and a hired patrol; and a small company of 25, or 30, men, had been formed out of the Customs employés, and drilled by the Commissioner, the present writer, and assistance had been written for to Hong Kong. It is to the great promptitude with which this appeal was responded to, by the instant despatch of H. B. M. Gunboats *Janus*, and *Flamer*, to the arrival of the *Bustard*, Lieut. John Tucker, from Foochow, who, on his own responsibility, brought his vessel here, on hearing that the city was menaced, and to the fortunate accidental arrival of H. B. M. S. *Pelorus*, 22 guns, that its safety may be attributed. This vessel, subsequently, by shelling the neighbouring turbulent and disaffected villages of Pan-t‘oo, 潘塗, Kwan-hsüne, 官潯, and Choo-t‘ou, 柏頭 for firing on her boats when searching for pirates, gave a great shock to the rebel cause. At the same time, 100 men of the Foochow Franco

召集几百名士兵，装配着生锈的长矛、叉子、火绳枪、旗帜和其他落伍的武器；给邻近两三个村发放六百两银子的补助，给城里的地痞每人每天发一钱银子，让他们维持秩序，他们一向人多势众，到处恐吓百姓。

与外国人的联系

真正可以为城市提供保护的，是刚好在海湾的勘探船“燕子”号和“鸽子”号。[44]外国人也没闲着，鼓浪屿等租界有志愿者和雇来的兵丁夜间巡逻。(二十五或三十个海关人员组成一小队)，接受税务司即笔者的训练。他们还写信向香港方面求助。后者迅速回应，立刻派遣炮舰“贾纳思”号和“弗拉默”号前去援助。约翰·塔克上尉听说漳州被威胁，出于责任，便将自己的船“巴斯塔德”号从福州开到厦门。并且，载有二十二门炮的“佩洛鲁斯”号也来了。正是它们确保了城市的安全。后来，“佩洛鲁斯”号在搜寻海盗的时候，被周围几个动荡不安且不友好的村子袭击，即潘涂、官浔和柏头，他们对此给予回击。同时，在福州海关税务司美理登的煽动下，福州将军命驻福州的中法混合军派出一百人，外加两门大炮，在德·默西上校带领下，登上武装的海关巡逻船“温德斯”号。这支队伍，外加之后的两支地面力量，本可以发挥不小的作用，不过却遭到妒忌，陷入阴谋之中，不得不在数周之后被遣回福州。

从台湾调来的部队在曾提督率领下，北面的部队在郭提督、王提督率领下，很快到达，并前往漳州附近。接下来便开始了一番漫长而乏味的三面围攻，双方围与被围、胜利与战败时常互换，从下面的话便可见一斑：“2月25日，大雾，两千名太平军袭击了丹州㊺(位于石码上方五英里)，但被曾提督、郭提督和王提督的军队击败，损失惨重。这次击退起义军的主要原因是丹州村民的正确判断，他们断了一座桥，导致起义军无处可逃。”据说，这次的战果包括捕获七十六名战俘，杀死二百五十四人，割掉二百三十一人的耳朵和辫子。需要说明的是，村民们的行为自始至终都与城里人形成鲜明对比；他们忠诚无比，愿意为贫穷的家园而战，并在

Chinese force, with two guns, under Colonel de Mercy, were sent down in the armed Customs cruiser, *Vindex*, by the Tartar General, at the instigation of the Baron de Meritens, Commissioner of Customs at Foochow. This force, afterwards supplied with two more field pieces, might have done good service, but its presence evoked nothing but intrigue and jealousy, and it had to be sent back to Foochow, in a few weeks.

Troops from “Formosa”, under the command of the Ti-tu, Tsên, and from the North, under the command of Ti-tu's Kwō, and Wang, also soon arrived, and were sent forward to the vicinity of Chang-chou; and now commenced a long and tedious investment of three sides of the city, during which the besiegers, were as frequently the besieged, varied by victories, or defeats, of which the following will serve as a fair specimen for all. “On the 25th February, during a fog, 2 000 rebels attacked Tang-chou, (5 miles above the city of Chioh-bei), but were repulsed with heavy loss, by the forces of Ti-tu's Tsên, Kwō and Wang. This repulse was greatly owing to the judgment of the Tang-chou villagers, in destroying a bridge, by which act, the rebels were caught as in a trap,” and 76 prisoners, 254 heads, and 231 ears, and queues, are reported to have been the fruits of this achievement. It should be stated that the conduct of the villagers throughout contrasted favourably with that of the dwellers in cities; they were loyal, willing to fight for their poor homesteads, and they displayed considerable intelligence in cutting up roads, opening sluices, destroying bridges, and in doing all in their power to embarrass the movements of the rebels. The rebels had with them at Chang-chou, some ten foreigners, at whose head was a Prussian, named Rhody, sometime a Colonel in the Imperial forces, under Gordon. This man succeeded in establishing communications with another Prussian, named Gerard, a storekeeper, and with another foreigner, a Swede, at Amoy, by whom he and his companions were visited, and supplied with whatever necessaries they required. These visits, although made clandestinely, were known to the authorities here, and were a cause of great disquiet, particularly as several foreigners had lately joined the rebels, and amongst them a Customs tidewaiter, named Patrick Shiel, formerly a plumber at Hong Kong, who was engaged to make shells. This man afterwards perished miserably, as did most of his companions, victims to the suspicions of their employers. In order to put a stop to these visits, and to prevent some sixty Shanghai, and Ningpo, foreign roughs, attracted here by the rebels, from joining them, the Customs lorcha, *Kiang Hoo*, was stationed at a narrow part of the river leading to Chang-chou fu, called Tin-tou, and armed junks were placed at the entrance of the Pechuiya a river, and at other points, leading in the same direction. These measures were successful, and it was no longer found possible to pass the Imperial lines, by donning some article of naval uniform, or by flying the Union Jack, or Naval Reserve ensign, (these flags were taken from

破坏道路、开挖水渠、毁坏桥梁中表现机警，竭尽全力给太平军制造麻烦。在漳州有约十个外国人投奔了太平军，为首的是一个普鲁士人，名叫罗第，他曾于戈登手下任常胜军将领。他成功地与另外一个来自普鲁士的名叫杰拉德的店主，还有一个在厦门的瑞典人取得联系。罗第及其伙伴见了这两人，并得到了他们提供的各种必需品。虽然这些会面是秘密进行的，但还是被当局发现，并引起了当局的忧虑。尤其是近来有几个外国人加入了太平军，包括一个名叫帕特里克·希尔的海关稽查员，他之前在香港做管道工，现在为太平军制作炮弹。这个人后来死得很惨，就像他的多数同伴一样，成了多疑的雇主的牺牲品。为了阻止他们往来，防止另外约六十名来自上海、宁波的外国暴徒被太平军吸引并加入其中，海关三桅帆船“江河”号被派去，停在通往漳州府的一个名叫亭头的狭窄河口处，一些武装船只则停在白水营河口处，还有些船停在通往漳州府方向的其他位置。这些措施很成功，不再发现有人穿着海军制服，或挥舞着英国国旗或者海军预备队旗帜（这些旗帜是2月25日太平军袭击丹州时从外国船上拿来的），越过官府设置的封锁线。

停在白水营的船首先捕获了三个美国人（其中一个是已故清朝副将华尔的侄儿），以及一个太平军军官。他们是晚上被抓的，当时他们坐在一艘狭窄的舢板上，里面放着武器和太平军的旗帜。一场剧烈的打斗之后，两名官兵受了伤。笔者当时刚从漳州府城墙前的清军大营拜访出来，回到石码。晚上十一点时，笔者听说这些人被带到了石码，担心他们会有生命危险，于是便写了一封信给曾道台。幸运的是，笔者与曾道台相熟，便在信中连忙请求他不要伤害这些人，并且请求参加审讯。这些请求得到了应允。第二天，这些人在石码衙门受审。首先受审的是太平军军官，他跪着，沉着地供认自己的罪行。他知道每条罪状都足以判他死刑，但他静静地嚼着甘蔗和糕点，有趣的是，这些是道台亲手从案桌上拿给他的。随后，这几个外国人被挨个审问，他们的供词被记录下来，然后几个人一起过堂。其中两个人的举止极为傲慢，他们的串通行为非常明显，供词也漏洞百出，道台好几次在案桌

foreign boats, which accompanied a rebel attack on Tang-pu, on the 25th February.）

One of the first captures made, was by the junks stationed at Pechuiya of three Americans, （one being nephew of the late Imperialists General, Ward,） and a Chinese rebel officer. They were taken at night in a sampan, in which were arms, and a rebel flag, after a sharp tussle, in which two Chinese soldiers were wounded. The present writer had just returned to Chioh-bei, from a visit to the Imperial camp, before the walls of Chang-chou-fu, when, at 11 o'clock P.M., hearing that these men had been brought to Chioh-bei, and fearing that their lives might be in danger, he caused a letter to be written to the Tao-t'ai Tsêng, with whom, fortunately, he was intimate, urgently requesting that they should not be injured, and that he might be allowed to be present at their examination. These requests were complied with, and on the following day, the men were examined at the magistrate's Yamên, at Chioh-bei; the rebel officer, first, who crouching on his knees, coolly told his story making admissions, each of which, he must have known, would consign him to certain death, and quietly munching sugarcane, and cakes, which the Tao-t'ai, himself, strangely enough, handed him from our table. The foreigners were next separately interrogated, their statements taken down in writing, and they were then questioned together. The behaviour of two of them, was so insufferably insolent, their complicity so apparent, and the falsehood of their statements, so gross, that the Tao-t'ai, touching the writer's knee several times beneath the table, made a short sharp significant chop with his hand. At last, at one outrageously mendacious and insolent statement, he sprung up saying: "If these men's ears can hear what their mouth say, they must know themselves to be liars," and again he made the significant gesture. The writer, thoroughly alarmed, then warned the men that he had come there to endeavour to aid them, but that, beyond persuasion, he was as powerless as themselves, and that an order given to the soldiers and Yamên runners, thronging the room, would be executed before human aid could reach them, and earnestly cautioned them against the folly and danger of their behaviour. This speech had its effect on all, but particularly on young Ward, who shed tears, and acknowledged that they were, when seized, en route to join the rebels, &c., &c., and who then pleaded earnestly not to be left in the Yamên. The writer succeeded in taking this man away with him, and in obtaining a promise that no injury should be done to the other two. The three men were afterwards sent to the United States Consul General at Shanghai, to be dealt with.

On the 13th February, just four months after the occupation of the city, an official party, with whom was the man Gerard, before mentioned, left in the gunboat Flamer, to visit Chang-chou-fu. They were well received by the rebels, and returned on the 15th bringing with them a rebel officer, who remained on board the *Pelorus* until the 19th, to the great consternation of the Chinese, who thought they saw in this, an intention on the part of

下拍了拍笔者的膝盖，并且比画了一个简洁明了的标志性的砍头手势。终于，当听到两人的一个令人无法忍受的虚假而傲慢的说法时，他一跃而起：“如果这些人的耳朵听到自己的嘴巴说了什么，一定也知道自己是个骗子。”说着，他再次做了那个标志性的手势。笔者也被彻底激怒了，警告这两人自己是来帮助他们的，但现在无法说服道台，他也就无能为力了；并且，道台给聚集在房间里的士兵和衙门听差下了命令，为防止有人解救这些人，先杀掉他们了事。笔者又真诚地告诫这些人别再做愚蠢和危险的行为了。这番话对所有人都起了作用，尤其是对华尔的侄儿，他哭着承认被抓时他们正想投奔太平军等等，并真诚地哀求把他放出去。笔者成功地将他带走，并获得了不伤害另两个人的承诺。之后这三人被送到美国驻上海总领事馆，交由他们发落。

2月13日，就在漳州城被占四个月之后，一个正式的团体，包括上文提过的杰拉德乘“弗拉默”号到访漳州。他们受到太平军的热情接待，15日返回时还有一个太平军军官同行，他在“佩洛鲁斯”号一直待到19日。这让中国人非常惊惶，他们由此认为英国政府打算支持太平军。当地的一位士绅发现，此人是他在香港时为他抬轿子的苦力；19日，当他被送回“弗拉默”号后，当地人揪起的心才放下来。有必要在此简要提及，就在此后不久，当杰拉德离开同伴，独自来到漳州时，被太平军在城门下残忍地杀害了。

1865年1月14日，傍晚六点左右，一个海关通事注意到，海关楼里的仆人们异常兴奋。询问之后，才知道原来是来了个外表光鲜的老人，他自称陈金龙，带着一封其结拜兄弟，即驻扎在漳州的太平军侍王李世贤给“海关”的信。英国领事和海关税务司都被称作“海关”，他错把海关楼当作了领事馆。通事没有告诉他真相，而是同平时对待有文化的中国人一样，按照礼节接待他，最后还邀请他在厦门城中的家里共进晚餐。这个老掉牙的诱饵，就像是英国乡巴佬受邀玩九柱游戏或者纸牌游戏一样，难以拒绝。陈金龙接受了邀请，半个小时后，他走到道台衙门去送死了。很快，道台把海防厅召集起来，经过简单调查之后，陈金龙连夜被斩了头。

the British government, to espouse the rebel cause. However when this man, recognised by a gentlemen here as his former chair coolie at Hongkong, was sent back in the *Flamer*, on the 19th, the feeling of disquiet abated. As Gerard's name will not be mentioned again, it maybe well to state that shortly after this, when visiting Chang-chou by himself, he was, after leaving his countrymen in their employ, cruelly put to death by the rebels at one of the city gates.

About 6 o'clock on the evening of the 14th January 1865, a linguist, residing at the Custom House, noticed great excitement amongst the servants attached to the building. On enquiry he found it caused by the presence of a fine looking old man, who said he was one Chên-chin-lung, bearer of a letter from his brother by adoption Li-sze-hsün, the Tze-wang, or rebel king at Chang-chou-fu, to the Haikuan at Amoy. Her Britannic Majesty's Consul, and the Commissioner of Customs, are both called Haikuan, by the common classes, and he had mistaken the Custom House, for the residence of the Consul. The linguist did not undeceive him, but offered him all those little courtesies, usual to educated Chinese life, and ended by inviting him to dinner at his house in the city. The old, old, decoy, which like the invitation to skittles, or cards, to the British yokel, seems irresistible. The invitation was accepted, and half an hour afterwards, Chên, was walking to the Taotai's Yámên, to meet his fate. It was soon decided; the Hai-fang-ting （local magistrate） was summoned, and after a brief examination, Chên was decapitated, by torchlight.

Burgevine

On the 13th May 1865, an American named Burgevine, formerly in command of the Imperial disciplined Chinese troops at Shanghai, and subsequently a leader of rebels at Soochow, arrived in the *General Sherman*. As this person had been deported some three months previously by the United States Consul General at Shanghai, and as his object in coming to Amoy was sufficiently apparent, application was made to the United States Consul here, Mr. Irwin, for his arrest; and the Consul issued a warrant for the apprehension of any suspicious person, claiming to be a citizen of the United States. This warrant was taken to the *General Sherman*, where there is reason to believe Burgevine was at the time. But the master of the vessel refused to allow search to be made. A search warrant was then applied for, this, the Consul for sufficient reasons no doubt, did not see fit to grant, and Burgevine, unfortunately for himself, remained unarrested. On the 14th it was known that Burgevine, and one or two other foreigners, had made arrangements to join the rebels at Chang-chou-fu, and orders were issued to the officers in command of the vessels stationed for the purpose of preventing supplies, and persons, reaching the rebel city, to keep a strict watch, and to examine every sampan that attempted to pass up the river; the result was that during the same night Burgevine, and an Englishman, named Crane, were found concealed under the bottom boards of a large native boat, and handed over to the safe keeping of the Commander-in-chief of the Chinese forces, Kwo-sung-ling, who had been directed, in the event of any foreigners being captured, to have them well treated, in addition to which, an European had been ordered to see that they were prop-

白齐文

1865年5月13日，一个名叫白齐文[46]的美国人乘坐“舍曼将军”号来到厦门。此人之前是驻扎在上海的清朝常胜军统领，后来成了苏州太平军首领。由于他大约三个月前被美国驻上海总领事驱逐，以及他来厦门的目的再明显不过，美国驻厦门领事欧文接到逮捕他的请求。随后，领事颁布了一道通缉令，抓捕任何声称自己是美国公民的可疑人员。当通缉令传到“舍曼将军”号时，有理由相信，白齐文当时就在船上。但是，船主拒绝搜查。于是又申请了搜查令，领事却认为有充分理由不适合颁发，所以还是没抓到齐白文。到了14日，才知道白齐文和另外一两个外国人已准备加入漳州府的太平军。负责阻止物资和人员到达太平军占据的漳州的官员，受命要严密监视，检查每一艘试图驶向九龙江的舢板。当天夜里，白齐文和一个名叫克兰的英国人被发现藏在一艘本地大船的舱底。他们被移交给总兵郭松林看管。郭松林接到命令，要善待抓到的外国人；此外，还有个欧洲人奉命前来，看抓到的外国人是否受到妥当安置和照顾。这两人后来被移交给厦门的道台。听说他们要来，海关代理税务司波特半夜到道台家等着，请求将这两人移交给其各自国家的领事馆。对此，道台说他恕不能从命，他接到的指令是将人转交给福州的总督。次日清晨，代理税务司听说两人确已离开厦门，就通知了英国和美国领事馆。与此同时，一个应该是“舍曼将军”号的船主和白齐文朋友的人，召集了二十来个暴民，赶到海防厅衙门，他们认为白齐文被关在那里，决心救出他。实际上白齐文并没有关押在此，这里关的是一个叫约翰逊的人，此人自称是美国人，大家强行把他救了出来。后来，白齐文在去福州的路上翻船溺亡的事，住在中国的多数外国人还记忆犹新。

官军夺回漳州府

在此期间，对漳州的封锁越加紧密。太平军发现无法维持下去，于是准备撤离漳州。5月14日晚，他们从东门撤离。然而直到17日，官兵才占领这里。15日和16日，太平军留下小部分人，在城东继续进

erly lodged and cared for. The two men were forwarded to the Taotai of Amoy. On hearing of their arrival, the Acting Commissioner of Customs, Mr. Porter, waited on the Taotai at midnight, and begged him to hand them over to their respective Consuls. To this he replied that he could not accede, his instructions being to forward them to the Viceroy at Foochow. Early next morning, the Acting Commissioner, hearing that they had actually left Amoy, communicated the fact to the British, and American, Consuls. In the mean time, a man supposed to be the owner of the *General Sherman*, and a friend of Burgevine, collected about twenty roughs, and proceeded to the Hai-fang-ting's Yamên, where Burgevine was supposed to be confined, fully determined to release him. Burgevine, as has been shewn, was not there, but another prisoner named Johnson, who stated that he was an American, was forcibly released. The subsequent death of Burgevine, by the capsizing of a boat, when *en route* to Foochow, will be fresh in the recollection of most residents in China.

Recapture of Chang-chou-fu by Imperialists

Meanwhile the investment of the city, had been growing steadily closer and closer; and the rebels finding it no longer tenable, made their preparations to evacuate it, which they did, on the night of the 14th May, by the East Gate. It was not, however, occupied by the Imperial troops, until the 17th, the rebels having left a small force to cover and conceal the retreat of the main body, by keeping up the usual skirmishing to the eastward of the city, on the 15th, and 16th. With the suppression, or, more properly speaking, the dissolution of the rebel movement at Ch'ang-chou-fu, the long chapter of bloodshed, in this department of the empire, for the present, closes.

行寻常的小规模战斗，掩护主力撤退。随着漳州的太平军被镇压，或者更确切地说，其在漳州的活动被彻底瓦解，大清帝国这一地区漫长而血腥的篇章才暂告一段落。

【注 释】

① 应为1279年。——译者注

② 应为1387年。——译者注

③ 洪武二年即1369年，朱元璋下令编纂《皇明祖训》，初名《祖训录》，宣布将朝鲜、日本等15个海外国家列为“不征之国”。见《明史·外国三·日本》：“后著《祖训》，列不征之国十五，日本与焉。”这15个国家是：朝鲜国、日本国、大琉球国、小琉球国、安南国、真腊国、暹罗国、占城国、苏门答腊国、西洋国、瓜哇国、湓亨国、白花国、三佛齐国、渤泥国。——译者注

④ 应为1405年。见《明史·外国三·日本》：“王发兵尽歼其众，絷其魁二十人，以三年十一月献于朝，且修贡。”永乐三年即1405年。——译者注

⑤ 刘荣，邳州宿迁人（今江苏省宿迁市），因替父参军而冒父名刘江。后来立功授广宁伯，才改用原名刘荣。另外，望海埚之战的时间为1419年。——译者注

⑥ 应为1439—1443年。——译者注

⑦ 《明史·外国三·日本》：“先是洪熙时，黄岩民周来保、龙岩民钟普福困于徭役，叛入倭。倭每来寇，为之乡导。”——译者注

⑧ 应为1553年。据《明史》载，此事发生于嘉靖三十二年，即1553年。——译者注

⑨ 原文“Chê river”直译为“浙江”，实际指钱塘江。作为浙江境内最大的河流，钱塘江因江流曲折而被称为“之江”“折江”，又称“浙江”。省以江名，简称“浙”。——译者注

⑩ 应为1555年。据《明史》载，此事发生于嘉靖三十四年，即1555年。——译者注

⑪ 摘自《海国图志》，这是一本中国地图集，内有对外国的简要描述。——原注

⑫ 应为1573—1620年。——译者注

⑬ 摘自《中国丛报》（*Chinese Repository*），第6卷，第584页。——原注

⑭ 此时，荷兰舰队指挥官为雷尔生，“Keizerroon”似为其荷兰语名称。——译者注

⑮ 即大员港（今台南安平区）。——译者注

⑯ 这个村子名叫石井村，在崎髻山的山脚下。——原注

⑰ 纽荷夫（John Nieuhoff，1618—1672），荷兰画家，曾为绘图员兼水手，1688年随荷兰东印度公司委派的使节到访中国，并到北京拜访皇帝，商谈同清朝间的贸易。他曾把在华见闻辑录成《荷使初访中国记》一书。——译者注

⑱ 杜赫德（Jean-Baptiste du Halde，1674—1743），法国耶稣会士，汉学家，历史学家。他没来过中国，但基于大量材料编辑而成的《中华帝国全志》影响很大。该书1738年被译为英文，其代表了当时入华耶稣会士对中国认识的整体水平。——译者注

⑲ 国姓爷姓郑，当地方言读作“Tin”或者“Teng”。他本名“森”，明朝最后一任皇帝（实为明隆武帝——译者注）为他赐名“成功”。承蒙皇帝的恩宠，赐予他国姓。因此，他以“郑国姓”的名字为人所知，人们称他为“国姓爷”。其家乡人以及同安和南安的百姓仍对“郑国姓”引以为豪，并十分敬爱。——原注

⑳ 海澄镇，福建历史上四大商港之一，位于今龙海市海澄镇西南九龙江下游江海汇合处。从海澄镇顺九龙江而下至海门岛的这段河道，其形如月，又称月港。——译者注

㉑ 从元代开始的官修地理志中，“江南”一词被用于行政区划，清代初期江南省即如今苏南和皖南的统称。此后，广义的江南包括了上海、江西、湖南、浙江全境，以及江苏、安徽、湖北三省的长江以南地区；狭义的江南多指的是长江中下游平原的南岸地区。——译者注

㉒ 1英里约等于1 609米。——译者注

㉓ 雅加达的旧称，为当时荷兰东印度公司总部所在地。——译者注

㉔ 范堡（Antonius Hambroek），荷兰早期来台的新教传教士。1648年抵台，

曾以当地土语重译了《马太福音》和《约翰福音》。——译者注

㉕ 温世缪（Arnoldus A. Winsemius），荷兰传教士，其到台湾传教的时间大概在1655—1662年。——译者注

㉖ 李率泰（1608—1666），顺治十三年（1656），任闽浙总督。两年后，闽浙总督分设为二，李率泰任福建总督，驻守福州。不久，郑成功率部袭扰福州，李派兵焚烧其兵舰一千多艘，将郑所部赶走。康熙元年（1662），郑成功去世，其子郑经继位，坚持抗清。康熙三年（1664）李率泰降服郑经手下大将，并向郑的部队发起攻击，大获全胜；李率泰因功，加秩一品。两年后，李率泰卒于任上。——译者注

㉗ 揆一于1662年因被郑成功军队包围而投降离台。后被审判，判处终身监禁，软禁于班达群岛。服刑十多年后，因家人付款而被保释，1674年在威廉亲王特赦下回到荷兰。——译者注

㉘ 据其他文献记载，荷兰人直到1668年，才放弃对位于台湾北端的基隆的控制。——原注

㉙ 郑成功收复台湾后，将其改名为“安平城”。——译者注

㉚ 郑经（1642—1681），一名郑锦，字贤之、元之，号式天，福建省泉州府南安县石井镇人。郑成功长子，台湾明郑时期的统治者，袭封其父延平王的爵位。其任内，台湾境内曾大治。但后来纵情酒色，怠闻军政，康熙二十年（1681），郑经去世，谥号文王。——译者注

㉛ 姚启圣（1624—1683），浙江会稽（今浙江绍兴）人。康熙二年（1663），因擅自开放海禁被弹劾罢官。康熙十三年（1674），靖南王耿精忠举兵叛乱，康熙皇帝命康亲王爱新觉罗·杰书率兵讨伐，姚启圣捐资募壮兵，受康熙皇帝下诏嘉奖，晋升福建总督。康熙二十二年（1683），施琅取澎湖，姚启圣为其筹措粮饷不遗余力，立下大功。同年十一月病故。在任福建总督期间，姚启圣最大限度地恢复因连年征战、清廷“迁界禁海”政策而遭受严重破坏的当地经济，保护了百姓的利益。——译者注

㉜ 卫三畏：《中国总论》，第529页。——原注

㉝ 郭富（Hugh Gough，1779—1869），一译卧乌古，枢密院成员。第一次鸦片战争时指挥英军进攻中国。1843年任驻印英军司令。1849年加封为子爵。1862年晋升为陆军元帅。香港的郭富街、郭富山道和郭富山里均以他命

名。——译者注

㉞ 1英寸约等于0.025 4米。——译者注

㉟ 江继芸（1788—1841），海坛候均区（今福建平潭潭城镇）人，清朝爱国将领。年轻时加入清军水师，后升任金门镇总兵，有“福建抗英第一人”之称。1841年，在第一次鸦片战争厦门保卫战中，江继芸指挥守军与英军浴血奋战，终因官兵伤亡殆尽，后援不继，壮烈殉国。——译者注

㊱ 应为1623年。——译者注

㊲ 此种行为只是为挑起战争而找的借口。——译者注

㊳ 文翰爵士（Sir Samuel George Bonham，1803—1863），英国东印度公司及殖民地官员，第四任海峡殖民地总督，1848—1854年间出任第三任香港总督，并兼任驻华全权公使及驻华商务总监、香港岛海军中将，全面管理对华的外交及贸易事务。——译者注

㊴ 张熙宇（1783—1853），四川峨眉人。历任广东多地知县，广西南宁知府；任福建兴泉永兵备道六日后，捕获小刀会首领陈庆真，即刻处死。后任甘肃署按察使、安徽署按察使。咸丰三年（1853），太平军攻入安庆，张熙宇奉命率军抵御，全军覆没，见大势已去拔刀自刎未果，被清廷以罪处死。——译者注

㊵ 根据何丙仲先生的提示，从杜文凯编《清代西人见闻录》（中国人民大学出版社1985年版）所收佐佐木正哉《咸丰三年厦门小刀会叛乱》中，照录此文献。——译者注

㊶ 原文作“5th moon”，即五月，应有误。——译者注

㊷ 锦州与盖州均为辽宁所属地区，位于渤海湾旁，不属于天津。——译者注

㊸ 巴夏礼（Sir Harry Smith Parkes，1828—1885），英国外交家，主要在中国和日本工作。1841年10月抵达澳门，拟任英国驻华全权公使与商务参赞的翻译、秘书。1842年开始，巴夏礼分别在舟山、福州、厦门、上海和广州担任翻译一职。1851—1854年，任驻广州和厦门领事，再次与钦差大臣、两广总督叶名琛打交道。1856年10月，英船“亚罗”号进入珠江后被清水军官员登上，巴夏礼以英国国旗被降下为由，对时任两广总督叶名琛表示抗议。双方爆发冲突，战事持续较长时间。1860年8月，英军突袭大沽炮台，巴夏礼不

久被清军俘虏。英法联军迅速兵临北京城下，皇帝和嫔妃仓皇出逃；圆明园落入联军之手，惨遭劫掠。

1861年1月，巴夏礼回到广州任原职。2—4月，在镇江、九江和汉口设立领事馆。1865年，被任命为英国驻日全权公使与领事，并任该职位长达18年。1883—1884年间任驻韩大臣。1885年3月因疟疾发热病逝。

㊹ 此处作者在为英国船舰的行为开脱，其做法实际上是在干涉中国内政，而不是保护城市安全。——译者注

㊺ 可能是如今位于漳州市龙海区颜厝镇的丹州村。——译者注

㊻ 白齐文（H. A. Burgevine，1836—1865），或译白聚文，美国人。他24岁成为常胜军统领，活跃于晚清战场，曾组织洋枪队镇压太平天国，后投奔太平军，对抗清政府。后被清廷拘捕于厦门，押往苏州途中被李鸿章下令溺杀，时年29岁。——译者注

第二部分

PART Ⅱ

厦　门

厦门，位于北纬24°28′，东经118°4′，坐落于一个方圆约25英里的人口稠密的岛上，属福建省管辖。该城只是个三流城市，但由于其作为贸易港口的重要性，却是道台所在地。道台是兴化府、泉州府、永春州的地方官。厦门隶属于泉州府同安县，位于九龙江口厦门岛的西南部，九龙江一直通往漳州府。走海路的话，就要穿过鳿屿和青屿之间（此处水深达11～14英寻①），这两个岛是六岛中的两个。一进入海湾或外港，扑面而来的是旖旎的风光，两边是连绵起伏、满是石头的荒芜山丘，呈灰色或棕色。其中的一座山是南太武，山上矗立着一座宝

Amoy

Hsia men 廈門（the Gate, Harbour of Hsia） or the Port of Amoy, is situated in Lat. 24°28′ N. Long 118°4′ E. on a thickly inhabited island about twenty-five miles in circumference, and of the same name, appertaining to Fuch'ien province. The city is of the third class only, but on account of the importance of the trade of the port, is the residence of a Taotai, who is Intendent of the circuit of Hsing-hua fu （興化府）, Ch'uan Chou fu （泉州府） and Yung ch'un chou （永春州）. It is in the district of Tung an, （同安縣） belonging to the department of Ch'üan chou fu, and is situated on the south western corner of the Island of Amoy at the mouth of the Dragon river, leading to the city of Chang chou fu （漳州府）. The approach from sea is between the Chih hsü（鳿嶼）and Ching hsü（青嶼）Islands, （in which passage there are from 11 to 14 fathoms of water）, two of a group called the Six Islands. On entering the bay or outer harbour, the scenery is picturesque and striking, ranges of savage grey, and brown barren, rocky hills and mountains rise on either side. One, the Nan t'ai wu（南泰武）, surmounted by a Pagoda, towers 1 720 feet in the clear blue sky. A ruined fort, and a long line of stone fortifications stretch away to the right; to the left are a pagoda topped Island and chain of hills, and in front the Island of Kulangsu, and the inner harbour, which is set, a sparkling gem, in a back ground of range upon range of the grey, brown, or misty blue, mountains, of the mainland. The inner harbour extends from a rock, called the Cornwallis Stone, on the S.E. at Hsia mên Chiang（廈門港 A mng kang Native dialect）, along the N.E. face of the city until it joins a large estuary running some four miles into the island and skirting the northern side of the city, which, consisting of a citadel and a city, lies on a neck of land with one-third of its circuit protected by fortified walls. The city is about eight miles in circumference, including the outer town, and the North eastern environs; it contains about 350 000 inhabitants. The outer town is called in the native dialect A mng kang（廈門港）and is separated from the city by a chain of rocks having a fortified wall along their summit, a paved pass connecting the two. Rugged and brown hills of barren rock, of from five to seven hundred feet in height skirt the city; and the dwellings and warehouses of the inhabitants are built in the valley.

Amoy was once exceedingly well fortified, as may be seen by the vestiges of batteries on the Islands of Wu su, and Ch'ing su, at

塔，高1 720英尺，耸入云天。一座废弃的炮台和一长排石砌防御工事一直延伸到右边；左边则是岛的最高处即宝塔和一排山丘；山的前面是鼓浪屿，以及犹如一颗闪耀宝石的内港，依托着大陆或灰色或棕色或雾蓝色的连绵群山。内港沿着厦门港东南方的一块称为白石的岩石伸展开来，到了城东北方向，与环绕城北边缘、流入岛内的长约4英里的河流相连；城北包括一座要塞和城区，坐落于一片狭长地带，其四周的三分之一都建有加固的城墙。厦门城周围约8英里，包括外城和东北面的近郊，人口约35万。外城被当地人称为厦门港，被一排排岩石隔开，岩石顶端建有加固的城墙；内外城之间，由一条铺设的小路相连。凹凸不平、光秃秃的棕色石头山，环绕着城边，高达500～700英尺；居民的住处和店铺建在地势较低的位置。

厦门曾经防卫极好，这从位于外港入口处的浯屿、青屿上面的炮台遗迹，鼓浪屿上的“红角”（Red Point）炮台（曾经架着42门大炮）和“白角”（White Fort）炮台，以及厦门港长达1 100码[②]、架设过96

门大炮的石壁炮台遗迹，便可见一斑，尽管遗留下来的大炮、炮眼甚至城墙都已经斑驳不堪，并将很快消失在沙堆里。城北的要塞周长约$1\frac{1}{3}$英里，鸟瞰城内，周围是带塔楼的城墙，高18～33英尺不等。要想了解当时海防炮台和防御工事的情况，也许从1841年英军侵略厦门时，麦克弗森的描述中可以找到线索："防御工事看起来范围广、力度强。厦门港炮弹射程内的每处，都派人值守，大力设防。从进入内港开始，海岸上排开的防线是一排排不间断的花岗岩炮台，延绵一英里。炮台外面覆盖着厚达几英尺的草皮和泥巴，从远处看，无法发现这些防御工事的踪迹。炮眼也是隐蔽的，石墙外盖着厚厚的草皮，用来掩护操作大炮的人。"[③]他称，英国军舰对着这众多的炮台连续开炮4个小时，一刻不停；单"伯兰汉"号和"威里士厘"号就各自发射12 000发炮弹，而这些防御工事依然完好无损。然而当英军攻击并占领炮台时，发现这些炮台连同500门大炮，已经被尽可能地毁坏而无法使用了。

外港为由于逆风不能航行或即将离港的船只提供了安全又宽敞的锚地，但对于

the entrance of the outer harbour; on Kulangsu, at Red Point (once mounting 42 guns), and at the White Fort; and from the strength and magnitude of the long line of sea batteries at A mng kang, 1 100 yards in length, and once mounting 96 guns, yet remaining, though denuded of their guns, and with embrasures, and even walls, fast disappearing under mounds of sand. The citadel, which is about a mile and a third in circumference, commands the inner town, and is surrounded by a turreted wall varying in height from eighteen to thirty-three feet. What the sea batteries and fortifications once were, may be gathered from Mr. McPherson's description of them at the time of the British attack in 1841. "The defences appeared to be of vast extent and strength; every spot from whence guns could bear on the harbour was occupied and strongly armed. From the point of entrance into the inner harbour, the great sea lines of defence extended in one continued battery of granite upwards of a mile. This battery was faced with turf and mud several feet in thickness, so that at a distance no appearance of a fortification could be traced. The embrasures were roofed and the slabs thickly covered with turf so as to protect the men while working the guns." And he states, that, for four hours the ships cannonaded these enormous batteries without a moment's cessation, the *Blenheim* and *Wellesley* alone firing upwards of 12 000 rounds each, and yet that the works were as perfect when they left off as when they began. The troops, however, assaulted and carried the batteries, when they, together with 500 guns, were rendered so far as then possible, unserviceable.

The outer harbour, affords a safe and commodious anchorage for ships windbound, or on the point of departure, but it is too distant for the shipment or discharge of cargo. The inner harbour, is capable of affording secure anchorage, within a short distance of the beach, to about 100 vessels. The hidden dangers, the Coker, Brown, and Harbour rocks, and Kellett spit are marked by five buoys, and the position of other rocks, by stone beacons and perches.

The rise and fall of the tide, is from 14 to 19 feet. The western boundary of the harbour, is formed by the island of Kulangsu, the channel being 675 to 840 yards wide. This island is about four miles in circumference, has two distinct ridges upon it, and is composed chiefly of granite and disintegrated granite. Its highest point is 280 feet above the sea, and it has detached rocks lying off nearly all its circuit. It is dotted about on all its best sites with handsome houses, the private residences of the Merchants, Missionaries and Officials worth, perhaps, in the aggregate $150 000. It contains four Chinese hamlets, and has an increasing population of probably 4 000 or 5 000 souls.

After the capture of Amoy in 1841, a garrison of detachments from the 18th and 26th regiments, and the Madras Artillery, occupied this island, until it was restored to the Chinese in December, 1845. They were encamped on its northern extremity in a hollow, shut out by high hills from the south west breeze, and facing a large bay, which, at low water, becomes a muddy flat. At one time the mortality amongst the troops from these

装船和卸货来说又太远了。内港可以为约100艘船只提供安全的锚地，离岸又近。长羊礁、户定内礁、港口礁及尾涂礁等隐患用5个浮标来标记，其他礁石的位置用石头灯塔和标杆来标记。

厦门的涨潮和退潮落差可达14～19英尺。港口西面是鼓浪屿，海峡宽675～840码。鼓浪屿周长约4英里，岛上有2条明显的山脉，主要由花岗岩和风化的花岗石构成。岛上的最高点高出海平面280英尺，到处是些凸起的石头。岛上最好的地方几乎布满了漂亮房子，那是些商人、传教士、达官贵人的私人住宅，总值可能达到15万元。岛上有4个小村庄，人口增加到四五千人。

1841年英军侵占厦门后，其第十八团、第二十六团和马德拉斯炮兵部队派遣兵力占据了鼓浪屿，直到1845年12月才归还中国。英军在鼓浪屿北面尽头的一片洼地扎营，高高的山丘阻挡了西南风，其对面是个大海湾，海水浅时，会变成一块泥地。英军一度出于这些原因而病死率太高，以至于要雇用中国人看守军需品仓库。英军撤退之后，他们占用的房子被推倒，他们修的路被破坏，英军存在过的所有痕迹被尽可能抹去。在岛的东北面尽头，有3块古老的墓碑，上面刻着铭文：

长眠于此的是约翰·杜菲尔德，“特朗布尔”号指挥官亨利·杜菲尔德之子，卒于1698年9月6日。

长眠于此的是斯蒂芬·贝克上尉，他是“胜利”号的前指挥官。卒于1700年10月18日，享年49岁。

这儿埋葬的两位是来自菲律宾的多明戈和印度的丝兰，卒于1759年10月。

第四块墓碑历时已久，墓的地点模糊不清。这些坟墓丝毫没被中国人毁坏，而是保存完好，上面的铭文清晰可辨，毫无疑问是出自某位好心人。希望这些墓碑不要被损毁。另外一处有块纪念碑，标示着那是罗马天主教一位主教的安葬之地，周围是一些西班牙人的坟墓，这些人逝世于

causes, was so great, that Chinese watchmen were employed to guard the military stores. After the departure of the troops, the houses they had occupied were torn down, the roads they had made cut up, and every vestige of their presence obliterated by the Chinese as far as possible. On the north eastern end of the island are three ancient tombstones, bearing the following inscriptions: "Here lyeth the body of John Duffield, son of Henry Duffield, Comm. of the *Trumbull* obt. Sept. 6th anno æt, XIII . An. Dom. 1698."

"Here lyeth the body of Capt. Step^{n}. Baker, who was late Comm^{l}. ofy[2] *Success*, who departed this life Octob. ye 18th Anno Dom. 1700, aged 49 years."

"Sepultura de Domingo de Pangasinan y otros dos Indios de Filipinas que fallecieron en Octubre ano 1759."

A fourth has succumbed to time, its site only being faintly marked. These graves have in nowise been desecrated by the Chinese, and are in a good state of preservation, with perfectly legible inscriptions, due no doubt to some kindly hand. It is to be hoped that they will not be suffered to fall into decay. In another spot a monument marks the resting place of a Roman Catholic bishop, and near are the graves of some Spaniards, buried during the early intercourse of Spain with China.

Amoy (continued)

The centre of the island of Amoy is in Lat. 24°30′ N. Long. 118°7′ E. It is of an irregular oblong square form, intersected on its south west face, by a deep estuary; its greatest length from North to South is somewhat under eight miles; its extreme breadth from east to west is about six and a half miles; and its circumference, measured from point to point, is twenty-five miles. Eight insignificant streams called the Kwei hsing ho 魁星河, Woong chai'ho 甕菜河, Kwan tao ho 關刀河, Yen ts'ao ho 鹽草河, Hsi ma ho 洗馬河, Hwang choo ho 黄厝河, Kuai Chih ho 鬼仔河, and Hsi pu ho 洗布河, form its water supply; and it possesses, besides the city of Amoy, one hundred and eight villages and hamlets; the principal of which are Hou cho 後厝, Tsêng cho an 曾厝垵, Mu hou 墓後, Tien chien 店前, Lew pan 劉坂, Ma chou 麻灶, Wu hoo 五後, Fêng shan Hse 鳳山社, and Pan wei hse 坂尾社. Its population has been variously estimated at from 350 000 to 800 000; but, including that of Amoy city, 550 000 persons will probably be about the correct number. Its surface is very uneven, huge and fantastic boulders frequently cropping out of the earth; and bluffs, hills, and brown arid granite mountains abounding.

Productions

All the valleys are most carefully cultivated, indeed no spot capable of production is wasted, and cultivation is carried, terrace above terrace, far up the sides of the rugged mountains; or if there be a natural ledge a few feet long and broad, its poor soil of sandy earth

西班牙和中国交往的早期。

厦门（续）

厦门岛的中心位于北纬24°30′，东经118°7′，呈不规则的椭圆形，西南面横贯着一个深水湾。全岛从北到南接近8英里，从东到西最宽处约6.5英里，周长25英里。由8条小河为厦门提供水源，即：魁星河、甕菜河、关刀河、盐草河、洗马河、黄厝河、鬼仔河、洗布河。管辖区域除了厦门城，还包括108个大小不一的村庄，其中主要的村子有后厝、曾厝垵、墓后、店前、刘坂、麻灶、五后、凤山社和坂尾社。根据不同算法，厦门人口为35万至80万不等。不过，包括城中的人口在内，55万大概是比较准确的数字。厦门的土地表面凹凸不平，经常有奇怪的大石头从地表冒出来，到处都是陡峭的悬崖、山丘、棕色且荒芜的花岗岩山。

粮食及果蔬

谷地尽皆利用，没有浪费一点可产出粮食的地方。人们在一层又一层的梯田上耕作，层层延伸到崎岖不平的山上；如果只是一块几英尺见方的土地，只有满是沙土和风化碎石的贫瘠土壤，肯定也会被人们种上了番薯。水稻、小麦、大麦、玉米、甘蔗、花生、黄豆、豌豆、番薯、山药、卷心菜、大头菜、洋葱、胡萝卜、白萝卜、生菜、瓜和其他蔬菜，都会得到最精心的培育。地里看不到一根野草，肥料都是人的尿和粪（对此有固定的圩场和赶集日），效果完美，虽然非常难闻。厦门及其周边地区种植柚子、菠萝、杧果、橙子、葡萄、香蕉、酸橙、杨梅、李子、桃子、荔枝、龙眼、梨子、柿子和其他水果。

and disintegrated granite, will surely be found to be planted with sweet potatoes. Rice, wheat, barley, maize, sugar cane, groundnut, beans, peas, sweet potatoes, yams, cabbages, turnips, onions, carrots, radishes, lettuce, melons and other vegetables are tended with the greatest care; not a weed is to be seen, and the system of manuring with human ordure (for which there is a regular market, and market day here) is to judge by results as perfect, as it is offensive to the nose. Pomeloes, pineapples, mangoes, oranges, grapes, bananas, limes, arbutus, plums, peaches, lichies, lungngans, pears, persimons and other fruits are cultivated here and in the surrounding districts.

灌　溉

人们精心灌溉。没有溪流的地方，就挖井，利用一个简单的装置，一个人就可以迅速地将水灌入稻田或其他田地的人工沟渠里，即竖起一根杆子，绑上一根长竹竿，在合适的角度再交叉绑上一根，一头挂只水桶，另一头是块重石头。如果水是从地势较高的堤岸上的一条小溪引入（这是节俭的农民利用河水把土地改造成肥沃良田的方法），那么可以采用同样简单、有效又廉价的固定在两根柱子上的木制水车，只要一两个人就能操作。

Irrigation

Irrigation is carefully attended to. Where streams are absent, wells are sunk, and a simple contrivance, an upright post, crossed see saw fashion by a long bamboo, with another at right angles, a bucket at one end and a heavy stone at the other, enables a single man to rapidly fill the little artificial channels leading to his rice or other field. If the water is to be conveyed up from a stream over the high embankment, wherewith the thrifty agriculturist has reclaimed his rich land from the river, an equally simple, efficacious and inexpensive wooden chain pump, fitted upon two cylinders and worked by one, two or three men, is used.

Agricultural Implements

The agricultural implements are few and rude, a strong hoeshaped pick serves as a spade; an iron sharepoint, attached to a rough piece of bent wood, without colter or wheel, and drawn by a pretty little Amoy cow or bullock, and not by an ass and two women as I have seen at Peking, serves as a plough; and a large tub, against the edge of which the stalk of the cereal is beaten, with a mat screen to keep off the wind, takes the place of the flail or threshing machine. The winnowing apparatus where one is used, is on the same principle and not unlike in form, that in use in England some twenty years ago. Notwithstanding these rude implements, the appearance of the crops and land, and the absence of waste of space or material, denotes excellent agriculture, such as would gladden the heart of Mr. Mechi, or any other scientific farmer. Grain is not cut but pulled up by the roots.

Farm Stock

The farm stock consists of very small and beautifully shaped cows and bullocks, hideous water buffaloes, pigs and goats, geese, ducks, and fowls, and on Kulangsu, created by a local want of the foreigner, a fine breed of turkeys; which however are not

农　具

农具稀少又简陋，一把结实的锄头模样的尖嘴锄被当作铁锹使用；铁质的铧尖，绑上一个粗糙的曲柄，没有犁刀或轮子，便是他们的犁了，由一头漂亮的小牛或者阉公牛拉着犁田，而不是像我在北京看到的那样由一头驴和两个女人拉着；一个大桶，外面挂一张席子挡风，人们在桶的边缘摔打谷物，便代替了连枷或脱粒机。这种脱粒装置，英国大约20年前也用过，原理相同，外观也大同小异。尽管使用的农具简陋，可农作物和土地的面貌，以及空间和物质的充分利用，说明这里的农业很出色，这将使梅齐先生④或其他任何使用科学方法耕种的农民感到高兴。最后，人们收获时不是割掉谷物，而是将其连根拔出。

牲　畜

本地有体格小、体形漂亮的母牛、公牛，丑陋的水牛，猪和山羊，以及鹅、鸭子和其他家禽。由于本地的外国人有需求，火鸡在鼓浪屿养殖得很好，但不是土生土长的，而是从马尼拉进口的。厦门的马很小，是非常漂亮的矮种马，从不用于农业生产。

indigenous, but were imported from Manila. The Amoy horse is a very small, and handsome pony, it is never used for agricultural purposes.

气 候

关于厦门的气候，有几个作家描写过，最近出版的一本蓝皮书也称此处的气候不利于健康。根据笔者个人及当地居民的经验，这肯定不符合实际。尽管夏天很长，这里的气候却非常有益健康。从11月初到来年3月末，跟中国的其他地方没什么差别。1871年，在海关阳台的树荫下，8月31日最高温度是96华氏度，12月13日最低温度是37华氏度，当时鼓浪屿有的地方结了半英寸的冰。此地结冰非常少见，虽然寒冷刺骨的日子不稀罕，却很少结冰。通常不怎么下雨，不过去年特别多雨，10月7、8、9、10日暴雨如注。

穆勒医生和曼森医生在截至1871年9月30日的厦门卫生情况半年报告中写道：

福建省的这个地区多山。山上全是花岗岩，部分是由于土壤不足，但主

Climate

The climate, I notice, is described by several writers, and in a recent Blue book, as highly insalubrious. From the personal experience of myself and other residents here, I think this is a mistake, and that, although the length of the summer is trying, the climate is exceedingly healthy, and that from the beginning of November to the end of March, it is equal to any in China. The highest temperature during 1871 in the shade, in the verandah of the Custom House, was 96° Fahr., on the 31st Aug. and the lowest 37° Fahr., on the 13th December; when there was ice half an inch thick on certain spots on the island of Kulangsu. To find ice here is very rare however, for although it is not unfrequently piercingly cold, it seldom freezes. Little rain usually falls, but the past year was exceptionally wet, the heaviest falls were on the 7, 8, 9 and 10th October.

Doctors Müller and Manson in their report on the health of Amoy for the half year ended 30th September 1871, write as follows: "This part of the province of Fokien is very hilly. The hills are of granite and partly from the want of soil, but principally from the false economy of the people, who cut down nearly every tree and shrub, and grub up the natural grass, they leave a bleak and uninviting appearance. Enormous masses of granite absorb and radiate the heat, storing it up during the day, to return it to the air during the night. Fortunately several large rivers and estuaries intersect the country, and open a road through the hills for the sea breezes and monsoons. These and the great rise and fall of tide facilitate the circulation of air, rendering what would otherwise be hot and unhealthy country, comparatively mild and salubrious. By the industry of the people every available spot has been brought under cultivation. The alluvial flats along the banks of the rivers and the narrow gorges among the hills, where water can be obtained, are occupied by rice fields, while in the drier soils, sweet potatoes, ground-nuts, sugar cane and a variety of suitable crops are raised. The rain fall is very capricious. For the most part the climate is dry, frequently several years passing without a sufficiency of rain, famine or great distress is the consequence, and epidemic disease of some form is sure to follow in their train. After three years of drought we have this summer had abundance of rain; and tanks and wells are again filled, after remaining useless or stinking for a long time. The following table will give an idea of the temperature for the summer months, though perhaps it represents a lower range than generally obtains for the season:—

要是由于当地人错误的经济观，他们几乎砍掉所有的树和灌木，挖掉野草，只留下荒凉、令人生厌的景象。大量的花岗岩吸收和释放热量，白天储存起来，晚上释放到空气中。幸运的是，有几条河流和海湾交汇，海风和季风穿越山峦而入。再加上潮起潮落，有利于空气循环，使厦门的气候变得宜人，而不是炎热、不利于健康。勤劳的人们充分利用了每块耕地。河流两岸淤积的平原以及山间狭窄的峡谷，只要有水就能开辟为稻田，而在相对干燥的地里则种植了番薯、花生、甘蔗和各类适合的农作物。降水也很不稳定。大部分时间气候干燥，经常是连续几年雨水不足，导致饥荒和极端困苦，传染病也会接踵而至。在三年干旱之后，今年夏天雨水充沛，长时间不用的或发臭的贮水池和水井又注满了水。下表显示了夏季几个月的温度，虽然它可能不足以代表整个夏季的时间段：

6个月间（4—9月）的温度一览表

月份	最高气温（华氏度）	最低气温（华氏度）	平均气温（华氏度）	降雨（天数）
4月	82	60	69.7	3
5月	89	67	77.5	13
6月	88	75	79.3	14
7月	91	76	83.3	3
8月	88	78	82.7	11
9月	89	72	81.3	7

注：数据来自鼓浪屿室内墙上、面向东北的温度计。

另外半年则凉爽了许多。清新凉爽的空气会让受尽了夏日高温的人精神为之一振，在这里的欧洲人可以进行户外活动了。户外活动是他们热衷的，且相对不会受到惩罚的高品质生活方式。厦门的寻常百姓虽然勤劳，却极其贫困，收入低微。普通劳动力一天的收入是60～100文铜钱，一般手艺人每天可挣120～150文。即便是最节俭的人，靠这点钱养活一家人也艰难。攒不下多少钱以防雨天、疾病或大米价格上涨，而这会带来难以估量的困苦。米饭或者掺了番薯的米饭，加上腌菜或者咸鱼，就是日常食物了。猪肉和牛肉是少数人的奢侈品。乡村地区，人们以务农为主。海边的人捕鱼、出海，偶尔兼做农活。

"During the other half of the year the climate is much cooler. Then the clear cool air goes far to reinvigorate the victim of the summer heats, outdoor exercise is possible, and the high living usually indulged in by Europeans can be borne with comparative impunity. The people though industrious are poor in the extreme, and their earnings small. From 60 to 100 cash a day for an ordinary labourer, to 120 to 150 cash a day for a mechanic are about the general wages. To support a wife and family on this, must be a hard task even for the most economical. Very little can be saved against the rainy day, and sickness or a rise in the price of rice, must cause incalculable distress. Rice, or a mixture of rice and sweet potatoes, flavoured with pickled vegetables or salt fish, is the staple food, pork and beef are the luxuries of the few. In the country the people are chiefly agricultural; along the coast they employ themselves in fishing and are sailors, occasionally combining these occupations with farming. In Amoy and other large towns, manufactures of various kinds engage large numbers. The town of Amoy, as most Chinese towns are, is superlatively dirty. The streets, narrow and irregular, are filthy in the extreme and redolent of every impurity. Pigs and dogs are the sole representatives of the elaborate machinery of sanitation in use in European towns, and a scientific sanitarian, with only home experiences to guide him, would confidently predict the reign of epidemics and death. Yet the Chinese manage to live and thrive, where he would hardly dare to lodge his pigs. There is no typhus, no typhoid, or other disease considered the inevitable consequence of defective sanitation, although Amoy is full of typical typhus dens. Luckily, filth overcrowding and bad food, are not the only factors necessary for the manufacture of a typhus epidemic, were they so, we should live here in perpetual dread. Typhus, and typhoid, are not the only fevers whose absence we have remarked. Indeed, with the exception of small pox, we have met with no representative of the class of continued fevers which claims so large a number of victims in Europe. We have never met a case of scarlet fever, measles, or relapsing fever, either here or in 'Formosa'. Diphtheria, so common in Peking, does not exist, or is very rare, yet other diseases of an epidemic character, such as mumps and whooping cough, are common enough. The petechial fevers are, we think, with the exceptions mentioned, entirely wanting. Considering this, and reflecting on the rarity of the atheromatous and fatty degenerations with the numerous dangerous diseases they entail, one may be at a loss to account for the mortality. When we consider, however, the prevalence

在厦门和其他大的城镇，很多人在各类作坊中干活。和中国其他城镇一样，厦门也非常肮脏。街道窄狭且不规整，脏乱不堪，弥漫着混杂的气味。在欧洲的城镇，猪和狗被用作环境卫生的专用检测仪，一位公共卫生学家只要有饲养猪和狗的经验，就能有效地预测传染病和死亡情况。但是，在甚至无法养猪的地方，中国人设法生息繁衍。尽管厦门是典型的能够引起斑疹伤寒之地，这里却没有恶劣卫生条件所必然引起的斑疹伤寒或者其他疾病。幸运的是，污浊且过于拥挤的生活环境、腐烂的食物未必会导致传染性斑疹伤寒，否则，我们在这里就会一直活在恐惧中了。我们注意到，厦门未曾见到的发热病，不限于斑疹和伤寒。事实上，除了天花，我们还没见过像欧洲那样，大量病人罹患连续性发热的典型病例。不管在厦门还是在台湾，我们尚未遇到一例猩红热、麻疹或反复发热的患者。流行于北京的白喉病在这里也不存在，或者非常罕见。但是，这里却有其他传染性疾病，如流行性腮腺炎和百日咳很常见。除了上面提到的那些，瘀热则根本没有发现。鉴于此，并且考虑到动脉粥样变性和脂肪变性所导致的危险性疾病发生率很低，也许有人会对当地的死亡率感到不解。然而，当我们想到天花在毫无疫苗保护的人群中肆虐流行，直到几乎每个人，在其一生之中注定会感染这种疾病，而三分之一不种牛痘的人会死于此，我们的困惑便会即刻消失。致命率第二的疾病可能是疟疾，它会带来间歇性的热症、发冷，脾脏和肝脏上的疾病，贫血以及并发症等。接下来可能是霍乱，然后或许是麻风病。这些都是导致死亡的主要原因。不过，和欧洲一样，当地常见的是既不会传染也不会地方性流行的普通疾病。肺结核、支气管炎、肺炎、肿瘤等在这儿十分普遍。

对于本地的欧洲人来说，他们既然在厦门定居了，便不再认为这里的气候不利于健康了。他们办公的地点，还有一些住宅，都位于城市的海滩边，那是相当抢手的位置，而他们多数人在鼓浪

of small-pox in a population completely unprotected by vaccination, and learn that almost every one, should he live long enough, is sure to contract the disease, while the mortality from the unmodified form is about one in three, we dispose at once of a part of the difficulty. Then, as second in fatality, we might rank malarial diseases, as remittent fever, ague, diseases of the spleen and liver, anæmia and their consequences. Cholera might come next; then perhaps leprosy. These are the principal causes of death, but ordinary diseases of neither an epidemic nor endemic character are common here as in Europe. Phthisis, bronchitis, pneumonia, cancer, &c., are rife enough.

"For Europeans, as they are now housed, the climate cannot be considered unhealthy. Their places of business, and a few of their residences, are situated along the foreshore of the town, —rather a hot locality, but for the most part they have their private houses on Kulangsu. This, a small rocky island quite close to Amoy, affords excellent situations for building. These have been carefully selected by the residents, and houses in every way suitable to the climate built upon them. In the summer they have the full benefit of the strong sea breezes blowing during the greater part of the day, and of the land winds at night. The cold of winter is never so intense as to make their exposed situations uncomfortable. Did the residents display as much wisdom in the furnishing of their tables as they have in the building of their houses, they might live as comfortably here—as far as health is concerned—for eight or ten years, as they could in Europe. The inevitable sherry and bitters, brandy and soda, and full animal diet indulged in three times a day, combined with want of exercise, and a rather high temperature, induce disease which is hardly climatic, although the victim may call and think it so. All do not err in this way, but most of those who sicken, have indulged in too high living. Those who are temperate and exercise discretion in exposing themselves to the sun and rain keep their health. A little languour by the end of summer, becoming more pronounced, as a rule, the longer one stays here, is perhaps the only climatic disease a sensible man need suffer from."

People

The characteristics of the people have by some been described to be boldness, pride, and generosity; and by others, to be quarrelsomeness, rudeness, and intense dishonesty. My own experience of them is that they differ but little from their fellow countrymen generally. I have ever found them civil, industrious and, according to

屿都有私宅。鼓浪屿是座多岩石的小岛，毗邻厦门岛，很适于建房。岛上居民精心设计，根据岛上的气候条件修建房屋。夏天，白天的大部分时间里，这些房子尽享强劲海风带来的凉爽，晚上也有从陆地上吹来的风；冬天，房子外露的部分也不会令人冷到不适。如果岛上的外国居民能像建房那样在餐桌上花心思，他们就能像在欧洲一样，在鼓浪屿健康舒适地生活八年或十年了。每天三餐必不可少的雪利酒、苦味酒、白兰地和苏打水，满满的肉类食品，加上缺乏运动，气温又高，引发的疾病很难说与气候有关，不过病人会这么想。虽然不是所有人都如此，但多数的病人是由于过于放纵自己。那些生活节制，不让自己过多暴露于日晒雨淋的人，身体都很健康。在此地待久了，夏末会有些疲倦，待得越久就越明显，这也许是敏感的人会感受到的唯一与气候相关的症状。

闽南人

有人说闽南人勇敢、骄傲、慷慨，而

有人说他们喜欢吵架、粗蛮、不诚实。基于和他们接触的经验，我觉得他们大体与其他同胞区别不大。他们文明、勤劳，根据中国人的标准，他们诚实。当然他们热衷于赚钱，把钱看得很重，甚至有些锱铢必较。他们是精明的生意人、勇敢无畏的渔民、优秀的水手；他们自由地移民国外，每年有成千上万的人去马尼拉、新加坡、槟榔屿和其他地方。大多数在爪哇、暹罗和海峡殖民地的中国人都是厦门人或闽南人。我曾经读到的一件事可以证明他们精力旺盛、野心勃勃，即18世纪曾有个闽南人当上了暹罗的国王⑤。从外表上看，他们个子适中，身体强壮，充满活力，吃苦耐劳。显然，他们能够忍受极端天气，而不会表现出不适。

杀　婴

考虑到他们的道德标准，一个最恶劣，同时也是最突出的家庭罪行就是杀女婴。这种罪行极为严重，不幸的是其真实性不容置疑。我曾经询问过在厦门及其周边地区被雇来给传教士做事的一些人，他

the Chinese standard, honest; they are certainly keen in pursuit of the dollar, and sight that coin from afar, leading up to it with unerring accuracy. They are shrewd traders, bold and fearless fishermen, good sailors, and they emigrate freely; tens of thousands going annually to Manila, Singapore, Penang and elsewhere. Most of the Chinese in Java, Siam, and the Straits Settlements, are Amoy, or Fohkien men, and, in proof of their character for energy and ambition, I have somewhere read that, during the last century, a Fohkien man ascended the throne of Siam. In appearance they are middle sized, and well built, strong, active and hardy, and they endure the extremes of temperature with, apparently, no discomfort.

Infanticide

Regarding their morality, one of the worst, and at the same time most prominent, crimes laid at their door is that of female infanticide. That this crime exists to a fearful extent, there is unfortunately no reason to doubt. I have inquired of gentlemen engaged in missionary labours in this, and the surrounding districts, and they all concur in stating that it is common, and generally committed by the women. One gentleman told me that, from statistics he had made, he calculated that not less than 25 per cent of female children were destroyed at their birth. Proclamations against the practice are issued by the authorities, but they are disregarded, and so little shame, or fear of punishment, is felt by the perpetrators of this atrocious inhumanity, that, I am told, in several instances ahmahs, or female nurses in foreign employ, have admitted that they have put to death one, two, or even three, of their children. One of these ahmahs, named Kioh—literally "the picked up one"—was herself cast out on some stones, on the night of her birth; but, being found alive and uninjured on the following morning, superstition, or some better feeling, induced her parents to save and rear her. Another woman, lately married here, was rescued from death about eighteen years ago by a Reverend gentleman, in a singular and providential manner. Soon after his arrival, seeing from his boat an earthen jar floating by and fancying he heard a wail, he asked his boatmen what it contained, and was unconcernedly told "piecy smalla girlee". That night the young and reverend occupant of the boat, had the pleasure of adding to his varied accomplishments, some of a character not embraced in his academic curriculum.

I, myself, a short while ago, met a stout, well to do looking man of the coolie class, carrying two neat and clean round baskets slung at either end of a pole he bore on his shoulder. Hearing the cry of a child, he was stopped, and it was found that he had two infants in each basket; which, he said, he was going to sell. A girl is saleable at the Foundling hospital only, and is worth but 100 cash or 10 cents,

们众口一词地称这种现象很普遍，且基本上都是妇女所为。一位绅士告诉我，据他的统计，不少于25%的女婴在出生时被杀。政府颁布公告，反对这种陋习，人们却视而不见，并对这种惨无人道之事毫无羞耻之心，也不担心受罚。有人告诉我，有几个奶妈或外国人雇用的保姆承认她们曾亲手弄死了一两个甚至三个自己的孩子。其中一个奶妈名叫“拾”（Kioh），字面意思是“捡来的”，她自己便是在出生当晚被扔到一块石头上，第二天早上有人发现她还活着，且完好无损，她的父母出于迷信或良知，才救了她并将她养大。另一个最近才嫁到厦门的妇女，18年前幸运地被一位牧师救了下来。这位牧师到当地不久，他在船上看到水里漂着一个陶罐，并隐约听到啼哭声，于是问船夫陶罐里装着什么，船夫满不在乎地回答：“一个小丫头片子。”当天晚上，这位年轻的牧师又多了一项功绩，那是他布道生涯中并不曾有过的。

不久前，我遇到了一个身材敦实、看上去还算体面的底层人，肩上的扁担两端挑着两只整洁光滑的篮子。我们听到了孩子的哭声，就将他拦住，结果两只篮子里各装着一个婴儿，他说正准备拿去卖。女婴只能卖给育婴堂，一个女婴卖100文钱，或者10分钱；而一个健康的刚出生两三天天的男婴，很容易以15元或3英镑以上的价格出手。自从雅裨理⑥牧师在这件事上发文关注以来，一位具有善心且有智慧的当地商人，即宝顺洋行多年的买办叶文澜⑦重建了一座育婴堂，并在同安和金门建了分堂，这使得被杀的婴儿数量明显减少。育婴堂靠向租用外国船只的中国商人收费来维持，每艘帆船或三桅船收8元，每艘方帆双桅船或纵帆船收6元，对鸦片的买家每箱收7元，对茶叶的卖家每半箱收1分，此外还有其他零星收费。据称，育婴堂每年接收两三千个孩子，每抱一个孩子来，育婴堂给对方100文钱。每名保姆照看2个孩子，报酬是包伙食，每月再得1 000文钱的工资。若孩子托给保姆照看，每名只需交500文钱。任何人想要从育婴堂领养孩子，不必交费，只需开张收条，再找一个熟人担保他是个可敬的人。据说，育婴堂每年开销约在3万元。但是，信息很难获取，我也无法确认

while a healthy boy, two or three days old, will fetch readily $15 or over £3. Since Mr. Abeel wrote on this subject, some considerable diminution in the number of children put to death, must have occurred, from the reestablishment of a Foundling Hospital here, with branches at Tung-an and Quemoy, through the exertions of Tuck-suey, a philanthropic and intelligent native merchant, for many years compradore to Messrs. Dent & Co. This hospital is supported by fees, charged to the Chinese charterers of foreign vessels, of $8 on a ship or barque, and $6 on a brig or schooner, $7 per chest on the buyers of Opium, and one cent per half chest on the sellers of Tea, besides other minor charges. It is stated that between 2 000 and 3 000 children are received annually, for each of which the institution gives the bringer one hundred cash. Each nurse has to nurse two children, for which she receives her food and 1 000 cash per month. For children put out to nurse, 500 cash only are paid for each. Any person desirous of obtaining a child from the hospital, can do so without charge, by giving a receipt for it, and lodging a guarantee from a known person, that he is a respectable man. The annual expenses of the hospital are said to be about $30 000. Information, however, is difficult to obtain, and I have been unable to ascertain the number of children who yearly die in it. Speaking of infanticide at Chüan Chou fu, and its five districts, in 1843, the Rev. David Abeel states:—"From a comparison with many other parts of the country, there is reason to believe that a greater number of children are destroyed at birth in this district （Tung An 同安縣） than in any other part of the province, of equal extent and populousness." He states that, he has enquired of persons from forty different towns and villages, and gives as a result that: "The number destroyed varies exceedingly in different places, the extremes extending from seven to eight-tenths, to one-tenth; and the mean of the whole number, the average proportion destroyed in all these places, amounts to nearly four tenths or exactly 39 percent." He adds that: "In seventeen of these forty towns and villages, my informants declare that one-half or more, are deprived of existence at birth." Of the seven districts in the department of Chang chou fu, he writes that, from enquiries he has made of the inhabitants of eighteen towns and villages, in the district of Lung hsi 龍溪縣, six in that of Chang pu 漳浦縣, four in that of Nan ch'ing 南靖縣, and from more limited enquiries in the other four districts, "there is reason to fear that scarcely less than a quarter of those born, about 25 per cent, are suffocated almost at the first breath;" and that in the course of his investigations, he has frequently questioned visitors from some of the other departments of the province, from Fuchow fu, Ting chow fu 汀州府, and Yen p'ing fu 延平府, who have all testified to the existence of the evil in their respective departments; but gave ground to hope that it prevailed to a less extent than in this vicinity.

育婴堂每年儿童死亡数。关于泉州府及所辖5县1843年的杀婴情况，雅裨理牧师称："参考全国其他很多地方，有理由相信，与福建省其他同等面积和人口密度的地区相比，该地区（同安县）有更多的婴儿在出生时被杀。"他询问了来自40个不同村镇的人，得出结论："不同地方杀婴的数量差别很大，从70%~80%到10%；而且总平均数，即所有地方死亡的孩子的平均数，几乎占40%，或者确切地说是39%。"他补充道："我的消息提供者宣称，在这40个村镇中的17个，一半或更多的婴儿一出生就丢了性命。"至于漳州府所辖7县，根据他对龙溪县18个、漳浦县6个、南靖县4个村镇的居民的询问，以及对其他4县居民的更有限的调查，他写道："有理由担心，不少于1/4即约25%的婴儿，几乎刚呼吸第一口空气时就给闷死了。"调查过程中，他常常询问省里其他地方，如福州府、汀州府、延平府来的人，他们证实了这种罪行在他们那里也存在，但是有理由相信，不如在闽南这么猖獗。他谨慎地补充道，得出这些结论的数据，其精确性可能值得怀疑，或许“言过其实”。而不幸的是，几乎不能质疑他辛苦得出的调查结果，因为这太接近事实。他还说，厦门海防厅提及在英国人到来之前，孩子一出生就被杀死的事很少发生；但自从1841年之后，育婴堂关闭，贫困人口增加，杀婴事件就泛滥成灾了。他举了几个例子，那些残忍的父母向他坦白，他们杀死过1～5个自己的女婴。不过，他补充说，这种可怕的罪行正在减少，在某种程度上是因为有识之士写文章劝诫该行为，这些告诫张贴在人口密集的公共场所。倪为霖牧师在回答我关于这个话题的问题时说：“在整个同安县，杀女婴现象极为普遍；然而，漳州府和泉州府的其他任何地方在这方面与同安没什么区别。一个会说当地方言的人，如果不了解这种几乎让人难以置信的野蛮行径，是无法和当地人相处的。经过大量仔细观察，我确信：第一，这种行为绝不限于穷苦家庭。在殷实的家庭里，如果连生两三个女孩，往往只有一个可以活下来。第二，尽管有文化的中国人交谈时会谴责这种行为，事实上，他们并不认为这事在道德上有错，且自己

He conscientiously adds that the data from which these results are obtained, may be fairly questioned as to entire accuracy, as being opinions rather than facts but there is, unfortunately, little room to doubt that his painstaking investigations, are too near the truth. He also states that the Haifangting of Amoy, (District Magistrate) mentioned that before the English came here, but few children were killed at birth; but since that time (1841) the Foundling hospital had been shut, poverty had increased, and infanticide, had prevailed to a far greater extent. And he cites several cases in which the inhuman parents admitted to him, that they had put to death from one to five of their female offspring; but he adds, that the horrible crime is declining, owing, in a measure, to the exertions of literary men who write against it, and placard the admonitions in the most public places. The Revd. W. McGregor, in answer to my enquiries on this subject, has favoured me with the following statement: “Throughout the entire Hsien, female infanticide is exceedingly prevalent. In this respect, however, Tung an does not differ from any other part of the Chang chew, and Chin chew prefectures. No one who speaks the language of the people, can freely mix with them, without learning that this is a barbarity practised to an almost incredible extent. A good deal of careful observation has convinced me: 1st. That this practice is by no means confined to the families of the poor. In well-to-do families, if two or three girls be born in succession, often only one will be saved alive. 2nd. That while educated Chinese will, in conversation, denounce the practice; they do not, in reality, look upon it as a thing morally wrong, and will very likely (after talking of it as an evil) practice, or allow it to be practiced, in their own families. 3rd. That although the mandarins, from time to time, issue orders for its discontinuance, they never take any steps to secure attention to such orders. 4th. That while educated Chinese will not defend the practice, the great mass of the population do not consider it in the least blameworthy, or a thing to be ashamed of. 5th. That women are still more ready to defend it, than men are. Few women of the labouring classes, feel any hesitation in answering, if asked whether they have put any of their female children to death, or not. Often women seem to think they have, in so doing, acted meritoriously. They would, of course, consider it a crime to put to death a male infant. 6th. That probably half the children born in these two prefectures, are either put to death at their birth, or die very soon, in consequence of the studied neglect with which a female infant is treated. Many Chinese give the estimate at two-thirds, but I am induced to think they err, through thinking only of families, where some have been put to death, and some spared, forgetting the families in which none have been put to death at all. The extreme prevalence of this crime, is most fully shewn by the callousness with which the Chinese talk of it to each other. Even those whom affection for their children has kept from this atrocity, do not seem to feel the hideousness of the practice as prevalent around them. It is evident that this crime is more

很有可能这样做（虽然在口头上称其为邪恶），或者允许这种事情发生在自己的家庭里。第三，尽管官员们时不时发布命令禁止这种行为，却从不采取措施确保其落实。第四，尽管有文化的中国人不会为这种行为辩护，但是大部分人认为这没什么可责备的，也不认为这是种耻辱。第五，比起男人，女人更维护这种行为。劳动阶层的妇女，当被问到是否曾杀死自己的女婴时，她们回答起来很少难为情。她们通常好像认为这样做是值得称赞的，当然，杀死男婴就是有罪的了。第六，在漳泉二府，可能有一半的孩子要么出生时就被杀死，要么由于是女婴，而被故意疏于照料，导致早夭。很多中国人估计约有2/3的婴儿夭亡。但是我认为他们错了，因为他们只考虑有杀婴行为的家庭，而忽略了没有杀婴的家庭。这种罪行极其猖獗，最充分地体现在中国人谈论此事时的麻木不仁。即便那些因为对孩子有爱而远离这种暴行的家庭，似乎也并不觉得周围盛行的暴行多么可怕。很明显，这种罪行在中国的一些地方、一些族群里更加普遍。在广东省，这种事在当地人中几乎没听说过，而在客家人和福佬人中却很普遍。这些事实提出了几个待研究的问题，例如：盛行于不同地方的杀婴行为与灵魂转世等信仰之间有何关联？母亲杀死自己的女婴，是否因为殷切希望她可以托生为一个男孩，还是出于愤怒，因为生女孩使她被人责骂？不同地区有该行为的中国人，其联系的本质是什么？例如在广东省，这种罪行在福佬人中很普遍。现在，结合考察福佬人的传统和语言相似性，表明其来自相邻省份福建的兴化府。通过我在汕头的个人观察，我发现其方言不与其在福建的近邻同源，而是与泉州以及更北面的地区同源。在汕头有一种陋习，其产生时间早于福佬人的迁入。”

为这些让人憎恶的行为找的借口，肯定是完全站不住脚的，但是当地人所用的借口，真是非常没有说服力的。贫穷；担心孩子被卖给或者送给没孩子的人，孩子可能被虐待，或者被不怀好意地养大；以及卑鄙地怕麻烦、担心送孩子去收容所的费用：这些都是杀婴的原因。穷人不以杀婴为耻，甚至富人也如此，因此每年就有成千上万

prevalent in some parts of China, than in others, and also among some Chinese tribes than in others. In the Canton province, it seems almost unknown amongst the Puntis, while it is prevalent among the Hakkas, and Hoklos. These facts suggest several subjects for investigation, such as what connection has this practice with the beliefs, prevalent in different localities, on such subjects as metempsychosis? Does the mother kill her female infant in the affectionate hope that it will again be born a male, or does she do it in anger, because the birth of female children exposes herself to obloquy? What is the nature of the connection between Chinese of different localities? In the province of Canton, for example, the crime is prevalent among the Hoklos. Now the traditions of the Hoklos, and linguistic affinities unite in indicating Hing hoa（興化府）, in Fokien（福建）, as the neighbourhood from which they came. From personal observation at Swatow, I have found their dialectical affinities to be not with their immediate neighbours in the Fokien province, but with Chinchew and the region to the north of it. Here then we have a barbarous custom indicated as dating from a period anterior to the Hoklo migration."

Excuses for this detestable practice, must be utterly insufficient, but those put forth by the people here, are weak to a degree. Poverty, fear that if the children are sold, or given to the childless, they may be illtreated, or brought up for immoral purposes, and the sordid dread of the trouble and expense, that might, hereafter, spring from placing them in an asylum, are amongst the reason given. The crime of infanticide reflects no disgrace upon the poor, if it does upon the rich even, and therefore thousands of human beings are annually abandoned to meet a cruel death by the roadside, or in a pipkin by the river; or perhaps, more mercifully, the foul deed is done by smothering the little atom in a jar of lime, or by slinging it into the water. There is a pool in Amoy at the Ching nan kuan gate called *the dead infants pond.*

This wholesale murder of female children has had the effect of causing a very great disparity between the sexes in Amoy, and, more especially, in the country around. Even though every Chinaman, here, were inclined, and in a position to marry, it would be impossible to do so, owing to the scarcity of woman. Another natural consequence is that the state of morality is exceedingly low, and adultery, which is committed to an enormous extent, has to be submitted to as a necessity by the husbands.

Antiquities

Amongst the still existing antiquities in this neighbourhood, there are, so far as I am aware, but few anterior to the present dynasty, if inscriptions on rocks, temples, memorial arches, and graves be excepted. Many of these inscriptions, date from the Mongol, and some from the Southern Sung dynasty. On the island of Amoy, on the Chin-pang-shan, 金榜山, are inscribed on the rock 金榜石 from which the hill takes its name, the following characters 談玄石, which are said to have been written by the celebrated Confucian commentator, Chu-hsi 朱熹. Belonging to the present dynasty are several inscriptions of some historical importance. In front of the Nan-pu-tó 南普陀, a Buddhistic temple of great beauty, though fall-

的婴儿被抛弃在路边，或被装在陶罐里丢在河边。或许，仁慈一点，将婴儿闷死在石灰罐里，或者抛入水中。厦门镇南关的门口有个池塘，就被称为“死囝仔池”。

大量杀害女婴，造成了厦门的性别失衡，尤其在周边的乡村。即使当地的每个男人都想结婚，却不可能做到这一点，因为女人太匮乏了。另外一个自然的后果就是道德低下，私通泛滥，丈夫们甚至认为这是必然的。

古　迹

据我所知，附近现存的古迹中，如果除去摩崖石刻、寺庙、牌坊、墓穴，只有一些是早于当朝的。很多摩崖石刻可追溯到元代，有些可以追溯到南宋。在厦门岛，金榜山上有金榜石，这便是金榜山名字的由来；金榜石上刻着“谈玄石”几个字，据说出自著名的大儒朱熹之手。当朝的一些石刻颇具历史意义。在厦门港的南普陀，一座非常漂亮但有些坍塌破败的佛寺前，有一排大石碑，上面用汉文和满文记载着清军收复澎湖列岛的事迹。附近的镇南关，路边也有一块石碑，上面记载着国姓爷将荷兰人驱逐出台湾的事迹。在同一条路上，有一座配有石人和石马的大墓，墓的主人是一位高级武官，国姓爷的堂兄弟。⑧从同安到泉州的路上，在大营和五陵之间，有一座更精致的大墓，这是国姓爷某位族叔的最后归宿。厦门岛上散落着大约16座佛寺，其中几座寺庙相当漂亮，尤其是刚才提及的南普陀。它有着一些迷人的八角形石制佛殿，雕刻着极为精美的花窗和雅致的装饰。虎溪岩、仙洞岩、万石岩寺，还有据说是这里最古老的寺庙白鹿洞寺，这些非常知名、保存完好的寺庙掩映在石山深处风景如画的榕树树荫里。另一座寺庙是董内岩，该寺庙之所以出名，是因为一个模糊的传说，即唐朝的一位皇帝曾喝过附近池塘的水。很多寺庙用"善生乐死""止于至善"等石刻题词来告诫观者，毫无疑问，所有这些极富道德教诲、劝人行善的话，对芸芸众生来说都具有教化提升的作用。在天气凉爽的季节，这些寺庙

ing into decay, at Hsia mên chiang, are a series of large stone tablets, on which is engraved in Chinese and Manchu, an account of the subjugation of the "Pescadores". Near here on the Ching nan kuan, 鎮南關, road is also a tablet containing some account of the expulsion of the Dutch from "Formosa" by Coxinga. A large grave on the same road, ornamented with stone figures of men and horses, as of a high military official, is that of a cousin of Coxinga; and a yet more elaborate tomb of the same description, on the road from Tungan to Chinchew between Ta Ying 大營and Wuling 五陵 is the final abode of one of Coxinga's uncles. Scattered over the island are some sixteen Joss-houses, several of which possess considerable beauty, particularly the already mentioned Nan pu to, this building contains some charming octagon shaped temples of stone, covered with carvings of most delicate tracery and exquisite finish. The Tiger's Mouth, the Hsin tung yén, or Grotto of the Hill fairies, the Temple of Ten thousand rocks, and the White stag temple, which is said to be the oldest here, are all noteworthy as fine, well preserved temples, nestling in picturesque Banyan shaded nooks far up the rocky hills. Tung lai yén, another temple, bases what claim it has to celebrity, on a hazy story of an Emperor of the Tung dynasty, having drank at a pool in its close vicinity. Many of the inscriptions in these temples enjoin the reader in phrases such as the following: "Live well and die happy," "The chief aim of life should be the practice of virtue," & c., all highly moral sentiments, and no doubt very improving to the artless beings to whom they are addressed.

During the cool season these temples are a favourite resort of the Barbarian for the performance of his rite of the picnic; here in the courts of Budha, amidst the images of Wu lai Shen, the scowling god of Thunder, Kuan yin, the goddess of Mercy, or the simpering Tien how, empresses of heaven, appear the long table and gay guests looking so incongruous and out of harmony with all their surroundings, except, perhaps, with the effigy of jovial old Budha, himself, who, in easy sitting posture, with vinous leer and ample stomach, looks, as I have sometimes thought, no unfitting presiding deity; the effect may be somewhat marred by his ears hanging down to his shoulders and his toes being as long as his fingers, but who has not seen other presiding deities who have, or ought to have, very long ears. It is only in the direction in which they grow that his are singular.

成了洋人最喜爱的胜地，他们在此野餐。佛殿里供奉着的怒目而视的雷神、慈悲为怀的观音、一脸笑意的天后，与长长的餐桌边快乐的游客们很不协调，与周围的环境也不和谐，除了天性快乐的老佛祖的雕像。他悠闲地坐着，睡眼迷离，大腹便便，我有时候会觉得这与主神的形象不大相符。他的威严可能被双耳垂肩、脚趾和手指一样长的形象破坏了，不过谁没看到其他主要神佛有长长的耳朵呢？只不过他耳朵的生长方向真是与众不同。

Local Peculiarities of Religious Beliefs

Upon the subject of the local peculiarities of religious belief, the Rev. J. Macgowan writes:

"Amid the multiplicity of gods worshipped in Amoy, there are two that hold a specially prominent place. These are the god Yuhwang 玉皇 and the goddess Ma tsaw po 媽祖婆 both of which belong to the Taouist calendar.

"The former of these is looked upon by the Chinese almost universally as the great Supreme Ruler, and by the majority is identified

当地宗教信仰的特征

关于当地宗教信仰的特征，麦高温⑨牧师写道：

厦门人信仰的众神中，有两位神仙地位显著。他们就是同属于道教的玉皇大帝和天妃妈祖婆。

玉皇大帝几乎普遍被中国人视为最高统治者来膜拜，大多数人认为他就是天，是上古之神。老百姓相信他法力无边，是宇宙万物的主宰。天地人三才之主的深奥思想，非常人所能领会；因此，人们对这位曾经以凡人的身份生活在凡间的玉皇大帝报以最坚定的信奉，欢天喜地定期庆祝其诞辰。人们相信他统管其他神仙，派众神仙代表他下到凡间，监督凡人的道德行为，并及时遏制恶人的恶念。这些神仙每年一度飞升上天，向玉皇大帝汇报所管事务。他们在天上度过一段时间之后，又返回凡间，回到各自的岗位，发挥其特殊职能。

妈祖也是船员们特别信奉的女神，厦门及其周边地区普遍信奉妈祖。这位女子起初生活在福建省，被认为拥有超凡的力量，可以帮助船员们在海上渡过劫难。据说她有四个在海上谋生的兄弟，有一天，他们的船被一场可怕的大风掀翻，危急之中，她施展法力入了定，灵魂便飞去帮助她在不同船上的兄弟们。在她把所有兄弟都救出来前，她从入定中被唤醒，结果是一个兄弟失踪，其他三兄弟平安

with the heaven and the god of the classics. His power is believed by the common people to be unlimited, and to him is assigned the control of the physical universe. The abstruse speculations of the leaders of the three systems, are entirely unknown to the people; and therefore we find the most unwavering faith in a being who once lived as a man upon earth, and whose birthday is celebrated with unusual rejoicing, as it periodically comes round. He is believed to have the control of all the other gods, who are commissioned by him to act as his deputies on earth, to watch the moral behaviour of men, and, to a certain extent, restrain the passions of the wicked. These gods ascend to heaven once a year, to give him an account of their stewardship; and after remaining a few days in heaven, return to their various posts, to carry out their peculiar functions.

"Ma tsaw again, is the goddess especially of the sailors; although she is very universally worshipped in Amoy and its neighbourhood. This woman originally lived in the province of Fokkien, and was believed to have miraculous power by which she was able to assist mariners in distress at sea. It is related of her that she had four brothers, who were engaged in seafaring life, and that one day having fallen into a trance, by some wonderful magic, her spirit went to the assistance of her brothers, who were each in distinct ships, and who were in danger of being wrecked by a terrific gale. Being aroused from her trance before she was able to render assistance to them all, the consequence was that one of them was lost, and but three of them passed through the gale in safety. The sailors never think of going to sea without invoking her blessing, and no voyage is ever supposed to be prosperous without the special intervention of this goddess.

"The worship of these two, whilst very extensive, must not be supposed to include all that is actually paid by the Chinese to their gods. To enumerate all that are worshipped on special occasions, would not only be extremely wearisome, but hardly possible within the limits of these pages. Standing out in bold relief, however, and almost apart from the endless ceremonies connected with the worship of the gods, we have what may be termed the religion of the Chinese, and that is the worship of ancestors, already alluded to. Their religious life, whilst developing itself and striving to obtain satisfaction in their various forms of belief, appears to find a more congenial resting place in this ancestral worship. It is practised, not merely by the respectable and well behaved, but also by the most vicious of the community, and whilst numbers profess their utter disbelief in the idols of the country, it would be impossible to meet with a single individual who would express a want of confidence in the efficacy of this worship. We can here but simply hint at the prevalence of this worship, and the amazing hold it has upon the entire nation. It will be for the missionary, in his residence among the people, to mark how the religious element manifests itself in an infinite variety of ways, and

地渡过了劫难。此后，船员出海之前都会祈求妈祖的保佑，海上航行在她的庇护下才能一帆风顺。

对这两位神仙的信仰虽然很广泛，但并不能代表中国人信仰的全部。若列举特定日子里拜祭的所有神明，不仅是极其乏味的，而且本书有限的篇幅也容纳不下。然而，最明显的信仰十分突出，而且其没有无穷无尽的拜神仪式，我们或许可以将其定义为“中国人的宗教”，即已经提及过的祖先崇拜。中国人的宗教生活自主地发展，人们在各种各样的信仰中得到满足，然而他们却在祖先崇拜中找到了适宜的心灵栖居。不仅受人尊敬、行为端正的人祭拜祖先，就连最邪恶的人也同样祭拜祖先。尽管有些人声称压根不相信乡下的神明，但是却没人怀疑崇拜祖先是否灵验。我们在此只是简单提及祖先崇拜的盛行，不过对举国都如此盛行祖先崇拜还是感到非常惊讶。牧师要在众人中观察这些宗教因素是如何以各种方式呈现的，并观察这些信仰的不安定之处，这些甚至也可以在大众更普遍信仰的神明身上观察得到。⑩

助航标志

奉海关总税务司的命令，由船主比斯比、巡灯司和笔者共同建造东椗岛的灯塔和建筑。灯塔于1871年11月16日第一次亮灯。⑪

从厦门出发，从水路驶向西南方向，经过因山顶有座坍塌佛塔的小岛⑫，进入一条两旁是陆地和一个小岛的航道，眼前的景象和苏格兰高地景观颇为相似。这个椭圆形的大海湾长约6英里，宽4英里。旁边是一些繁荣而美丽的乡村，掩映在美丽的林间。村落之间是一片片良田，多是围江造田而成，一直延伸到蓝灰色的山脚下。当季的时候，海湾里满是鹅，水鸭、野鸭等各种各样的鸭子，以及鹈鹕、苍鹭和其他野禽。这里是厦门狩猎爱好者最喜爱的狩猎场。九龙江的两条支流和北溪流入此湾。沿着漳州河方向前行约3英里，便抵达一座围着城墙的大城镇海澄县。再往前2英里是另一座城镇，它更大、更繁忙富庶，

to observe the restlessness of the faith, which is observable even in reference to these gods, which are more universally trusted in."

Aids to Navigation

Chapel Island Lighthouse and buildings were erected by Captain Bisbee, Divisional Inspector, and myself, by order of the Inspector General of Customs, and the Light exhibited for the first time on the 16th November 1871.

Proceeding from Amoy by water in a South westerly direction, past Pagoda Island, topped with a crumbling ruin, that gives it its name, and entering a passage formed by the mainland and a small island, a view, equal to some in the Highlands of Scotland is disclosed. It is a large oblong bay, perhaps six miles long, by four broad, whose margin is fringed with thriving and pretty looking villages embowered in fine trees, and whose boundaries are highly cultivated plains, most of which have been reclaimed from the river, stretching to the base of blue and grey mountains. In the season this bay abounds with geese, teal, widgeon, ducks of almost every description, pelicans, herons and other wild fowl. It is the favourite shooting ground of the sportsmen of Amoy. Into this bay are discharged two branches of the Dragon River, and the North river. Following the course of the Chang Chou River for about three miles, a large walled town called Hai têng hsien 海澄縣 is reached, and two miles further on, a second, larger, and more busy, more prosperous town or city, called in the local dialect Chioh bei（石碼 Shih ma）, which is densely populated ashore and afloat, and maintains a large and brisk foreign and native trade, with Amoy.

Winding through a charming, thriving and well populated country rich in corn, rice, and sugar cane, and in hill and plain, for ten miles further, the city of Chang chou fu is reached.

当地人称石码。这里人口密集，人们住在岸上和船上，和厦门做着大宗且兴旺的洋货和土产生意。

穿过一个弯弯的航道，两边都是漂亮繁荣、人口众多的村庄，山丘和平原上盛产玉米、大米和甘蔗，再前行10英里，就抵达了漳州府。

Chang Chou Fu

The prefecture of Chang chou fu 漳州府 contains seven districts or Hsiens, namely Lung chi 龍溪縣, Chang pu 漳浦縣, Hai têng 海澄縣, Ping ho 平和縣, Chao an 詔安縣, Chang tai 長泰縣 and Nan ching 南靖縣.

Its chief city Chang Chou, is in Lat. 24° 31′ 12″ N. and Long. 117° 59′ E. of Greenwich, or 1°24′ E. of Peking. It is approached by several broad and well made, partially paved roads, and by a bridge some 750 feet long, built upon 25 piers about 30 feet apart, and 25 feet in height; pieces of heavy timber stretch from one abutment to another, and are again crossed by smaller pieces, which are covered with earth and paved with brick and stone; some of these stones are over 40 feet long.

The entire structure is of the rudest description; and at either extremity there are hucksters' shops extending, perhaps, one-fourth of the length of the bridge.

Chang chou fu, following the

漳州府

漳州府辖区内包括7县：龙溪县、漳浦县、海澄县、平和县、诏安县、长泰县和南靖县。

漳州府的主城漳州，位于北纬24°31′12″，东经117°59′，往北京的东面偏1° 24′。有几条宽阔且路况良好、局部铺设路面的道路，以及一座长750英尺的桥可以通往漳州。这座桥有25个高25英尺的桥墩，相邻桥墩间隔30英尺。很多块重木板横架在桥墩之间，再交叉铺上小一些的木板，之后覆盖上泥土，砌上砖和石块，有的石块超过40英尺长。

有关整座桥结构的介绍极为粗略。桥的两端有一些小摊铺，可能占据桥长的1/4。

沿着九龙江的河道，漳州府在厦门以西24.5英里，位于九龙江畔。漳州城以前肯定是一座十分漂亮的城市，它被城墙环绕。据说漳州城建造得很好，街道铺着花岗岩，一些石板有12英尺宽。现在却一片荒芜，简直就是一堆满是砖头和烧焦物的废墟。1864年漳州城落入长毛手中，据说有20万～25万人惨遭屠戮或死于疾病，大约价值2 000万元的财物被掠夺。1865年5月长毛撤离漳州城，此后的7年间，人们耗费巨大的人力财力，在城前重修了一条蜿蜒的沿江街道。漳州城周围的景色，跟闽南地区的很多地方一样，果真极为优美。劳里先生在《中国丛报》第11卷第506页有恰如其分的描写："想想看！一个长30英里、宽20英里的近圆形谷地，周围都是荒芜的、尖尖的小山丘，一条河流横穿而过，一座大城就在我们脚下，稻田、甘蔗地、参天大树，还有无数村庄，向四周延伸。这是多么壮美的中国景色！脚下的这座城呈四方形，河岸处稍有弯曲，建筑密集，四下都是多得让人惊奇的大树。向导告诉我们，在明朝，这儿有70万人口，他认为

course of the river, is distant 24$\frac{1}{2}$ miles due west from Amoy, and is situated upon the banks of the Lung or Dragon river. It must have been a very fine city, it is walled, and is described as having been well built, and its streets paved with granite, some of the slabs being twelve feet wide. It is now a picture of the abomination of desolation, literally a heap of bricks and charred ruins. When the city fell into the hands of the Chang mao rebels in 1864, from 200 000, to 250 000, persons, are said to have perished by the sword. or from disease; and some $20 000 000 worth of coin and property, to have been the spoils of the rebels, It was vacated by them in May 1865, and during the succeeding seven years, sufficient energy has been found to repair or rebuild, one long straggling street along the river front of the city. The surrounding scenery, as in many other spots in this district, is really beautiful. It is thus aptly described by Mr. Lourie in the *Chinese Repository* Vol. XI p. 506: "Imagine an amphitheatre 30 miles in length and 20 in breadth, hemmed in on all sides by bare, pointed hills, a river running through it, and an immense city at our feet, with fields of rice, and sugar cane, noble trees, and numerous villages, stretching away in every direction. It was grand and beautiful beyond every conception we had formed of Chinese scenery. Beneath us lay the city, its shape nearly square, curving a little on the river's banks, closely built, and having an amazing number of very large trees within and around. The guide said that in the last dynasty, it had numbered 700 000 inhabitants, and now he thought it contained a million, probably a large allowance. The villages around also attracted our attention. I tried to enumerate them, but after counting twenty-nine of large size, distinctly visible in less than half the field before us, I gave over the attempt. It is certainly within the mark to say that within the circuit of this immense plain, there are at least one hundred villages, some of them small, but many numbering hundreds and even thousands of inhabitants."

This city was, prior to its capture, famous for its sugar, and sugar candy, manufactures, tea, silk, velvet, silk and cotton manufactures, and iron manufacture; and was the richest and most important in this vicinity.

It is the residence of a Taotai, Prefect, the Magistrate of Lung Chi 龍溪縣, a Chen-t'ai or General, a Colonel, and other military mandarins. On the north, and northeast, is the district of Chang-t'ai 長泰, Tiohto'a, locally, in which exists coal in undeveloped abundance. The specimens seen are very poor. This is no doubt owing to the fact that the people are allowed only to use what may be easily procured on the surface; and are not permitted to open mines. Quantities are brought down in baskets to Chioh-bei（石碼 Shih-ma）for sale, and are purchased by native blacksmiths.

To the northwest, is the district of Nan-ching. The district of Hai-téng, is between Lung-chi and the sea, and its chief city stands upon an island. Nearest to Changt'ai on the coast, is the district of Chang-pu, next to Yune siau, while Chao an, lies to the extreme south. North of the last named district, is that of Pingho. The inhabitants of the department, once had a most evil

现在有100万人，也许这个数字已经是大打折扣的了。周围的村庄也引起了我们的注意。我试着去数，但是数完我们眼前能看得见的29个大村子之后，还没数到一半，我就放弃了。看来估计得没错，在这个大平原上，至少有100个村子，有的比较小，但很多有几百甚至几千的人口。"

漳州城在被太平军占领之前，以糖、冰糖、茶叶、丝绸、绒制品、丝制品、棉制品和铁制品而闻名。它曾经是邻近地区中最富有、最重要的。

漳州城是道台、龙溪县县令、镇台或总兵、参将以及其他武官的驻地。漳州城的北面和东北面是长泰县，这里拥有大量没有充分开采的煤矿。煤矿样品看起来品质很差。毫无疑问，这是因为官府只允许百姓开采能轻易挖掘的表层煤炭，而不允许他们开采整个矿。当地人用篮子将大量煤炭运到石码售卖，多由那里的铁匠买去。

南靖县位于漳州城的西北面。海澄县位于龙溪县和海岸之间，主城在一个岛上。漳浦县在靠近长泰的海边，云霄县在其隔壁，而诏安县位于最南面。最后是北边的平和县。这里曾经因为杀女婴、野蛮残忍而声名狼藉。据说，这里的杀婴行为比大清帝国的任何地方都更加猖獗。

漳州府位于福建省的南面，呈三角形，北面与汀州、龙岩、泉州交界。南面靠近大海，西面毗邻广东的潮州府。漳州府的海岸线从南澳延伸至厦门。

江东桥

在龙溪县有一奇观，即江东桥，又名浦南桥。此桥距厦门19.5英里，是茶叶运往厦门市场的必经之地。这座桥风景如画，位于九龙江的一个急转弯处，这里石头密布，水流湍急，河水在此处看起来没有出口。靠近江东桥的几英里都风光迷人。肥沃的冲积平原，满是刚种下的水稻、麦子和甘蔗，点缀着数不清的繁荣的大村庄，它们掩映在一片片肃穆的榕树林里，放眼望去，一片绿色。远处的平原连绵不绝，延伸到那美丽的、层层叠叠的山峦之中。

桥长354步，宽6步，中间有个小建筑物。桥有20个桥墩；3个桥墩一组，构成2个小拱门，第四个桥墩则距离其他桥墩3倍

reputation for destroying their female offspring, and for rudeness and cruelty. Infanticide was said to be more prevalent here, than in any other part of the empire.

The prefecture of Chang-chou, constitutes the southern portion of the province of Fuh-kien, and is of a triangular shape, having the departments of Ting-chou, 汀州, Lung Yen,龍岩, and Chuan-chou,泉州, for the northern line, the sea coast for the southern, and the department of Chao-chou-fu 潮州府, in Kwan-tung, for the western. The line of coast stretches from Namoh（南澳）to Amoy.

Chiang-tung Bridge

In the district of Lung-chi, is one of the curiosities of this neighbourhood; it is the Chiang-tung-chiao, 江东桥, or Polam bridge 浦南橋. This bridge is distant nineteen and a half miles from Amoy; through it must come all the Teas destined for the Amoy market. It is very picturesquely situated at a sharp angle of the North River where it turns into a savage, rocky, gorge, with seemingly, no outlet. The approach to it is for miles charming. Rich alluvial plains, bright with young paddy, wheat, and sugar cane, dotted about with numerous large, prosperous-looking villages, set generally in clumps of venerable banyan trees, greet the eye on every side, and in the distance the plains swell up, with easy sweep, to the base of a chain of fantastic and many-hued mountains.

The bridge is 354 paces long, by 6 broad, and has a small building on its centre, it is built of stone on 20 buttresses; three grouped together to form two small arches, while the fourth is placed at nearly treble the distance, and forms an arch of good span; these buttresses are spanned by huge blocks of roughly hewn granite, mostly from 54 feet to 66 feet long, and from 3 to 6 feet thick. The largest block, from a rough measurement, we calculated to weigh 80 tons. By what means these enormous stones, were got into their position, it is difficult to imagine. Although they are polished with the footsteps of seven centuries, much of their original inequalities yet remain. The ends of the arkshaped buttresses, are being forced upwards by the enormous weight resting on their centres, and two huge cross blocks of stone, have already slipped from off one of their end supports into the water. The bridge was once defended at its southern end, by a well built stone battery, and by a circular stone fort, on the top of a steep bluff some 350 feet high, covered at its base with handsome copperbeech, banyan, lung-ngan, and other trees, festooned, here and there, with gorgeous red hued creepers. No guns are now in these fortifications. It is the station of a small military mandarin, and of a taxing establishment, at either end there are a few wretched shops and houses. On the occasion of the visit of myself and party, the inhabitants, both male and female, told us, with much gesticulation, that large tigers frequently crossed the bridge at night, perhaps as often as 40 or 50 times a year; that one carried off a dog two nights before from the house against which we were standing; and also that a short time previously, a man had been killed near there, and they urgently

远，形成一个漂亮的单跨拱门。桥墩之间横架着切割粗糙的大块花岗岩，多数花岗岩长54～66英尺，厚3～6英尺。粗略算起来，最大的石块约重80吨。很难想象这些巨石是如何放置上去的。尽管700年来，这些石头已经被行人的脚印磨平了，但昔日的凹凸之处仍依稀可辨。由于中间部分承重过大，拱门两端被挤得往上凸起，两块巨大的横石已经从支撑的一端滑落，掉入水里。桥南有牢固的石炮台和圆形石堡，守卫着这座桥。石堡建在350英尺高的陡峭断崖上，崖下是姿态优美的山毛榉、榕树、龙眼树和其他树，四处长满漂亮的红色爬藤类植物。眼下，这些防御工事里已没有火炮。这里有一个下级军官的驻地和一座饷馆，桥的两端有少量破旧的商店和房屋。我和同伴去参观的时候，碰到的居民，不论男女，都比画着夸张的手势，称夜间桥上经常有大老虎经过，每年四五十次呢；就在我们所站在的房屋对面，前两天晚上，有老虎叼走了一条狗；还说不久前，有个人在附近被老虎咬死。他们迫切地希望我们能去打死老虎，提出可以在一个庙旁拴上一头小山羊，用羊的叫声来引诱老虎。

他们还说附近山上有野猪。

浦南镇

过了桥10英里就到了浦南镇，属江东司管辖，是一处军事汛地。

这儿的居民有两三千人，他们买卖的主要货品是当地和周边地区的物产：茶叶、糖、纸、橙子和柚子。尤其后面两种水果因其特有的美味而知名，成了每年进贡给朝廷的贡品。在被太平军攻占之前，据说这儿大概有一万人。现在这儿成了一片废墟，之前完好的货栈再没重修。大部分地方依然一片荒芜，无人居住。

浦南过去25英里，就进入了产茶区，要经过不少于70个急流才能到达这里。之前，有人向我说过，这里林木茂密，风景绝佳。迄今为止我还没机会探索这一带，但在探索过后，我会再写一篇相关文章。

以下对漳州府的有趣记述，是由麦高温牧师好意提供给我的：

据说，早至夏朝（前2169—前

begged us to come and shoot them, offering the use of a small temple, and to tether a young goat near it, to attract the tigers by its bleating.

They also stated that there are wild pigs in the adjacent mountains.

Polam

Ten miles beyond this bridge, is the town of Polam, Polam, which is under the jurisdiction of the magistrate of Chiang-tung-ss'u 江東司, and is the residence of a military mandarin.

The number of its inhabitants, is estimated to be from two to three thousand. Its principal articles of trade, are those produced in the neighbourhood, and surrounding districts, namely: tea, sugar, paper, oranges, and pomeloes; the two latter are celebrated for a peculiarly delicious flavour, and form one of the articles of tribute sent hence, annually, to the throne. Before its capture by the rebels, this place was said to contain a population of about 10 000 inhabitants. It is now in ruins, and its formerly fine warehouses, have never been rebuilt. The greater part of the place is still desolate and uninhabited.

Twenty-five miles distant from Polam, is the commencement of the Tea district. No less than seventy rapids have to be ascended in this region, and the richly wooded highland scenery, has been described to me as beautiful in the extreme. I have not yet had an opportunity of exploring this part of the country, but when I do so, it will form the subject of another paper.

The following interesting account of the Prefecture of Chang Chou, has been kindly furnished me by the Rev. John Macgowan.

"The region embraced under this name was known to exist as far back as the time of the Hea dynasty（B.C. 2169-1756）. At that period it was a wild uncultivated district, inhabited mainly by the natives of the country, who ... were altogether uncivilised, and who maintained themselves by the chase. Very few of the Chinese had penetrated thus far, and we may presume they were the more daring and adventurous spirits of the age, who acting as pioneers had pushed their way into the wild and unexplored regions that lay to the South.

"The history of these early times is necessarily of the vaguest possible character. The accounts of them are scanty, and, moreover, mixed up with so much that is fabulous, that we cannot rely upon them very much for giving us an insight into the state of things then existing, or of the process by which the country finally became cleared. All we know for certain is that ... Mandarins were appointed by imperial authority, so that this region became, to all intents and purposes, a portion of the kingdom of Tsin. Matters continued in this state until the time of Woo te,（B.C. 81）of the western Han dynasty, when a change in the mode of government took place. The people of Chang chou region, like most people inhabiting a frontier country, were of a turbulent and independent character. The fierce conflicts in which they were continually involved with the original inhabitants, had necessarily developed a spirit within them, that made them very unwilling to submit to the control of the

1756）⑬，这个地区就以现在的名字命名了。那时，这里还是未开垦的蛮荒之地，居住的主要是当地土著，尚未开化，他们靠打猎为生。当时只有很少的中原人来到如此遥远的地方，我们猜想他们是那个年代里勇武且富有冒险精神的人，披荆斩棘，深入这南方蛮荒之地。

早期的历史难免模糊不清。有关土著的记述较少，且混杂着很多杜撰的成分，不是很可靠，难以据此了解当时的事件，或者这些地区最终是如何开垦的。我们所能确信的是，朝廷任命官员到这个地方，于是，这里实际上成为秦朝的属地。直到西汉的武帝时期（前81），政府的管理模式发生了改变。⑭漳州地区的居民，与多数边疆地区的民众一样，勇猛好斗，不受管束。他们与土著持续爆发激烈的冲突，这必然使他们生出藐视法律的对抗精神。彼时的状况和现今也迥然不同。当时，很多地方仍是蛮荒之地，还没怎么开发。人们认为土地很贫瘠，不适合耕种，且人们的耕种方式很粗放，以至于从未想到过土地中储藏着巨大的资源。不像现在，这里可以产出养活几百万人的粮食。由于当地民众不受管束的个性，加上其上缴的税收微乎其微，武帝决定放弃对此地的直接统治权。于是，武帝在当地望族中择选一人，并封他为王，将福建、广东两省交给他管辖。⑮此人除了向皇帝进贡之外，还被赋予了全权管辖属地的权力，作为诸侯，他实际上拥有独立的统治权。

这位被任命的诸侯，很快就被证实是个野心勃勃、不择手段的人。多年之后，他不仅对皇帝不忠，还胆大妄为意图不轨，伺机侵占其他诸侯的领地，意在窃取王权。皇帝觉察到了他的阴谋，于是集合一支大军，将其彻底击溃。汉武帝的主力残杀了整个地区六成以上的人口。汉武帝在位期间四处布防，目的就是压制不服管束的百姓，他认为保全其领土的绝佳办法就是把这个地方的人赶尽杀绝。⑯那

law. The region, moreover, was nothing like it is now. Many parts were still uncleared. Very little comparatively had been done to develop the resources of the country. The soil was considered poor and unfruitful, and the country instead of producing the rich harvests that now sustain millions of people, was so poorly cultivated, that the vast resources that lay dormant within it, had not yet even been suspected. In consequence of the character of the people, whom it was found almost impossible to restrain, and of the fact that the revenue to be derived from the district was almost nothing, Woo te determined to relinquish the direct government of it by himself. He consequently selected a man belonging to one of the principal families in the district, and appointed him Prince, giving him the provinces of Fohkien, and Canton, as the territory over which he was to reign. He allowed him the fullest control within his dominions, and excepting that he was obliged to pay tribute to the Emperor, as his liege lord, he was to all intents and purposes an independent sovereign.

"The Prince thus appointed, proved before long to be an ambitious, and unscrupulous character. Before many years had elapsed, he had not only determined to ignore the allegiance he had promised the Emperor, but he had also formed a bold scheme for invading his dominions, in order, if possible, to gain possession of his kingdom. The Emperor when he became aware of his designs, assembled an army, and having utterly routed the forces of his antagonist, carried off by main force no less than six tenths of the inhabitants of the whole district. These he distributed, in various directions, throughout his own dominions. He was prompted to this act, by the utterly unruly character of the inhabitants, and because he deemed that nothing but an utter depopulation of the country, would secure the safety of his own dominions. Those of the inhabitants who had escaped this wholesale seizure, had taken refuge amid the hills, and forests, where the soldiers of Woo te, could not follow them. After the departure of the invading forces, the people ventured out from their hiding places, and gathered once more around their former homes. Little indeed was now left them. Their houses had been burned, their property had been either plundered or destroyed, and their friends and kindred, had been ruthlessly carried off, without the remotest hope that they should ever see them again. The destruction had been very thorough and complete. The Imperialists, indeed, were under the impression that they had cleared the whole region of inhabitants, for they relinquished the government of it; and abandoned it to the care of itself for the future. The miserable remnant that had escaped, being unmolested from without, began again to grow and flourish. During the two succeeding dynasties, viz. the Eastern Han, (A. D. 30-226) and the later Han, (A. D. 226-260) we have very few authentic details concerning them. Whatever rulers they may have had must have been of their own election, for none of the sovereigns of the above two dynasties, claimed allegiance from them in any respect.

"At the beginning of the Western Tsin dynasty, (A. D. 260-313) the place had grown so much in importance, and the inhabitants had become so numerous, that it was deemed valuable enough to be

些在这些大劫难中得以幸免的百姓便藏身于深山老林中，逃到汉武帝的士兵追不到的地方。等到军队撤退之后，百姓们才冒险从藏身之处出来，重返家园。他们现在几乎一无所有，房子被烧毁，财产被抢夺或毁坏，亲友们也惨遭杀害，天人永隔。所有的一切都被彻底破坏。统治者以为已经扫清了整个地区，于是便放弃了对这个地区的管治，任其未来自生自灭。那些幸免于难之人，不再受到外来烦扰，整个社会重新发展并逐渐兴盛起来。在接下来的两个朝代，即东汉（30—226）和之后的朝代（226—260），⑰我们对这里所发生的事情的真实细节知之甚少。该时期此地统治者都自立为王，从未宣称要效忠朝廷。

西晋（260—313）⑱之初，这一地区变得非常重要，人口激增，被认为足够有价值并再次并入中央王朝。于是，皇帝将此地收归统辖，并任命合适的人来掌管。在西晋和接下来的朝代，此地保持着对最高权力的服从，除了令普通读者毫无兴趣的有关内部管理规章的简单描述外，并没有发生任何足以引起历史学家特别关注的历史事件。

唐朝（622—897）⑲伊始，这里发生战乱，中原移民和已开化的土著之间冲突不断。战争持续了30多年，其间战事多有反复，最后中原移民发现他们对付不了这些对手。紧急关头，他们祈求唐太宗（654）⑳指派一位智勇双全的官员来结束这里的战争，并采取英明措施来恢复此地的和平和安宁。皇帝同意并任命陈政为王，授予他与之前的汉朝委派的诸侯同等的权力。㉑事实证明，陈政是一个十分聪慧又意志坚定的人。在他的英明统治下，战乱得以平息，整个地区的资源也逐渐得到开发。他获得了百姓的爱戴，朝廷似乎放心大胆地授予其家族以权力。接下来的三百年间，他的后人一直统治着这一地区。后来，由于陈政的后人太过无能腐败，人们便从另外的家族选了一位统治者，此后该

once more annexed to the empire. It was accordingly taken possession of by the emperor, who delegated suitable men to take charge of its government. During this, and the succeeding, dynasty, the country remained in quiet submission to the supreme authority: nothing of any special note occurred, sufficient to attract the notice of the historian for we have no record beyond the simple statements regarding its internal regulations, which are of no interest to the general reader.

"At the commencement of the Tang dynasty, (A. D. 622-897) we find the whole region involved in civil war. This was waged between the purely Chinese inhabitants, and the civilized natives of the country. The war continued for upwards of thirty years, with varying success, but in the end, the Chinese were beginning to find themselves unable to cope with their half civilized antagonists. In this emergency they prayed the emperor Tae tsung, (A. D. 654) to appoint a wise and powerful mandarin, who would have authority to put an end to the intestine struggle going on, and who would be able, by his wise measures, to restore peace and tranquility to the country. The Emperor consented and nominated Chèn Chêng, 陳政 to be a Prince, with the same powers, and under the same conditions, that governed the appointment of the first Prince during the Han dynasty. The man appointed, proved to be one of great wisdom and firmness. The civil war was put an end to, and the internal resources of the country, under his wise management, were gradually developed. He gained such a strong hold upon the affections of the people, that the supreme government seemed by right to be securely vested in his family. For a period of three hundred years his descendants ruled as Princes in the country. At the end of that time their incapacity, and their corruption, became so marked, that the people chose a prince from another family. From the time that this change occurred, there began to be dissensions in the state. Political parties gradually arose in the country. The most powerful families, naturally, thought that they had as much right to rule, as the one that had lately been selected. The consequence of all this was that the minds of men were exceedingly unsettled, and the aspect of affairs was anything but satisfactory. Chên hung chin, 陳洪進, who happened to be Prince at the beginning of the Sung dynasty, (A. D. 950-967) , seeing that a struggle was inevitable, and that he would have to succumb before the various powerful parties that were aiming at dominion, placed his territories at the disposal of the Chinese emperor. He proposed that they should no longer be held independently of the empire, but that they should come under its direct government. The proposition was accepted by the emperor, and Chên hung chin was reinstated in his authority, with powers very similar to those of a Governor General. At once peace was restored to the country. The various parties, seeing that they would now have to cope with the whole force of the empire, silently melted away, and during the next two dynasties, no serious event marks the history of this region. After it came under the control of the Sung dynasty, the present city, which up to that time had been an open town, was surrounded with a mud wall, four li in circumference.

地区便纷争不断，慢慢地出现了不同的政治派别。那些最有权势的家族自然认为他们也一样有权统治这里，结果人心躁动不安，人们对社会局面极为不满。宋朝初年（950[22]—967），军阀陈洪进[23]看到此地将不可避免地发生战争，他只好在各方势力争夺统治权之前归顺朝廷，将自己的领地交由朝廷处置。他提议各方势力不再自立为王，而是应该处于朝廷的直接统治之下。皇帝接受了他的提议，陈洪进也跻身高位，其权力与总督相当。这一地区也恢复了和平。各方势力也知道无法对抗整个朝廷，无形中消散了。之后的两个朝代里，这一地区未发生重要的历史事件。归入宋朝统治后，漳州城已是一个方圆4里的土墙环绕的开放城镇。150年之后，残颓的土墙被石墙替代，因为这更具有防御和实用功能，是对旧城墙的一次巨大改进。

入清之前，漳州城没发生什么大事。当国姓爷公开反抗清廷之时，他占据了厦门及其周边地区。顺治十二年（1655），国姓爷轻取漳州，但他并不打算长期占领。听闻有一支大军正从福州赶来，准备向他发起进攻，他清楚自己无力抵抗，于是毁掉城墙，据说还把建城墙的石头扔到了海里。第二年，清军重修了城墙，而且规模比之前更大。之前的城墙只有方圆4里，现在却有9～10里。12年之后，国姓爷再次包围了漳州城，但这次他面对这座城却束手无策。㉔清军因善于守城而出名，他们固守漳州城的两三处地方，证明了他们在守城方面的成就确实是实至名归的。据说在最后一次围城中，漳州城中有不少于七十万人死于饥饿。我想这些数字未免过于夸张，但这也说明困苦的程度和死亡率肯定是前所未有的，才会有此一说。

历史的潮流奔涌向前，直到1864年，富庶的漳州城再次遭到突然袭击，这次是被长毛攻陷。在被占领期间，漳州城被起义军破坏殆尽。最先被破坏的是寺庙、公共建筑、官邸，大半个城区成为废墟。约40万人失去家园，

One hundred and fifty years after, the mud walls, which had fallen into serious decay, were replaced by stone ones, which for purposes of defence and general utility, must have been a vast improvement upon the old ones.

"Nothing eventful occurred in the history of Chang chou till the beginning of the present dynasty, (A. D. 1643). At the time Amoy, and the surrounding districts, were held by Koksenga, who was in open rebellion against the rulers of the new dynasty. In the 12th year of Shun che, (1655) Koksenga attacked Chang-chou, and took it with the greatest ease. He was not destined, however, to keep it long. Hearing that large bodies of troops were on their way from Foochow, for the purpose of attacking him, and knowing that he was in no condition to withstand them, he demolished the city walls, and, it is said, carried the stones of which they were built, and threw them into the sea. The Imperialists rebuilt the walls again next year, but on a much larger scale than previously. Formerly they had a circumference of only four li, now they extended to between nine and ten li. Twelve years after, it was again besieged by Koksenga, who, however, was unable to make any impression on the place. The early soldiers of this dynasty, have the reputation of having been exceedingly skillful in repelling attacks upon their walled towns. The ability with which they successfully defended two or three places in the Chang chou prefecture, would seem to prove that their reputation on this point, was well deserved. It is said that, during this last siege, no fewer than 700 000 persons, died of starvation within the city. I fancy that these numbers are greatly exaggerated. Still they imply that there must have been an unprecedented degree of distress and mortality, to have given rise to such a statement.

"Again the tide of history rolls on till 1864, when the prosperity of Chang-chou, again received a sudden shock, from the capture of the city by the long haired rebels. During their occupation of it, they seem to have been filled with a spirit of destruction. Temples, public buildings, and official residences, were the first to feel the effect of their presence. Large portions of the town were reduced to ruins. The population, which was reckoned at 400 000, was scattered in every direction. Immense numbers of them were murdered, and the whole business of the place was completely paralysed. It will be long before the town will recover its old prosperity. Even now (1872) it is in many places a vast heap of ruins. The former inhabitants have either been killed, or they have been so impoverished, that they have not the means of rebuilding. It is only in the more business quarters, that there is any sign of a return to the state of things that existed before its capture by the rebels.

"*Size.*—In reference to the size of the Chang-chou prefecture, it is difficult to speak with extreme accuracy. I should say, that it is about 70 miles in length, and 240 miles in circumference. Very much of this area, however, is unavailable for the cultivation of the cereals. It is intersected in every direction, by ranges of hills, some of them rising to a considerable height. Many of these are exceedingly barren, and are comparatively of little value to their owners, others, again, are

数不清的人被杀害，这里所有的商业活动都停滞了。而要恢复漳州城以前的繁荣，则需要很长的时间。即便到了时下（1872），很多地方依然是一片废墟。这里的百姓要么被杀，要么太穷，没法重建家园。只有一些更商业化的区域，才恢复了一点起义军攻占之前的迹象。

关于漳州府的范围，很难说得准确。可以说，它长约70英里，方圆约240英里。但是，这里的大部分地区都不能耕种谷物。它四面八方都被群山切割，有的山非常高。很多山极其荒芜，对于它们的所有者没有什么价值。另外一些山上布满了树，是作为柴火种的，将卖往漳州府各处。这种情况下，这些山成了很多人可观的收入来源。

关于物产。漳州府居民的生活水平总体看起来好于周围地区。在相邻的泉州府，人们的生活比起更受恩惠的邻居来更加贫困，生存也更加艰难。毫无疑问，这主要是因为漳州府是一个十分多产的地方这一事实。日常消费的很多重要物产都是这里产出的。而卖出这些物产的税收给大多数本地人带来了财富。主要有如下物产：大米、茶叶、糖、油、生姜、蜂蜜、麻、烟草、纸、清漆、染料、樟脑、木料、木炭。这里水果种类繁多，有荔枝、龙眼、橙子、瓜类、香蕉、柿子、桃子、梨子、橄榄、枣、葡萄、桑椹、柚子、石榴等。

关于人口。整个漳州府的人口估计有三四百万。

关于古迹。漳州府有价值的古迹不多，就好像人们根本不在意保护那些可以解释过去风俗，或者那些有助于阐明遥远的历史的任何特定史事、人物的遗迹。在漳州，我们看不到宋朝以前的文物，那些保留下来的，之所以能逃过常见的衰颓命运，仅仅因为它们是普通大众必不可少的东西。我指的是他们的城和桥。而其他任何大家觉得不影响生活的东西，都可以被破坏，变成废墟。有些好玩的或奇

covered with trees, which are specially cultivated, with the object of being cut down for firewood, to be sold throughout the prefecture. In this latter case, the hills are a very fruitful source of gain to great numbers of the population.

"*Products.*—The people of this prefecture, seem, on the whole, to be much better off than those outside of it. In the neighbouring prefecture of Chinchew, the people are much poorer, and seem to have a harder struggle for life, than their more favoured neighbours. This is owing, no doubt, to the fact that the Chang-chou region, is an exceedingly productive one. Most of the most important articles of general consumption, are produced in it, and the revenue derived from their sale, brings in wealth to vast numbers of the community. Its chief products, are as follows: rice, tea, sugar, oil, ginger, honey, hemp, tobacco, paper, varnish, dyestuffs, camphor, timber, charcoal. The fruits are very abundant, viz: laichi, dragon's eye, oranges, melons, plantains, persimmons, peaches, pears, olives, dates, grapes, mulberries, pomeloes, pomegranates, &c.

"*Population.*—The population of the entire district, is estimated at between three and four millions.

"*Antiquities.*—In the prefecture of Chang-chou, there are scarcely antiquities of value. ··· There seems to have been no care taken to preserve anything that would have explained the customs of the past, or that would have served to illustrate any peculiar fact, or feature, of their remote history. In Chang-chou, we seem to have absolutely no relics of anything in existence before the time of the Sung dynasty, and those that do remain, have escaped the general decay, simply because they were essential to the general community, and, therefore, must be preserved, I refer to their cities, and bridges. Anything that the public could get along without, has been allowed to fall into ruin, and decay. Wherever the conservation of anything interesting, or curious, has been left to private enterprise, the result has been most disastrous. The only relic in the prefecture, really worth mentioning is the very fine bridge called the Chiang-tung-chiao, or Polam bridge, which spans the North River. The point at which this bridge has been built, is an exceedingly beautiful one. It is a kind of gorge, through which the river finds its exit from the great Chang chou plain, the opposite side of the hills. The hills at this place, rise very high on both sides of the river, which, of course, add much to the grandeur of the scene. As there are no villages, and no inhabitants, in the immediate vicinity, the scene around the bridge is one of quiet beauty.

"The first notice that we have of any bridge at this place, is at the beginning of the Sung dynasty. In the year 1190, a floating bridge was erected, which did service for 35 years, when it was replaced by a permanent wooden one. This was burnt down in the year 1265, that is 30 years after its erection. The prefect of Chang-chou headed a subscription list with five hundred thousand cash, in order to the building of a stone one. The requisite funds having been subscribed, a stone bridge was built. It was 2 000

特的东西，如果由私人保存，其结果肯定非常糟糕。漳州府唯一值得一提的历史遗迹就是一座保留完好的桥，名叫江东桥或浦南桥，它横跨在九龙江北溪之上。建桥的地方风景非常优美，是一个峡谷，江水流过广阔的漳州平原，从那里流出，对面是群山。河两岸高耸的群山当然也让这里的风景更加壮观。由于没有村庄和村民，桥周围的风景更显一派静谧之美。

此地的所有桥中，我们首先注意到的就是建于宋初的那座桥。[25]1190年，人们在这儿架了一座浮桥，使用了35年，之后人们建了一座木桥。1265年，也就是建桥30年之后，桥被火烧毁。漳州知府带头认捐50万文铜钱，用来修建一座石桥。募集到所需要的资金后，就建了石桥。这座石桥按照中国的计量法，长2 000尺，相邻桥墩之间的距离是80尺。此桥在今后的300年间，经历了一些小修，直到1565年才经历了一次大修。1590年，桥的两边修了石栏杆。桥的两端还各建了一个牌楼。西面的牌楼上题着4个大字——“三省通衢”。在国姓爷起兵期间，这座桥毁坏得很严重。1673年，为了切断清军的进攻，这座桥的4个地方被毁坏。之后很快又用木材重建，但是在1678年，国姓爷手下的一个将军再次纵火烧毁了这座桥。1679年，福建总督又用木材重修，但是这已不能满足人们的日常使用。于是1685年，厦门的水师提督用石头重修了这座桥。之后，这座桥也重修了好几次。它是一个非常了不起的杰作。它的桥拱不是圆的，而是由一块块巨大的石板架在桥墩上。有些石板长76英尺，厚8英尺，宽3英尺。遗憾的是，我们没有造桥人的相关记录，也没有夯打桥墩地基的方法的记录。通常来讲，九龙江是一条相当湍急的河流。雨季时，它经常发洪水，河面会上升12～15英尺。在这种情况下，河水汹涌地咆哮着冲上桥，甚至会漫过桥面，而这些桥墩也许1265年时就存在了，如今依然坚固如初。

feet long, and the distance between each of the piers, 80 feet, Chinese measurement. With very slight repairs this lasted for 300 years, when it had to undergo a thorough repairing in the year 1565. In 1590 a stone railing was built along each side of it. Two archways were also built, one at each end of the bridge. On the western one were inscribed four characters 三省通衢, 'a public road for the three Provinces.' In the great rebellion under Koksenga, this bridge suffered very severely. In order to cut off the advance of the Imperial troops, the bridge was destroyed in four places. This happened in 1673. Soon after it was rebuilt of wood, but in 1678, one of Koksenga's generals destroyed it again with fire. In 1679, the Governor General of the Province rebuilt it of wood, but this was found so unsatisfactory for general use, that in 1685, it was rebuilt of stone by the Admiral of Amoy. During the present dynasty it has been repaired several times. This bridge is an exceedingly remarkable one. Its arches are not round, they are simply immense slabs of stone reaching from one pier to another. Some of these slabs are seventy-six feet long, eight feet in thickness, and three feet in width. Unfortunately we have no history of the builders of the bridge, or of the manner in which they laid the foundation of the piers. The river, generally, is a pretty rapid one, and during the rainy seasons there are freshets, which cause a rise of from twelve to fifteen feet. On such occasions the waters absolutely roar as they rush down upon the bridge and even over it, and yet, though these piers have, probably, been in existence since the year 1265, they appear as strong and as firm as ever.

"*Roads.*—One of the great roads of China, that passes through the Canton, and Fohkien, provinces, runs through the plain on which the city of Chang-chou is situated, and crossing one of the spurs of the hills, passes over the bridge just described. This road is in fact the only practicable one, for commerce, which exists in all this region. The mountains are so high and inaccessible, that nothing but bye paths are found on them. The great stream of people that moves North, and South, must necessarily pass along this great road, as the only convenient one the Chinese have yet constructed.

"*Literary.*—The prefecture of Chang-chou, has not yet attained a very high literary reputation. In this respect it ranks far below the neighbouring prefecture of Chinchew. The number of scholars that assemble for the literary examination, cannot be less than 11 000, but of course comparatively few of these could, by any possibility, obtain their degree at any one examination. The number that can pass each time is absolutely fixed. Of the seven heens, or districts, within the prefecture, five are allowed twenty each, and the remaining two, fifteen each. In addition to these the city of Chang-chou, has the privilege of having twenty of its scholars graduate at each examination. Although

关于道路。中国有一条很好的连接起广东省和福建省的大路，它经过漳州城所在的平原，穿过一个山嘴，经过刚提到的那座桥。事实上，这条路是所有当地商贸往来的道路中唯一切合实际的。山太高，难以越过，山上只有羊肠小道。大量走南闯北的人必须经过这条大路，因为这是迄今修筑的唯一便利的路。

关于文化。漳州府迄今为止还没有取得非常高的文化成就。在这方面，它的排名远远低于邻近的泉州府。每年应试的人数不少于11 000人，却很少有人能在任何考试中获得名次。通过考试的人数是绝对固定的。漳州府有7个县，其中5个县各有20个名额，另外2个县各有15个名额。此外，漳州城有特权，可以有20个名额。虽然，漳州府在文化上没有取得很高的成就，但也不是说这里绝对没有出过名人。漳州的一个考生通过了各级考试，并以优异的成绩通过了翰林院的考试，最后成了六部的一位官员。1864年，他出访漳州，正好遇到起义军攻陷漳州城，不幸遇害。另外一个来自浦南的人也一样成功地获得了最高的文誉，名列诸翰林之首。长泰也有这样的传奇人物。当地人偶像崇拜的特性让他们永远被人记住。在漳州这一带，人们尤其崇拜一位被称为“王爷”的偶像，其非常出名。这位偶像，除了在一些寺庙中有专门的塑像，在一些特定的日子也会被搬到喜气洋洋的彩船上进行巡游。每当船靠近，人们就会以最大的敬意和热烈的仪式来表示欢迎。人们坚信他具有治愈疾病和祛除恶灵等能力。跟其他县相比，长泰倒是个例外。在长泰，这尊偶像得到的尊重最少，人们提到它必然伴随着最恶毒的言语。通常情况下，中国人非常害怕说偶像的坏话。但是在这一例中，长泰人好像并未被那源远流长的恐惧感所束缚。主要原因如下：这个王爷在成神之前，只是一个进士，而与此同时，长泰出了一个状元。因此，在地位上，这个王爷远不如他们出名

the prefecture does not stand high in a literary point of view, it still is not absolutely without some celebrities. One graduate from Chang-chou, succeeded in obtaining every degree the empire could confer. He passed with distinction the examinations at the Hanlin college, and finally became a member of one of the Six Boards. He was on a visit to Chang-chou, in 1864, when the rebels took the city, when he was unfortunately murdered by them. Another from the town of Punan 浦南 has been equally successful in attaining the highest literary honours. His name stood the first among the candidates for the Doctor's degree. Chang-t'ai 長泰 similarly can boast that one of its citizens has risen to the same proud position. This fact is perpetuated in one peculiar feature of their idolatrous worship. In all this region the worship of a particular idol named Wang yeh is very widely celebrated. This idol, besides having a regular place in some of the temples, is brought around at certain periods in a gaily painted boat. Wherever this boat approaches, it is received with the greatest honour and ceremony, and there is the most unbounded faith in its efficacy to heal deseases, drive off evil spirits, & c. The city of Chang-t'ai is an exception to all this. There this idol is held in the lowest possible estimation, and it is never mentioned without the vilest epithets being launched against it. Usually the Chinese are terribly afraid of saying anything against their idols, but in this case they seem to be unrestrained by the remotest feeling of dread. The reason of this is as follows: This Wang-yeh before he was deified, was simply a Chin shih

進士, that is a scholar of the third literary degree, Ch'ang-t'ai in the mean time, however, had produced a man who had gained the highest degree, the Chuang-yuen 狀元 in the empire. Wang-yeh must therefore, in point of position, be far inferior to their celebrated townsman. Officially, therefore, he has no standing in their town. The spirit of their townsman, they believe to be presiding over their district, and can it be supposed that one who is his inferior, would presume to come in to exercise an authority, which rightly belongs to his superior. They have no dread of his power, since a stronger than he stands by to defend them. We have in this fact, a singular illustration of how the Chinese believe that there is an exact analogy between the present world, and the world of spirits, and that the same gradation of rank, &c., prevails equally in them both.

"The only really world wide celebrity that the prefecture can boast of, is the famous Chu-wĕn-kung, 朱文公.

"This man is the celebrated commentator of the Chinese "Four Books." His family really belong to the province of Honan, but as he was born in this province, he is claimed as one of its worthies. He was prefect of Chang-chou and died there."

Chüan Chou Fu

The prefecture of Chüan-chou-fu 泉州府, Chinchew local dialect, lies to the north east of, and is distant by sea, 60 miles, and by land, 40 miles, from Amoy. It possesses five districts,

的同乡。按理说，王爷在长泰是没有地位的，因为人们相信他们的同乡就能够保佑这个地方。而一位地位较低的人怎能擅自行使地位比他高的人的职权呢？这里的百姓不害怕王爷的权力，因为他们有一位权力更大的人保护他们。通过此事，我们可以简单地解释中国人如何精确地对照阳间和阴间，阳间的等级制度在阴间也同样流行。

漳州府唯一一位值得炫耀的世界知名人士就是著名的朱文公。

朱文公著有《四书章句集注》。他祖籍河南，但是因为他在福建出生，也被认为是这里的知名人士之一。他曾任漳州知府，并在漳州去世。㉖

泉州府

泉州府位于厦门的东北部，距离厦门海路60英里，陆路40英里。泉州有5个县：晋江县、同安县、南安县、惠安县和安溪县。泉州位于东南沿海，北面靠近兴化府，西北面与永春州毗邻，西面与漳州府接壤。泉州位于一片狭长的陆地，周围有几条河流，水源充足。主城叫泉州府，建在晋江北岸的平原上，位于距离入海口10英里的一个海岬，北纬24° 56′ 12″，东经118° 47′ 40″，北京往东2° 22′ 40″。以茶叶出名的安溪位于泉州府主城的正西面。去安溪要走陆路，并经过一条极其狭窄的河流，这条由山间溪流汇集而成的河流叫北溪。惠安县位于泉州的东北面。南安县位于西北面。同安和马巷厅位于西南面，一同构成泉州的南部。金门岛、厦门岛和鼓浪屿隶属同安管辖。

托W.T.斯旺森牧师的福，我得以了解泉州府的诸多情况：

> 大多数中国城市的早期历史都包含了诸多神话和传说，因此，要弄清任何事情的真相就变得尤为困难，几乎不大可能从神话中推测真相。这尤其符合泉州城的情况。这是一座府城，这里的居民对它的美丽感到十分自豪，常常谈论这里的卓越人物。对于任何了解中国和中国人的人来说，以上情

or Hisens namely Chin-chiang 晋江縣, Tung-an 同安縣, Nan-an 南安縣, Hui-an 惠安縣, and An-chi 安溪縣. It is bounded on the south and east, by the sea, on the north by Hsing-hua-fu 興化府, on the northwest by Yung-ch'ing-chou 永春州, and on the west, by Chang-chou-fu 漳州府. It is on a narrow tract of land, exceedingly well watered by several rivers. Its chief city is called Ch'uan-chou-fu and is built on a plain on the northern bank of the Chin-chiang, about 10 miles from its mouth, on a cape, in Lat. 24°56′ 12″N. and Long. 118°47′ 40″ E. of Greenwich or 2°22′ 40″ E. of Peking. An-chi（Ankoi）, known for its teas, lies due west from the chief town of the department, and is reached by road, and by an extremely narrow river, fed by mountain streams, called the Pei-chi 北溪. The district of Hui-an, is situated to the north-east from Ch'üan-chou; and Nan-yan to the north westward. Tung-an, and Ma-chiang-ting, lie to the southwest, forming the southern portion of the department. The islands of Chin-mên（Quemoy）, Hsia-mén（Amoy）and Kulangsu, fall within the jurisdiction of Tung-an.

The Revd. W. T. Swanson, has favoured me with most of the following account of this prefecture. "A mass of myth and fable, surrounds the early history of most Chinese cities, and in consequence it is exceedingly difficult to ascertain anything definite regarding their founding, and almost impossible to eliminate the real from the mythical. This seems to be specially the case in regard to the city of Chin-chew. It is a prefectural city, and its inhabitants are very proud of its beauties, and are much given to talking of its eminence. To those who know anything of China, and the Chinese, the fact just stated, will be seen to increase the difficulty of ascertaining definitely and exactly, the facts of the early history of the city. It is stated that it was certainly in existence during the Tung dynasty, but all that can be gathered about its history, in the remote past seems to be shadowy in the extreme. It appears certain, however, that during the reign of Sun-te, the first Emperor of the Ching dynasty, the city was much enlarged and its wall almost entirely rebuilt. The wall was then made 20 feet broad at the base, and 23 feet high. These are its present dimensions, and it looks as strong to-day, as when it was first built. Its circuit is 20 li, or about 6 English miles. The people say that it is somewhat more than the circuit of the city wall of Fuhchow, and that it was made so, that Chin-chew might excel even the capital of the province. This magnificent wall encloses a large space, which has not been, hitherto, entirely occupied by buildings, and there seems little prospect of its ever being so. At the north and northwest corners

况只会增加进一步了解泉州这座城市早期历史的难度。据说，唐朝时泉州就存在了。但是我们能收集到的所有有关泉州遥远历史的文献看起来都极其模糊不清。可以确定的是，顺治（即清朝的第一个皇帝）年间，泉州城得到很大的扩建，几乎所有城墙都修缮过。当时的城墙基座有20英尺宽，23英尺高。它现在的尺寸仍是如此，看起来还很坚固，俨然刚刚修建好一样。城墙周长20里（或6英里）。老百姓说这里的城墙的周长比福州的还要长。泉州在城墙建造方面也许超过了福建的省府。这座雄伟的城墙围起来一块很大的空间，迄今为止，这里还没完全盖满建筑物，未来看起来也不大可能。泉州城内的北面和西北角，还有一大片空地没有被建筑物占用，这里常年有人耕作。在南门和晋江之间一英里的地方是人口稠密的居民区。从南面进城，要经过一座跨江大石桥。从桥上看去，晋江差不多有300多码宽。作为一座中国城市，泉州非常干净。城里街道很宽，铺着花岗岩石板。从南门到北门的街道看起来是城里唯一繁忙的地方。其他地方都很安静，只有为数不多的几块招牌代表着那里正在营业。这里没有重要的制造业。由于国家政策方面的原因，本该经过这个城市的通路被改到别处。目前，致仕的、现任的政府官员和数不清的文人或对仕途颇有雄心的人及其随从，构成了这里的大部分居民。现有的房屋并没有完全住满，因此泉州的房屋比这个地区其他的地方便宜。泉州曾经是省会城市，现在这里驻有一位知府、一位将军和晋江知县。泉州城里连同周边的人口，在20万～25万之间。著名的国姓爷在攻占厦门、金门、同安和漳州府的海澄县之后，继续攻打泉州，但他未能占领这座城市。于是，国姓爷只好退到他已经占领多年的地方。最终因为没有补给，他只能从这些地方撤往台湾。清廷随后占领了国姓爷留下的这块地盘。小刀会对泉州的影响也只到同安，并且其也只占领

of the city, inside the walls, there is a considerable space of ground which has never been built upon, and is constantly under cultivation. Between the south gate and the river, a distance of one mile, there is a densely populated suburb. The approach to the city from the south, is over a massive stone bridge spanning the river, which, at this point, appears, as nearly as can be judged, to be over 300 yards wide. The city, itself, is for a Chinese city, remarkably clean. The streets are wide, and well paved with granite slabs. The street leading from the south, to the west, gate, seems to be the only busy one in the city. The others are remarkably quiet with few, if any signs, of business being done in them. There are no manufactures of any importance, and from reasons of state policy, the traffic that naturally should have passed through the city, has been diverted to other channels. At present retired mandarins, the acting government officials, and an innumerable host of literary men, or rather aspirants to office, and their dependants, form a very large proportion of its inhabitants. The existing house accommodation is by no means fully occupied, and, in consequence, house property in Chin-chew, is cheaper than in any other part of this region. Chin-chew was at one time the provincial city, it is now the residence of a prefect, a general and of the magistrate of Chin-chiang. Its population, together with that of its suburbs, number between 200 000 and 250 000 persons. The celebrated Koxinga, after obtaining possession of Quemoy, Amoy, and Tungan, in the Chin-chew prefecture, and of Hai-têng, in that of Chang-chow, pressed on to the gates of Chin-chew, but he failed to take the city, and was forced to fall back upon what he had already won; and of these places, he held possession for years. Inability to get supplies ultimately compelled him to evacuate them, and he went to 'Formosa' and took the Manchus quietly coming, and occupying what be left. The 'small knife' rebels never approached nearer to Chin-chew than Tungan, which place they held for only a few days. Chin-chew has produced many officials of ability and note. Among the latest is Huang-tsung-han 黃宗漢, at one time Governor General of the two Kwangs. He and seven other mandarins, were appointed guardians of the present Emperor. At the time of Prince Kung's *coup d'état*, two of these were executed, and Huang-tsung-han, with others, was disgraced. The usual number of women have had memorial arches erected to them for their chastity, filial piety, and devotion to deceased husbands.

"At Tang-chioh 東石, a small port lying at the head of Hui-t'tou bay, there is a brisk trade in salt, carried on in junks, with Full-chow, the return cargoes are poles, charcoal, and bamboos. At Siong-si 祥芝, a port at the mouth of the Chin-chew river, and on its southern bank, there is a large trade with 'Formosa'. Rice, in considerable quantities, is carried

了同安数日。泉州出了很多功勋卓著的官员。其中最近的一位是黄宗汉，曾担任两广总督。他和其他七位大臣被任命保护当今皇上。[27]恭亲王发动政变，八位大臣中的两位被杀，黄宗汉和其他人则失势。[28]这里有很多为妇女立的牌坊来表彰她们的贞洁、孝道以及对去世丈夫的守节。

东石是围头湾前面的一个小港口，有活跃的食盐贸易，商人们在去福州的货船上装满食盐，在回来的船上装满桅杆、木炭和竹子。位于晋江入海口的祥芝港，其南岸有着与台湾的大量贸易。大量大米从台湾的高雄装船出发，在祥芝港转船运至泉州、厦门和其他地方。类似的对台贸易虽然规模没这么大，但同样在永宁和深沪进行。这两个港口距离祥芝港南面几英里。在鸦片船被允许在厦门港停靠之前，有零星鸦片船就停在大坠岛，这是晋江入海口北岸的一个锚地。安溪有很多茶叶出口。其他出口物产包括盐、花生油和糖。同安县出口少量靛蓝。同安在最近几年种植了大量罂粟，据称每年数量都在增加。在泉州上面10英里靠近江边的地方，有大量花岗岩。这些石头质量很好，整个泉州府都在使用。从北京到广州的大道经过泉州府，中间途经惠安，到达泉州，然后经过同安到达漳州，再到南方。这条路上交通拥挤，行人络绎不绝，上至最高级别的官员，下至社会底层的苦力都奔走在这条路上。这条路维修状况良好，每隔一段距离就有中国常见的小客栈。很长一段时间，这条路上盗匪横行，普通老百姓外出旅行几乎变得不大现实。但是，六七年前，罗将军被任命为提督。他以前参加过太平军，是一个精力充沛的果敢的人。[29]他夜以继日地将危害这个地方的所有匪患清除干净。不管何时何地，只要能抓住他们，他就烧毁他们的村寨，杀死寨里的居民。这种强硬有力的措施很快就收到了效果。现在大路上没有盗匪了，即使是偏僻的小路也非常安全。罗将军被调离后，

over from Takao, in 'Formosa', and transhipped at Siong-si, for Chin-chew, Amoy, and other places. A similar trade, but not by any means so extensive, is carried on at Eng-leng 永寧 and Chim-ho 深滬, two ports a few miles to the south of Siong-si. Before the opium ships were allowed to anchor in Amoy harbour, one or more of them were stationed at Ch'uan-t'ou, an anchorage near the mouth of the Chin-chew river, and on its northern side. From the districts of Ankoi, there is a large export of Tea. The other productions, are salt, peanut oil, and sugar. From Tungan district, there is a small export of indigo. In this district, during late years, there has been a considerable cultivation of thc poppy, and it is stated, that it is annually on the increase. There are extensive granite quarries, about 10 miles above Chin-chew, and quite close to the river. The stones are of a superior kind, and are used all through the prefecture. The great road from Peking, to Canton, passes through the Chin-chew prefecture. From Hui-an, it goes to Chin-chew, and thence through Tung-an, to Chang-chou, and the South. Over this road there is an immense traffic. An endless concourse of passengers, from the highest mandarins, to the lowest coolies, are constantly using it. It is kept in a fair state of repair, and there are inns, of the ordinary Chinese kind, at regular intervals. For a long time this road was so infested with robbers, that travelling for ordinary passengers had become almost impracticable. But about six or seven years ago, General Lo, was appointed Thetok.

He was an old Taiping, and a man of great energy and resolution. He rested neither night nor day, till he had cleared the whole district of these pests. He burnt their villages, and killed their inhabitants, whenever, and wherever, he could lay hands upon them. This vigorous action was soon followed by the most beneficial result. There are no robbers on the great road now, and even the bye roads, are perfectly safe. General Lo has been removed, and his successor does not seem to possess either his activity, or his resolution, and it is said that there are indications that would lead one to infer the possibility of a recurrence to the old state of lawlessness. From the five districts of the prefecture, the numbers of literary candidates, and graduates, are, approximately, as follows:—

Chin-kang	about	2 500
Lam-an	...	1 800
Hui-an	...	2 500
Tong-an	...	1 800
An-khoe	...	1 200

"The fixed number of graduates for the whole prefecture is 180.

"Amongst the most notable objects in this prefecture is the bridge of Wu-hai, which is over a mile long, and most substantially built of granite."

Tea Plantations

The spots where the Tea is cultivated at An-chi 安溪（An-koi）in the Ch'üan-chou prefecture, are scattered over a great part of the country, but there are no hills appropriated entirely to its culture. The ground of the

他的继任者似乎没有他的积极性和决心，据说种种迹象表明，之前那种无序的状态有可能会死灰复燃。

泉州府5个县童生的大概人数如下：晋江县大约2 500人；南安县大约1 800人；惠安县大约2 500人；同安县大约1800人；安溪县大约1200人。

整个府的秀才固定名额是180人。

泉州府最引人注目的东西就是五里桥。㉚此桥有一英里多长，由花岗岩建造而成，非常坚固。

茶园

泉州府安溪县的茶园占据了该县的大部分土地，但是没有一座山是完全适合于种植茶叶的。茶园不是在梯田上，而是在一些精心耕种的小块土地上，每块茶地种植着少量茶树，四周是低矮的石头围栏和地沟。种植地点都不是背阴处，但通常位于山里的凹地，两边都有大量的遮蔽物，而且坡度相对较缓。最高的茶园比平地高700英尺。但是那些只有700英尺一半高度，或者更低的茶园，看起来长势更加旺盛，也许因为这里土壤较好，尽管最好的土壤也不比沙地好多少。然而，人们没有施肥，也没有浇水。茶树不是朝东栽种，尽管这些茶树极不耐寒。在冬季，这里常有霜冻，偶尔会下雪，但是下雪时间不长，雪也不厚，不超过三四英寸。虽然以前的茶树种子产自武夷山，但现在的种子都来自当地。往一个三四英寸深的土坑里丢入几粒种子，3个月之后，嫩芽就会长出来，之后再移栽，因为随着树苗长高，其根部周围就要用土堆上。3年后，就可以采摘茶叶了。大多数茶树一年可以采摘4次。烘干的茶叶的重量大约是新鲜茶叶的1/5。每株茶树每年可产出一两（约1/12磅）左右的烘干茶叶，一亩地可以栽种300～400株茶树。一株茶树需要六七年才能长到最大，可存活10～20年。茶树有时候会被害虫吃掉木髓，茎和枝就变成了空管子，还有一种灰色苔藓会专门破坏老茶树。

有的茶树只有几英寸高，但是长得却很茂密，手几乎无法穿过树枝，这些枝上长满了约3/4英寸长的茶叶。同一块茶地里，有的茶树树干有4英尺高，枝叶稀疏，

Tea plantations is not terraced, but formed into carefully tended beds, each little plantation, being surrounded by a low stone fence and trench. There is no shade, but the places selected for cultivation, are generally in the hollow of hills, where there is a good deal of shelter on two sides, and the slope comparatively easy. The highest plantation is computed to be 700 feet above the plain, but those at half, and even less than, that height, appears to be more thriving, probably from better soil, although the best is little more than mere sand. No manure is, however, used, nor are the plants irrigated. The plant is not cultivated on an eastern exposure, although it is sufficiently hardy to bear a severe amount of cold. Hoar frost is common here in the winter months, and snow falls occasionally, but does not lie long, nor to a greater depth than three or four inches. The seed now used for propagating the plant, is all produced on the spot, though the original seed was brought from Woo-e-Shan（武彝山）. Several seeds are put in a hole three or four inches deep, and the sprouts appear three months afterwards, they are subsequently transplanted, and as the plant grows, the earth is gathered up a little round the root; the leaves are taken from the plant when they are three years old, and there are from most plants, four pickings in the year; the green leaf yields about one fifth of its weight in dry tea, and each shrub may yield about a tael of dry tea annually,（about the 12th of a pound）and a mow of ground may contain about 300 or 400 plants, The plant attains its greatest sizes in 6 or 7 years, and thrives from 10 to 20 years. It is sometimes destroyed by a worm which eats up the pith, and converts both stem and braches into tubes, and by a grey lichen, which principally attacks very old plants.

Some of the plants are but a few inches in height, yet are so bushy that the hand can scarcely be thrust between their branches, they are thickly covered with leaves about 3/4 of an inch long. In the same beds are other plants with stems four feet high, far less branchy and with leaves 1.5 to 2 inches long. The produce of great and small is said to be equal. The distance from centre to centre of the plant is about 4.5 feet, and the plants average about two feet in diameter.

The other productions of this district, are salt, peanut-oil, and sugar.

Tung-an-hsien

Tung-an-hsien, 同安縣 (local dialect Tung-oa) containing another somewhat important city, is situated at the bottom of an inlet about 30 miles to the northwest of the island of Amoy. I am indebted to the Revd. William McGregor for the following particulars: "This hsien extends southwards to the island of Wu-sew 浯嶼 near the foot of the Tai-wu-shan 太武山, and includes the belt of islands that guard the entrance to Amoy harbor, the islands of Quemoy, little Quemoy, Amoy, and Kulangsoo. Inside the island of Amoy, a shallow creek runs up to Tung-an city. The hsien thus consists of a border of mountains towards the north, a strip of level

叶子有1.5～2英寸长。据说大茶树和小茶树的产量差不多。茶树之间的间距是4.5英尺，每棵的平均直径是2英尺。㉛

这个县的物产还有盐、花生油和糖。

同安县

同安县，以及另外一个比较重要的城镇，位于距离厦门岛西北方约30英里的一个小海湾的末端。感谢倪为霖牧师提供以下详细资料：这个县向南延伸到了太武山山脚下的浯屿，包括围绕着厦门港入口的群岛以及金门、小金门、厦门和鼓浪屿等一些岛屿。厦门岛内，有一条浅浅的小溪流向同安方向。这个县包括北面的群山，一片狭长的、河流交错的平原，一个有着很多岛屿的大海湾。连绵群山形成同安县的北部边界，将它与北面的安溪县和东北面的南安县隔开。这条山脉向东延伸的尽头是鸿渐山和崎髻山，它们分别是英国海图上的西山峰（West Peak）和东山峰（East Peak）。一条从同安到安溪的路穿过群山之中，然后沿着江水而下抵达泉州，但是这条路的行人不多。产自安溪山上的茶叶，要么运到泉州，要么经过北溪运到厦门。从漳州到泉州的大路要经过同安城；也可以选择水路，从漳州先到厦门，再跨过厦门岛，由沙溪的另一条路转往泉州。这条路本来应该很多人走的，但实际上却没有。直到前些年，从同安到泉州的路上都频遭盗匪滋扰，附近村民也向路过的人勒索敲诈。1864—1865年太平军占据漳州期间，官府派遣北部的军队镇压缉拿这些盗匪，从那天起，这条路就安全了。

同安城的历史可以追溯到南宋时期。但是，关于同安城的具有史学价值的最早文献只能追溯到元朝。元朝时，同安被称作大轮，名字取自附近一座形似车轮的山，现在此山名为梵天山。在国姓爷和清军交战之际，同安城几经易手。有一次，这里的百姓被清军屠杀殆尽；还有一次，这里的城墙被国姓爷推倒。许顺之是大儒朱熹的门生和助手，据说他于南宋时出生在同安。还有《易经存疑》的作者林希元也是同安人，他是明代的名士。同安近年最出名的人物是苏廷玉，大约40年前，道光年间，他官至四川总督。他晚年退居泉州，

ground, indented by creeks along their base, and a large bay containing a number of islands. An extensive range of mountains bounds the district towards the north, separating it from Ankoi, and on the northeast from Nan-an. The extreme spurs of this range to the eastward, are the Hun-chien Shan 鴻漸山, and the Chi'chi-shan 崎髻山 laid down in the Admiralty charts as West Peak and East Peak, A road passes from Tung-an to Ankoi, through the intervening mountains, and thence down the river to Chin-chew, but it is not much frequented. The teas grown on the Ankoi hills, either go down to Chinchew, or come to Amoy, by the North river. The high road from Chang-chou to Chinchew, passes through Tung-an city. As there is an alternative road by water from Chang-chou to Amoy, and thence to Chin-chew, over Amoy island, (joining the other road at Sha-chi 沙溪) this one is not so much frequented as it otherwise would be. The road from Tung-an to Chinchew was, up to a recent date, much infested by robbers; the villages in the neighbourhood levying blackmail on all passers, but the number of northern soldiers at the disposal of the mandarins, during the rebel occupation of Chang-chou in 1864-5, enabled them to suppress this brigandage, and from that date the road has been free from danger.

The city is said to date from the time of the Southern Sung 南宋, but the first notices of it which seem to possess any historical value, do not go further back than the Mongol dynasty,元朝. Under the Mongols it was known as Talun, 大輪, a name derived from a wheel shaped hill in its neighbourhood, now generally called Han-tien-shan 梵天山. During the conflict between Coxinga and the present dynasty, the city of Tung an, changed hands several times. On one occasion its inhabitants were all massacred by the Manchus, and on another the city wall was demolished by Coxinga. Kho-sun-chi 許順之, a disciple and assistant of Chu-hi 朱熹, the celebrated commentator on the Confucian writings, is said to have been born here under the Southern Sung; and Lim-hi-goan 林希元, the author of a commentary on the Yih-king 易經存疑, who flourished under the Ming dynasty. The only man of note that this destrict has of late produced, is So-ting-yueh 蘇廷玉, who, some forty years ago, in the reign of Taukwang, was viceroy of Szchuen. In his old age he retired to Chinchew, where members of his family still reside. Of persons, not natives of the district, who have lived in it, the most noted is Chu-his 朱熹, who, in his younger days, held office in Tung-an as 主簿 under the Southern Sung. In character the natives of Tung-an, are more energetic and violent, than their neighbours of the Chang-chou prefecture, to the west. This applies especially to the people of the villages on the Tung-an creek, and on the coast inside Quemoy, and Amoy, Islands. These villages were, up to a recent date, more or less nests of pirates. On the coast of the mainland, inside Quemoy islands, a considerable quantity of salt is manufactured, but of the ordinary products of the country, rice, sugar, indigo, &c., this hsien does not produce more than is required for local consumption; indeed the rice crop is never sufficient for local necessities. Of late years, however, there has been a considerable cultivation of the poppy for the manufacture of opium; and it is stated that this is annually on the increase. At Shih-hsien 石潯,（Chi-oh jeim local dialect） the sea port of Tung-an, there is considerable local traffic.

As compared with the Chang-chou prefecture, Tung-an stands

他的家人至今仍住在那儿。也有一些名人，他们不是当地人，而是在这里住过。其中最著名的就是南宋的朱熹，他年轻时任同安主簿。与西边的漳州人相比，同安当地人的性格比较富有活力，也比较粗暴。这一性格特征尤其体现在汀溪边以及金门岛和厦门岛等海边的村民身上。直到前些年，这些村庄多多少少都是盗薮。沿海地区和金门岛盛产盐，此外，普通的物产包括水稻、糖、靛蓝等，但是这些物产的产量还不能满足当地人的需求。确实，大米永远都不够吃。然而，近年来人们种植了大量制作鸦片的罂粟；据说，罂粟种植数量每年都在增长。在同安的港口石浔，当地货运量很大。

和漳州府相比，同安在文化方面比较突出；但是与泉州府晋江县相比，又显得黯然失色。因为晋江有一个文学流派，不逊色于帝国的其他流派。截至咸丰三年小刀会起义时，同安的秀才名额固定为22人。泉州各县的名额为：晋江县32人、同安县22人、南安县22人、安溪县22人、惠安县22人。但是，由于同安县（包括厦门）筹集了很多钱财帮助平定太平天国起义，贡献巨大，这一年的秀才名额增加到了72人，之后固定为32人，并一直维持在这个固定数额。当时，增加秀才名额，推动了同安县的教育发展，直到现在它都还受益于这种推动。同安县参加考试的童生人数有一千六七百人，真正答卷人数只有五六百人，而有机会中榜的为100～150人。同安县的有些村子风俗很奇怪，正月十五日左右，人们来到田野，向彼此投掷石子、土块、棍子或者其他任何捡到手里的东西。有一个姓叶的家族，住在领下叶村，定期在祠堂里举办祭祀，之后就开始相互打斗。㉜这个做法似乎是因为今年苦难注定要降临在这个家族或者村子，所以他们宁愿以打破头的方式来避灾，否则他们就有可能患上热病、霍乱或者遭遇饥荒。同样的风俗在漳州府的石码也非常盛行。七月下半月至八月上半月，会县的人都会去南安县的凤山寺㉝朝拜。

这座寺庙位于郭圣王㉞的墓边，此人在世的时候好像也没丰功伟绩（他十三四岁就去世了），但是他的墓却不知为何出名

high in regard to literature, but its reputation in this respect is quite eclipsed by Chin-kang-hsien 晉江縣, in which is situated Chinchew city, which, as a literary school, is inferior to few in the empire. Up to the time of the small knife rebellion, 小刀會, in the third year of Hsien-Fêng, 咸豐, the number of literary graduates was fixed at 22. The number for the various hsiens in the prefecture, being Chin-kang 晉江 32, Tung-an 同安 22, Nan-an 南安 22, An-koi 安溪 22, Hui-an 惠安 22; but on account of the large contributions in money raised by Tung-an, (including Amoy) to put down the local rebellion, the number of graduates was for one year made 72, and afterwards fixed at 32, which still continues to be the fixed number. The addition to the number of graduates at that time, gave an impulse, to education, which is to some extent still felt. The number of candidates attending the examination is about 1 600, or 1 700, of these, the number that really write essay, is about 500 or 600, and the number of those so proficient as to have a chance of success, is about 100, or 150. Some villages in this hsien, have a curious custom of going out to the fields on or about the 15th of the first moon, and then pelting each other with stones, lump of earth, sticks, or whatever comes to hand. One clan, 葉 residing at, 領下葉, regularly set thus to maul each other at the close of a feast in the ancestral hall. The idea seems to be that a certain amount of suffering is fated to fall on the clan, or village, during the year, and they prefer to take it in the form of broken heads, lest otherwise it may come in the shape of fever, cholera, or famine. The same custom prevails at Chioh-bei 石碼 (Shih-ma) in the Chang-chou prefecture. Throughout the whole of this district there is during the latter half of the 7th moon and the first half of the 8th, a great pilgrimage to a temple called Tung-shan-sen 銅山汛 in the district of Nan-an 南安.

This temple is at the grave of a certain sacred King Kwoh 郭聖王 who seems to have done nothing remarkable during his life, (he died when only 13 or 14 years of age), but whose grave has somehow become famous. As his birthday approaches (in the 8th moon) pilgrims arrive from north and south, to the number of several hundreds of thousands, attracted by the fame of this grave, from the province of Canton on the one side, and from Chehkiang, on the other; and at such times the roads in the neighbourhood of Chinchew, get quite populous with pilgrims in companies of from 10 to 40, marching gravely along, distinguished from ordinary travellers by then carrying a number of small flags, and having a small idol tied in front of their persons. Large numbers also pass through Amoy, crossing from the south by boat. Some add to their pilgrimage (which seems in many instances to be undertaken in fulfillment of a vow) other hardships, such as kneeling down once every three or ten steps of the journey. The temple at the grave contains a large number of priests, who improve the occasion of the pilgrimage to carry on a flourishing trade in small flags, lamps, candles, incense sticks, &c.

Quemoy

To the eastward of Amoy, and separated from it by a channel of from five to seven miles wide, in the middle of which is little Quemoy island, is situated in Lat. 24° 20′ 30″ N. Long. 118°16′30″ E.

了。快到他诞辰时（八月）[35]，成百上千的朝圣者就会慕名从南面的广东省和北面的浙江省赶来。每当这时，泉州附近的路上到处都是前来朝拜的人，他们10～40人一群，神情庄重地前行。与普通行人的区别就是他们手里拿着一面小旗子，身前挂着一个小人偶。很多人也会乘船从南经厦门而来。有些人给他们的朝拜（很多情况下似乎是还愿）之路增加了额外的难度，例如在途中每三步或者十步就要跪下叩拜。墓边的寺庙有很多神职人员，他们抓住朝拜的机会，做一些小买卖，例如卖小旗子、灯笼、蜡烛和篾香等，生意非常红火。

金　门

金门位于厦门以东，二者之间被一条宽5～7英里的海峡隔开，中间是小金门。其位于北纬24°20′30″，东经118°16′30″。金门岛上的城镇与其同名，那里进行着少量的本地贸易。据说，岛上居民约1万人。该岛西南面即金门湾（东北面对着大陆）。

蔡清宪[36]出生于金门，是一位历史名人。他在明朝嘉靖年间当过高官，统辖过明朝13个省中的5个。

动　物

厦门及其周边地区的动物，除了老虎，很少为外国人所知。我对此的调查可以为已有的信息做一点补充。

据我所知，这里的动物包括老虎、豹，当地人所说的豹，我猜想应该是大山猫。在永春的原始森林里，据说有人发现了狼。从浦南延伸出去的多石的山丘和大山，形成了附近的高地，据说那里有野猪。在几乎所有这些山里，都有不少野生动物，如狐狸、野猫、獾、犰狳、豪猪、刺猬、白鼬、耗子、豚鼠等。

以前，老虎的活动范围只限于人烟稀少的山中多石地带。之后，它们数量激增，也变得非常大胆，几乎每周我们都会收到消息说老虎常在天亮后两三个小时到耕地众多、满是人烟的平原袭击当地人。山脚下小村庄的人感到非常害怕，于是他们抛弃家园，逃到更加安全的人烟稠密的村子里。值得注意的是，中国人晚上看守庄稼时躺着休息的小棚子，以前建在地上，现

the island of Chin-mên or Quemoy, on which is a city of the same name, carrying on a small native trade, and containing, it is said, about 10 000 inhabitants. This island forms the south western side of a harbour（having the mainland on the north east of it） called the bay of Quemoy.

Ts'ai-ching-hsien 蔡青獻, a man famous in history for having held high office in the reign of the Ming Emperor, 嘉靖 as ruler over five of the thirteen provinces into which the empire was then divided, was born at Quemoy.

Fauna

The fauna, with the exception of the tiger, in this and the regions around, is but little known to foreigners, and my investigations on this subject, enable me to add but slightly to the information already possessed.

It consists, so far as I have been able to ascertain, of tigers, leopards or panthers, called by the natives pal, an animal, I believe, to be the lynx ; and in the large natural forests at Yung-chün 永春, wolves are stated to be found. The rocky hills or mountains, extending from Polam, and forming the highlands of this vicinity, are said to contain wild pigs. In nearly all the hills, foxes, wild cats, badgers, armadillos, porcupines, hedgehogs, stoats, rats, guinea pigs, etc., are more or less numerous.

Formerly, tigers confined their depredations to the sparsely populated neighbourhoods of their rock fastnesses amidst the hills. Of late, they have become so numerous and daring, that scarcely a week passes without some account reaching us, of attacks made on natives, on the cultivated and peopled plains, sometimes two or three hours after daybreak. Such is the terror that they have inspired, that the inhabitants of one small hamlet, at the foot of the hills, have deserted it, and sought the safer shelter of a populous village; and it is significant that the little matsheds, formerly on the ground, in which the Chinese lie to watch their growing crops at night, are now all raised many feet above it, on bamboo poles. When moving about, or travelling at night, torches, and braziers full of lighted wood, are carried. I am informed by several gentlemen, whose duties as Missionaries, constantly take them into the surrounding districts, that on an average one man in five days, is killed by these ferocious beasts, while goats, pigs and dogs are continually being carried off, by them. Last year the Rev. W. McGregor, at early morning, was unable to leave his Chapel for some two hours, owing to a tiger, which had apparently "set," his coolie, when outside, prowling and roaring round it. I have before me, several instances of men, and women, being attacked by these animals, some instances occurring only a few days, or weeks since. The first, is the death of a military mandarin of low rank, and the wounding of two men near Chang-chou, in their endeavour to kill a tiger; the beast escaped. The second refers to the finding of his wife dead, and

在需用竹竿架高几英尺。晚上走动，或者出行时，人们都带着火把和燃烧着木头的火盆。有几个常常在周边地区传教的人告诉我，几乎平均每五天都有一个人被这些凶猛的野兽咬死，而山羊、猪和狗经常被拖走。去年的一天清晨，倪为霖牧师被困在他的小教堂里两小时，因为有一头老虎明目张胆地“坐”在外面，他的苦力在房子外面围着老虎踱步并大叫。我也有听闻几例人被老虎袭击的事件，有的就发生在几天或几周以前。第一例是漳州附近军营里的人去打老虎，结果一个下级军官被老虎咬死，另外两个人被咬伤，而老虎却逃跑了。第二例可能只是推测，一个人干活回家，发现他的妻子死了。此时老虎还和受害者在同一间屋子里，随后援救的人来了，老虎才从屋顶跑走。第三例是，据称在鼓浪屿对面靠近海门的石坑村，有两个人被老虎袭击。一个人被老虎咬住肩膀，当时他的妻子和其他人也在场，她奋不顾身地冲去帮助她的丈夫。她抓住老虎的两只耳朵，试图把它拉开。老虎猛然转身冲向她，咬住了她的肩膀。最后，村民一拥而上才合力把老虎打死。第四例是，最近在浯屿（进出厦门外港的出入口）一个人丁兴旺的村子，发现了两头老虎。村民给老虎的巢穴（一个洞穴）做了记号，把洞口堵死，用烟熏了老虎一晚上。第二天早上，两个人进入洞内，希望看到这两头野兽已经被呛死了，但是它们还活着。两人开枪打死了一头老虎，但另外一头逃到山洞更深处，失去踪迹。第五例是，前几周，有人在山顶的断崖上看见三头老虎（也许是母老虎和它的幼崽）一起朝一块田走去，而田里有农民正在干活。他朝这个人呼喊，刚开始没有引起农民的注意，后来农民听见了，却为时已晚，来不及逃跑了，因为有一头老虎已经进入田里，盯上了这个人。全然绝望中，他站定，抡起干活用的锄头重重地砸向袭击他的老虎。据说老虎四次扑向农民，之后他成功一击，将老虎打死在自己的脚下。第六例是一个可怕的故事，黄昏时刻，一个妇女在自家门口被老虎拖走，并在不远处被老虎可怕地胡乱撕咬，惨不忍睹。在这个事例中，老虎也被打死了。有一个叫坑尾的地方，距离厦门大约

in such condition as may be supposed, by the husband on his return from work. The murderer was still in the room with his victim, and assistance being procured, was subsequently despatched, from the roof. Two men are reported to have been mauled by a tiger at the stone quarry village, near Haimên, on the mainland opposite Kulangsoo. A man is reported to have been seized by the shoulder, in the presence of his wife, and others, she with great courage and devotion, flew to his aid, and seized the tiger by the ears, and tried to pull him off; it instantly turned on her, and bit her also in the shoulder. It was surrounded by the villagers, and killed. In a populous neighbourhood, at the back of the island of Wooseu, (the entrance to the outer harbour) two tigers were lately seen, their lair, a cave, was marked, the entrance blocked up, and the tigers smoked throughout the night; next morning two men went in, expecting to find the animals suffocated, they were however alive; the men fired killing one, the other retreated further into the cave, and was not followed. A man on the top of a hill, or bluff, a few weeks since saw three tigers (probably a tigeress and her cubs) advancing parallel to a field, in which a man was working. He shouted to the man, without at first attracting his attention, at length he was heard, but too late for escape, for one tiger had turned off into the field and made at the man. In utter desperation, he stood his ground, and met the attack with a swingeing blow from the heavy hoe shaped pick he was working with; the tiger is said to have come at the man four times, when the latter by a providential blow, succeeded in laying him dead at his feet. Next follows a dreary story of a woman being taken from her own door, in the gloaming, and horribly mangled, within a short distance. In this case the tiger was also killed. A place called K'he be 坑尾, about fifty miles distant, is said to be infested with them; and it may be that, owing to this region being devastated and nearly depopulated, by the Tai-ping rebels, in 1864, and 1865, they have so increased, as to be driven by want of food, thence to this neighbourhood. Certain it is that they have been met with near Peh-Chui-ya, Wo-seu, on the Nan-tai-wu, near Hai-mên, and at other places, where they have rarely, if even, been seen before. Tales of their depredations at Hai-ching 海滄 just at the head of the inner harbour, are also common. I have, myself, on several occasions tracked the foot prints of tigers, along the damp sandy beds of the nullahs, among the inner range of mountains at this place, and also found their excrement. There are some caves said to be their lair, near, but I never found a guide who could, or who would, point them out.

That tigers are numerous may safely be inferred from one, two, and sometimes three, of their cubs, being brought here, occasionally, for sale. The animal is described as being marked in the same manner as the Bengal tiger, but longer in the legs, and shorter in the body. Judging from one which I have seen, and from a cub, I once possessed, I should say that this description is generally correct.

There are in the interior, pheasants, a kind of partridge, called by the Chinese, Chuh Chi, or Bamboo fowl, quail, pigeons, snipe,

50英里，据说也有很多虎患。也许这是因为1864—1865年此地被太平军破坏，几乎人迹罕至了。随着数量激增，迫于食物短缺，老虎便跑到坑尾附近。可以肯定的是，白水营附近、涪屿、南太武山上、海门附近和其他地方都有人看到老虎的踪迹，而这些地方之前几乎没人见过老虎。在内港上面的海沧，有关虎患的故事也很多。笔者有好几次沿着大山中潮湿峡谷的沙质河床，循着老虎的脚印追踪过它们，也找到了老虎的粪便。据说，有些山洞就是它们的巢穴，但是从来没有向导能够或者愿意带我去找老虎。

从偶尔被带到厦门售卖的一两头，有时甚至三头小虎崽，可以推测出老虎数量很多。这种动物被描述得跟孟加拉虎属于同一种类，只是腿更长，身子更短一些。根据我之前见过的一头老虎和养过的一头虎崽来对比判断，应该说这种描述大体上是正确的。

在内陆，有野鸡，中国人称它为雉鸡或竹禽，还有鹌鹑、鸽子、鹬、鹅、各种各样的鸭子，麻鹬、鸦鹕、苍鹭等各种各样的水鸟，以及我不时看到的海鹰。那些不被当作猎物的鸟类，多是白嘴鸦、麻雀。这些鸟在中国和英国都很常见。戴胜，一种对我们来说非常珍稀的漂亮鸟儿，在这儿却很多。这儿也有鹞鸢、老鹰、鹩哥和画眉等鸟类，就像中国的其他地方一样。

据我所知，厦门市场上差不多有100多种不同鱼类和贝类在出售。上个月发生了一件怪事，人们发现大量死鱼漂浮在厦门外港的海面上。起先，人们不知道这是怎么回事，后来发现这是由一种水蛭所致。很多水蛭吸附在鱼身上，吸干血之后就跑掉去寻找下一个猎物。这种水蛭没吸血的时候长1.5英寸，但是它有能让自己变成两倍长的能力。除了口腔，水蛭的尾端也有一个吸盘，可以牢牢地吸住猎物。这种害虫的出现，被没受过教育的百姓视作当朝的一个不祥之兆。

爬行动物包括蛇，从一些被杀的蛇制成的标本来看，这些蛇长6英尺，甚至8英尺。大多数蛇是无毒的。一种像鞭子一样的小蛇，以及一种数量特别多的水蛇，据说都有毒。还有一种毒蛇，中国人因它的

geese, duck of almost every description, curlew, pelicans, herons, and an endless variety of water fowl, including, as I have now and again seen, the sea eagle. Amongst the birds which are not game, are most of those varieties, from the rook down to the sparrow, common alike in China and England. One beautiful bird, rare and valuable with us, the Hoo-poo, is found here in numbers; kites, hawks, minas, and the hwa-me-chéao, or painted eyebrow'd thrust, are also here, as elsewhere in China.

Of fish, and shell fish, I am informed there are nearly one hundred varieties sold in the Amoy market. Within the last month, or so, a curious circumstance has been noticeable. Large numbers of fish, have been found floating on the surface of the water in the outer harbour, either dead or dying. At first this was difficult to account for, but latterly it has been discovered that a kind of leech has been the cause. In many instances these leeches have been found attached to the fish. After sucking the blood of the fish, they detach themselves from it, to go in pursuit of other prey. This leech, when at rest, is about an inch and a halt in length, but it has the power of elongating itself to fully twice that length. In addition to its mouth, it is provided with a sucker at the other extremity, with which it holds on to its prey with great tenacity. The presence of this creature is looked upon by the uneducated classes, as an inauspicious omen to the reigning dynasty.

The reptiles consist of snakes, some specimens of which have been killed, and found to be six, and even eight, feet, in length. They are mostly harmless. A small whiplike snake, and a particular variety of the water snake, of which there are great numbers in these seas, are said to be venomous, as is also a snake, called by the Chinese from the shape of its head, the spoon headed serpent, (probably the cobra) and another known as the banded adder. The centipede, and the scorpion, are common.

头长得像一把勺子，而称其为“饭匙蛇”(可能是眼镜蛇)，另外一种名为金环蛇的也有毒。蜈蚣和蝎子在这里也很常见。

【注 释】

① 1英寻约等于1.828 8米。——译者注

② 1码约等于0.914 4米。——译者注

③ 见麦克弗森《征华二年记》（*Two Years in China: Narrative of the Chinese Expedition*）。——译者注

④ 梅齐（John Joseph Mechi，1802—1880），伦敦金融城的银匠、银行家、发明家和市议员，实验农民。梅齐出身平平，青年时代在伦敦金融城当文员，26岁时开店成为零售刀匠，生意蒸蒸日上，在全国家喻户晓。中年后，他斥巨资创建了Tiptree Hall农场（后发展为Tiptree公司，即“缇树集团”），并展示农业生产的新设备和新方法。他一直关注农民，《如何使耕种有利可图》一书颇具影响；他推进成立了农业慈善机构，帮助陷入困境的农民。随着知名度和社会地位日益提高，梅齐进入政坛，成为市议员，并有望成为市长。然而，商业版图的问题导致他破产，他被迫退出竞选，转而坚定地从事农业活动，成为农民俱乐部的主席。为了感谢梅齐在农业领域的巨大贡献，英格兰农民踊跃认捐，希望帮助他摆脱财务破产困境。然而，他还没来得及从中受益，就于1880年去世。幸运的是Tiptree Hall公司得以保存，2010年公司成立125周年之际，英国女王伊丽莎白二世到访表示祝贺。公司还委托制作了一部舞台剧，讲述梅齐传奇的一生。——译者注

⑤ 应指郑信（1734—1782），建立吞武里王朝，但其祖籍为广东澄海。——译者注

⑥ 雅裨理（David Abeel，1804—1846），美国归正会传教士。1830年即清朝道光十年抵广州，同年底被派往南洋考察。1839年再抵广州，后迁往澳门。1842年抵鼓浪屿，建立布道所，成为最早进入厦门的基督教新教传教士，也是闽南教会的开创者与奠基者。次年，迁至厦门本岛传教，两年后回国；1846年去世于纽约。著有《旅居中国及其邻国纪事（1830—1833）》。——译者注

⑦ 叶文澜，厦门同安人，字德水，号清渠，著名慈善家。——译者注

⑧ 此墓即民间所称“太师墓”，墓主人为郑成功堂叔郑芝鹏的两个儿子，即长子郑广英、三子郑海英。——译者注

⑨ 麦高温（Daniel Jerome Macgowan，1814—1893），美国浸礼会派遣来华的医疗传教士。1843年2月抵香港，9月抵达宁波。在宁波期间，他常对中国人传教。1854年，因妻子健康问题，移居厦门、香港、澳门。1893年病逝于上海。——译者注

⑩ 摘自厦门的麦高温牧师所著《论中国人的社会生活和宗教观念》。——原注

⑪ 此处略表。——译者注

⑫ 应为圭屿，又名鸡屿，其在明代时建有镇水塔。——译者注

⑬ 据夏商周断代工程报告，夏朝时间为公元前2070—前1600年。——译者注

⑭ 此处叙述有误，公元前81年为汉昭帝始元六年，汉武帝统治时期为公元前141—前87年。公元前220年，秦朝在福建设立了闽中郡，但实际上，只是派守尉令长到闽中来，废去闽越王的王位，改用“君长”的名号让其继续统治该地。公元前202年，汉朝刘邦封无诸为闽越王，闽越国复国。因此也并非汉武帝时期才改变政府管理模式，而是入汉之后即改变。——译者注

⑮ 此处应指闽越王（或称东越武帝）余善。公元前135年，闽越王郢攻打南越国，于是汉武帝派兵讨伐闽越。郢死后，汉武帝命当地宗室繇君丑和余善分别统治越繇国和东越国。实际上，闽越大部分地区掌握在余善手中。此外，此处所说的“广东”当时应处于南越国而非闽越国统治之下。——译者注

⑯ 公元前111年，余善反，汉武帝于是派兵攻打闽越。次年，余善死，闽越灭国。此后，汉武帝“尽徙其民于江淮间”，此地成为空虚之地。——译者注

⑰ 东汉的统治时间为25—220年，之后的三国时期曹魏统治时间为220—266年。——译者注

⑱ 西晋统治时间应为260—317年。——译者注

⑲ 唐朝统治时间应为618—907年。——译者注

⑳ 唐太宗统治时间为627—649年，此处应为唐总章二年（669）唐高宗命陈政入闽。——译者注

㉑ 陈政并未获封为王，而是任朝议大夫，统岭南行军总管事。其子陈元光被民间尊称为“开漳圣王”。——译者注

㉒ 宋朝建立时间为960年。——译者注

㉓ 陈洪进（914—985），五代十国时期割据军阀。他出身贫寒，才干勇气俱佳，屡立功勋，曾主政泉、漳二州。他改革田赋，兴修水利，推进泉州地区经济发展，持续海上贸易。宋太平兴国三年（978）四月，陈洪进入朝觐见，纳土归降，献出泉、漳二州及其所辖县，标志着闽南地区正式归入宋朝版图。——译者注

㉔ 此处关于郑成功两次围漳州城的描述与历史不符。在郑成功与清军多年的拉锯战中，顺治六年（1649）攻漳州未克；九年（1652），围漳州府，粮尽撤围；十一年（1654），攻克漳州府。其中，1652年围城导致城中军民大量饿死。——译者注

㉕ 即江东桥。江东桥始建于1190年，而非宋初。江东桥又名通济桥、虎渡桥。1214年，浮桥改为石墩木面桥；1237年，木桥被火烧毁，改建梁式石桥。之后屡毁屡修，其中最大的一次修建在明嘉靖十八年（1539）。——译者注

㉖ 原文中关于朱文公的描述，有许多与史不符之处。朱文公即朱熹（1130—1200），祖籍徽州婺源（今江西婺源），生于南剑州尤溪（今福建尤溪）。其祖籍并非河南。朱熹曾任漳州知府，但其并非在漳州去世，而是在建阳考亭（今福建南平）。——译者注

㉗ 此处与史实有出入。原作者误以为黄宗汉为“顾命八大臣”之一，其实“顾命八大臣”为载垣、端华、景寿、肃顺、穆荫、匡源、杜翰、焦佑瀛，黄宗汉为载垣一派人物。——译者注

㉘ 实际上，祺祥政变（即辛酉政变，慈禧太后与恭亲王联合发动）后，载垣、端华赐白绫自缢而亡，肃顺被斩首，其余或发遣，或革职。——译者注

㉙ 此处的“罗将军”应为罗大春（1833—1891），贵州施秉县人，曾任福建陆路提督、代理福建水师提督等。原文中说他“参加太平军”，与史不符。其非但没有参加太平军，反而在镇压太平天国运动中，屡建奇功，被清廷授予“冲勇巴图鲁”称号。不过，罗大春军中有不少太平天国降将。——译者注

㉚ 此处原文“Wu-hai”应指五里桥，即安平桥，泉州十八景之一，横跨晋江安海镇与南安水头镇之间的海湾。始建于宋绍兴八年（1138），历时13年建成。长2255米，是我国古代首屈一指的长桥，素有“天下无桥长此桥”之美誉，被国务院颁布为全国重点文物保护单位。——译者注

㉛ 摘自哥登（G. J. Gordon，英国东印度公司植茶问题研究委员会秘书——译者注）在《中华丛报》上发表的到访安溪茶叶产区的备忘录。——原注

㉜ 此处可能指流行于当地的“宋江阵”武术表演，其现为福建省省级非遗项目。当地人以迎神赛会化装形式进行表演，保持练武习俗和武术套路。原作者可能将其误认为是打架斗殴。——译者注

㉝ 此处原文为“Tung-shan-sen”，并注以中文“铜山汛”。据下文，此应为供奉广泽尊王的“凤山寺”，作者按当地发音误作“铜山汛”，实是与漳州的铜山汛（铜山水寨）混淆。——译者注

㉞ 郭圣王即广泽尊王，姓郭名忠福，泉州府南安县人。——译者注

㉟ 此处有误。郭圣王出生于后唐同光元年（923）二月二十二日，八月为所传郭圣王成佛之月，乡民议定为“祭墓月”，并于八月初一日行“开墓门”礼。——译者注

㊱ 此处原文作“蔡青献”，有误，应为“蔡清宪”，即蔡复一（1577—1625），字敬夫，号元履，福建泉州府同安县金门人。明代名宦，节制五省，死后赐谥“清宪”，后世尊称“蔡清宪”。——译者注

第三部分

PART Ⅲ

宋元明清时期的闽南贸易概述

厦门开始与外国通商的确切时间很难确定，不过卫三畏在《中国总论》第418～419页写道："西方国家对中国人的最早记载，应归于著名的地理学家托勒密，其本人这方面的知识好像得益于一位名叫马瑞纳斯的提尔人。但是，在托勒密时代之前，人们对这片孔夫子所生活的土地的描述，以及对这里生产的精美丝绸的欣赏和需求，在欧洲已经存在了。试图去确认那些早期文献中所提到的地名，是非常困难的事，而且几乎是徒劳无益的。例如文献中提到的名为'Cattagara'的商业中心，或许是广州，也可能是福州或者厦门，因为

General Sketch of Its History under Sung, Yuan, Ming, and Tartar Dynasties

It is difficult to fix a precise date to the opening of trade at Amoy with foreign countries, but Dr. Williams, in his *Middle Kingdom*, p. 418-9, writes, "The first recorded knowledge of the Chinese, amongst the nations of the West, does not date further back than Ptolemy, the celebrated geographer, who seems also himself to have been indebted to a Tyrian author, named Marinus. Previous to this period, however, the account of the existence of the land of Confucius, and an appreciation and demand, for the splendid silks made there, had reached Europe. It is a difficult, and almost profitless, endeavour, to attempt to identify the names of the places mentioned in these early records. The emporium called Cattagara, may have been Canton; it may also have been Fuhchou, or Amoy, for the places are all natural entrepots." Sir John Davis, p. 19, says, "Abundant evidence is afforded by Chinese records, that a much more liberal, as well as enterprising, disposition, once existed in respect to foreign intercourse, than prevails at present. It was only on the conquest of the empire by the Manchus, that the European trade was limited to Canton." He further speaks of Chinese junks being seen as far West, as the coast of Malabar, about the end of the 13th century; and adds, that even before the seventh century, it appeared from native records, that missions were sent from China, to the surrounding nations with a view to inviting mutual intercourse. The earliest attempt at intercourse between Great Britain, and China, was in the year 1506, when three ships, bearing letters from Queen Elisabeth, to the Emperor of China, were despatched, but they were lost on the way, and the project was not then renewed; and the oldest record of the East India Company at Canton, is dated the 6th April, 1637. It is, however, certain that tradal relations have existed from a remote period, between Amoy, the Philippines, the Dutch and English settlements of Batavia, Sourabaya, the Straits of Sunda, Padang, Sumatra, and in fact with the entire Malay Peninsula, the Gulf of Siam, the coast of Borneo, and even as far as Timor, in the far east of the Sunda Islands, and Dutch possessions. At this date, it appears that the port of Amoy was at Haitêng, (Haitien), a large town up the Nanchiang, or Southern river, about fourteen miles from the present port, for

这些地方都是天然的贸易中心。”德庇时①在《中国人：中华帝国及其居民概述》第19页称：“中国文献提供的大量证据表明，在对外交往方面，中国曾经出现过一个比现在更加自由、更加进取的局面。只是在清朝统治之下，中国与欧洲的贸易仅限于广州。”他还提及，大约13世纪末，中国的帆船曾出现在远西的马拉巴尔海岸②。他继续补充道，根据当地记载，甚至在7世纪之前，中国曾派使团前往周边国家，希望彼此之间能相互往来。中英之间交往的最早尝试发生于1506年，英国派遣3艘船前往中国，带着伊丽莎白女王写给中国皇帝的信，但是他们却中途迷路了，因此这项计划半途而废。东印度公司在广州的最早记录，可以追溯到1637年4月6日。然而，可以确定的是，很早以来，厦门贸易往来的对象就有菲律宾、巴达维亚的荷兰人和英国人据点、泗水、巽他海峡、巴东岛、苏门答腊岛，以及事实上整个马来半岛、暹罗湾③、婆罗洲④，甚至东到巽他群岛的帝汶岛，以及荷兰人控制的岛屿。当时，厦门地区的港口似乎位于海澄，南溪上游的一座规模较大的城镇，距离现在的厦门港14英里。《厦门志》中记载，在开放厦门作为贸易港之前，海上来的帆船进港时需经过大担岛，直达海澄；禀告地方官以后，在遵守当地洋行规定的前提下，才能继续驶向石码，并卸载货物。至于这种贸易的性质和贸易额，我们无法获得真实可靠的文献。石码和海澄港的淤塞，很可能使得港口迁至厦门。

中国历史、地理著作和游记中关于闽南的记载，是罗马天主教传教士到来之前，西方关于该地区的历史和地理信息的仅有来源。这些记载表明，厦门作为贸易港，是较为晚近的事情，大概在190年前。而在此之前，这一地区极其出名的海上贸易和对外贸易，是分别在漳州府和泉州府开展的。

宋元祐年间⑤，即宋朝第七位皇帝（在位时间为1085—1100年）任上，福建省首次开放对外或海上贸易，政府指定了专人监管（从其官职“市舶提举司”便可明了），他的主要职责是对外国货物征税及负责与之相关的其他事务。这种贸易曾经遭遇的阻碍已被清除，人们发现了一种新的且刺

in the Hsia-men-chih (Chinese History of Amoy,) the following passage occurs: Before the opening of Amoy as a port of trade, junks from seaward, on entering, passed the island of Taitan, and proceeded to Haiteng, where, after reporting to the District Magistrate, they were allowed to move up to Shih-ma (Chioh-bei) , when compliance with the port regulations being secured, by certain native hongs, they were allowed to discharge, and load cargo. Of the nature and value of this trade, no authentic record is obtainable. The silting up of the estuary below Chioh-bei (石碼) and Haiteng, probably necessitated the removal of the port to Amoy.

The notices of this region contained in Chinese histories, topographical works, and itineraries, which alone form the source of the information, historical, and geographical, possessed by occidentals, for the ages preceding the visit of the Roman Catholic propagandists, shew that the existence of Amoy, as an emporium of trade, dates but from a, comparatively, recent period, some 190 years. The maritime and foreign trade, for which this portion of the empire has been so preeminently distinguished, was, prior to that date, divided between the two prefectural cities of Chang-chou, and Chuan-chou.

During the reign of Yuan-yu, 7th emperor of the Sung dynasty (from 1085 to 1100 A. D.) , the province of Fuckien, was first opened to foreign, or oversea, trade, and an official was appointed to superintend (as is evident from his title, 市舶提舉司) the collection of duties upon, and other matters relating to, the commerce in, goods brought from abroad. The trammels by which this branch of trade had been confined, having been now removed, the people found a new, exciting, and, though dangerous, highly profitable, means of gaining wealth. They flocked to it, intercourse increased, and traders came in such numbers, that this single official, was quite unable to maintain anything like a useful surveillance. To remedy this state of things, the government entrusted the examination of goods, to the ordinary local officials at the various ports of entry, (viz. the 知州,通判, 知縣,監官) who acted under the supervision of an officer specially appointed to watch the transport and shipment of goods, whose title was 轉運司.

The trade appears to have gone on developing in much the same manner, under the succeeding dynasty of Yuan. And about the commencement of the 13th century, it had attained such proportions that the local authorities found it impossible, while attending to their own duties, to superintend the collection of the revenue, and legislate on the matters incidental to such extensive commercial transactions. They were, therefore, relieved of this burden, and replaced by a staff of seven officers, specially appointed to take cognizance of all such matters.

Under the Ming dynasty, owing probably to the depredations committed on this portion of the seaboard, in the first instance, by the Japanese, and subsequently by Chêng-chih-lung, and his son Cheng-kung (Koxinga), this trade appears to have declined. For the three superior officers of the staff, established by the preceding dynasty, were dispensed with, and three subordinate officers were found sufficient to maintain an effective control. And when an entire cessation of trade was caused by these troubles, this small staff was removed to Fuchow, from Chüan-

激的赚钱方式，虽然有风险，却能赚取高额利润。人们蜂拥而至，贸易量大幅提高，客商人数剧增，以至于这位官员单枪匹马很难行使有效的监管。为了扭转这种态势，政府指令货物抵达口岸的当地官员（即知州、通判、知县、监官），在转运司（一位专门任命来监管货物运输的官员）的监督下，检查进入口岸的货物。

在接下来的元朝，对外贸易在很大程度上以相同的方式进行着。大约13世纪初⑥，贸易规模急剧扩大，地方官员不可能在履行自身职责的同时，既监管税收，又制定法则，规范如此大规模的商业贸易带来的各种事务。因此，他们卸下了这副担子，相关职责被交给了专门任命来处理此类事务的七位官员。⑦

到了明朝，或许因为东南沿海地区遭到劫掠，首先是来自日本的倭寇，后来是郑芝龙和他的儿子郑成功，这里的贸易开始萎缩了。前朝制定的七位官员制中的三位高级别官员被裁去，三位属官足以进行有效的管理。⑧当这些麻烦导致贸易完全中断时，这个小小的市舶司就被上头从泉州府迁往福州，而该机构原本就是派驻在福州的。

根据记载外国概况的汇编材料《东西洋考》，宋朝有一个风俗，即每次船离港时，都会有一位官员上船，去查看船是否违规。之后会在附近的一块石头上刻上碑文，标着船名、离港日期、目的地，等等。这种做法在后面的两个朝代得以延续，但是后来渐渐废弃不用了。

chow-fu, known to foreigners as Chinchew, to which it was originally appointed.

It is stated in the Tung-hsi-yang-káo, a sort of compendium of notices of foreign countries, that it was the custom under the Sung dynasty, to send an official on board every vessel leaving the port, whose duty it was to see her beyond its limits. An inscription was then cut upon some rock in the neighbourhood, giving the vessel's name, date of departure, her destination, &c. This practice would seem to have been maintained under the two succeeding dynasties, but gradually fell into desuetude.

最早来访的欧洲商船

最早注意到来访的欧洲商船，可以追溯到15世纪初。据称，在明朝的第八位皇帝成化年间（1465—1486）和第九位皇帝弘治年间（1486—1506）[9]，来华的外国船只中，有的体量巨大。在获利最大的当地人的帮助下，这些船的货主似乎建构起了庞大的走私网络，直到与倭寇爆发冲突时所有征税活动都停止了。不久，政府再次颁布了海禁通告。

明确地指出这些船是欧洲商船的最早记载，是在一些年后。1548年[10]（即明朝第十一位皇帝嘉靖任内的第二十六年），葡萄

First Arrival of European Vessels

The first notice of the arrival of an European vessel, would appear to date from about the commencement of the fifteenth century. As it is stated that, during the reigns of Chêng-hua（成化）, and Hung-chih（弘治）, the 8th, and 9th, emperors of the Ming dynasty, whose reigns dated from 1465-1486 and 1486-1506, respectively, amongst the foreign vessels that arrived, some were observed of an immense size. Aided by the natives, who were of course the chief gainers, the supercargoes of these vessels, appear to have carried on an extensive system of smuggling, till the outbreak of troubles with Japan put a stop to the collection of all revenue. Soon afterwards the prohibition of oversea trade, was promulgated afresh.

The first notice of their arrival, expressly stating them to be European vessels, does not appear, however, until some years later. In 1548（26th year of Chia Ch'ing, the 11th emperor of the Ming dynasty）Frankish vessels arrived with foreign merchandise at Wu-hsü, an island situated some 7 miles seawards of Amoy, at Chuan-chou-fu, and Chang-chou-fu. A brisk trade sprung up with the natives, but it was looked upon with unfavourable eyes by the officials, who, it would appear, conceived the idea that these attempts on the part of foreigners to effect an opening for then commerce, were but the prelude to further and more forcible designs of possessing themselves of the country, and therefore, determined to crush it in embryo. A force was, therefore, despatched by Ho-chiao 柯喬, the Hsün-hai-tao, or Intendant commanding the Coast guard contingent, to put a stop to the trade; but as this produced no result, a censor named Chu-wan 朱紈, seized over 90 of the merchants, and struck such fear into the mercantile body, generally, by their summary execution, that all commercial operations were suspended, and trade brought to a stand still. It was, however, merely a temporary cessation, and we find about twenty years later, the native officials, themselves, awakening to the importance of international commerce, and of the advantage to be derived from it. In 1567 T'u-shih-min, 涂澤民, a Censor, and Governor of the province, addressed the throne praying that the prohibition restricting the coast-landers from the free use of the sea, be abolished, and commerce with all foreign nations, Japan alone excepted, be legitimised. The request was granted, and a large trade was again created, which appears to have been carried on viâ Meiling, in Nanchao, 南詔之梅嶺, until the frequent piratical depredations compelled a change of course to Hai-têng. The new port prospered so rapidly, with this fresh influx of trade and wealth, that, say its chronicles, in 1564, a Tung-chih, a magistrate, of very subordinate rank, it is true, but still the superior of any the district had yet been able to boast of, was added to the staff of collectors, and two years later,

牙[11]商船携带外国商品抵达浯屿，该岛位于泉州府和漳州府之间，距离厦门海路7英里。欧洲人很快与当地人建立了活跃的贸易关系，但是官员们对此却看不顺眼。他们认为这些外国人来此地开启商业贸易，只不过是为进一步强占中国领土拉开了序幕，因此决心将其扼杀在萌芽期。于是，作为指挥海防部队的官员，巡海道柯乔派兵前往阻止这些贸易；但该行动收效甚微，于是监察都御史朱纨抓捕了90多个商人，并将他们迅速处死。商人们感到非常恐惧，便暂停了所有商业活动，贸易陷入停滞状态。然而，这只是暂时的，大约20年之后，当地官员开始意识到对外贸易的重要性，以及由此带来的好处。1567年，福建巡抚、都御史涂泽民上奏朝廷，呼吁废除限制沿海百姓自由出海的禁海令，建议与日本以外的国家的商业往来应该合法化。皇帝批准了他的奏请，于是经往南诏之梅岭进行的贸易再次大兴，后因频繁招致海盗劫掠，才被迫改道海澄。随着贸易量的扩大和财富的大量涌入，新的港口迅速繁荣起来。根据地方志记载，1564年，新设立了作为地方官的同知，他也被列入收税的官员队伍中，因此，虽然他的品级很低，但也是当地可以拿来夸耀的“高官”了。两年之后，海澄升级成了县。

关税的管理委托给了海防官员

1573年[12]之前，对外贸易的征税事务并没有委托给内务方面任何常见的分支机构，而是交给专门任命的官员，只是其主管部门经常更换。这一年，漳州知府罗青霄建立了负责征收关税的督饷馆，并将督饷权交给负责海防的同知。

6年前，根据时任督饷官王起宗的建议，在海澄对面的小岛圭屿建立了一个分馆，这扩大了海防官员的职权。[13]尽管并未明说，事实上这个变化的部分原因是为了免去在海澄较近的一个地方设立类似机构的维持费用，主要原因是督饷官渴望拥有军事指挥和部署部队的权力，以终结本地区一贯猖獗的走私活动，清除海盗对港口的滋扰，而且要确保他达成这些目的的权力；之前由于权力分散和利益冲突，此权力是无法保障的。

Hai-têng was erected into a Hsien, or district town.

Superintendency of Revenue on Oversea Trade, Entrusted to Commandant of Coast Guard

The collection of duties on the foreign trade, does not appear to have been entrusted to any regular branch of the Civil Service, prior to 1573, but to have been handed over to a set of officials, appointed, certainly, for this express purpose, but now under the control of one chief, and now of another. In this year, however, a Custom House, charged with the collection of these duties, was established by Lo-ching-hsiao 羅青霄, the Prefect of Chang-chou, and its superintendence handed over to the subprefect commanding the Coast guard.

This addition to the duties of Commandant of the Coast guard, had been made six years earlier, in consequence of a proposal made by Wang-chi-tsung, 王起宗, the then controller of Customs, to establish a branch office at Kuia-hsü 圭嶼 a small island lying nearly opposite Hai-têng. This change appears, though such is not stated to be the case, to have been decided upon, partly, to avoid the expense of maintaining another establishment in such close proximity to that of Hai-têng, but chiefly, from a desire to ensure, as Superintendent of Customs, by the appointment of an officer holding a military command and entrusted with the disposal of troops, a person not only whose interest it would be to put a stop to the smuggling, always prevalent in this district, and to clear the approaches of the port from the piratical craft which infested it, but who would, at the same time, have the means at his disposal for effecting these ends, which hitherto with divided authority and conflicting interests, it had been impossible to secure.

Institution of a Tariff, Amount of Collection

In 1576, it was decided, at the proposal of the Governor, Liu-jao-hui, 劉堯誨, to devote the shipping duties, to the payment of the troops. In order then, to bring the total collection as much as possible under control, and to fix a sum, upon the receipt of which they could depend, the authorities drew up a sort of tariff, consisting principally of three descriptions of duties. Amongst these, first comes the license fee, which is subdivided into two classes, according as the license includes, or not, the right to trade with the northern "Formosa" ports of Tan-shui, and Chilung (Keelung.) ··· For a license to trade with any foreign port, ··· a fee of 3 taels was levied. Were it desired to include the two ports of Tan-shui, and Chilung, as well, an endorsement to this effect was made on the original document, (both documents being the same in the first instance,) and an additional fee, of 2 taels, collected. The most important of these duties, as returning the largest sums to the treasury, are the Export duty 水稅 and Import or Inland tax 陸稅. It is exceedingly difficult to trace, accurately, the nature of these taxes after the lapse of so many years, and with the sparse records kept in statistical works. But as far as can be judged, the Export duty would appear to have been levied upon the owner, or charterer, of the vessel, and to have been computed according to her size, so that, as far as the manner of levying be regarded, it would correspond more

税制的设立及税收的金额

1576年，朝廷采纳了中丞刘尧诲的建议，以船税充军饷。为了尽量控制所有关税，并且达到可以依赖的固定的税收额度，当局设计了一套关税制度，主要包括3种类型的税收。首先是引税，细分为两类，区别在于是否有与台湾岛北部港口淡水和基隆的贸易权。一个能与任何外国港口进行贸易的文引，每引要缴纳3两纹银。如果要加上淡水和基隆两个港口，需要在原来基础上再交2两纹银。[14]其次，这些税收中最重要的，也是国库收入中最大金额的税，是水饷和陆饷。多年之后，因数据资料着实有限，要追溯这些税收的确切性质，难度极大。但是目前所知道的是，水饷是根据船的体量向船主或者船的承租人征收的，这种征收方法与船舶按吨位征税非常相似。陆饷是对货主征收的，根据所装货物的数量比例征收。因此，似乎就是对每艘出入港的船只都粗略地收税。对于出港的船，只向承租人收税；对于进港的船，则根据购买数量向货物的买家按比例征收。最后，还有一种税叫“加增饷”，对每艘进出口岸的船额外征收150两，不过我无法确定事实是否如此。此举是为了弥补朝廷向菲律宾和日本的商船征税时，由于后者缴纳的白银不纯或成色较差而带来的损失；正如1860年《天津条约》批准之前，在华洋商必须缴纳关税总额的1.2%，作为耗羡。

官员侵吞税款

当时，关税总额是固定的，每年为白银6 000两；接下来的4年里，总额增加到10 000两；1594年，数额几乎是10 000两的3倍，达到大约29 000两。但是，这种固定税额的机制容易导致大范围的腐败；饷官向国库缴纳每年的定额税收之后，便不向上级官员汇报剩下的金额，而是留下作为自己的额外收入。随着贸易的扩大和繁荣，这就成了一笔非常可观的收入；而法定征收的额度，多半只是实际征收金额的一小部分。因为，尽管征收的总额曾有一次达到过去的3倍，但饷官积累的大量财富证实了一件公开的丑行（在执行“缩赢”时期达到了巅峰），即当局不得不严格执行一项法

nearly with our Tonnage dues, than Export duty. Import duty, on the other hand, was levied on the salesman, and the amount proportioned to the quantity of goods disposed of. It would thus seem probable, that a lump sum was levied roughly, on each vessel leaving, or entering, the harbour, the dues in the former case, to be paid by the charterer alone; and in the latter, by the purchasers of goods, in proportion to the amount purchased. An "Additional tax," 加增餉, of 150 taels, would appear to have been levied on every vessel, probably, though I have been unable to discover whether such is the case or not, upon her entering and leaving the port, in addition to those above mentioned, in order to recoup the government, for the loss they would, otherwise, have sustained from impurities, or alloy, in the Philippine, and Japanese silver, which had to be received in payment of duties from vessels coming from those countries, just as, previous to the ratification of the treaty of Tientsin in 1860, a meltage fee of 1.2 per cent, was levied on the total amount of duties, from the foreign merchants established in China.

Misappropriation by Superintendants

The amount of duties to be accounted for annually, was, at the same time, fixed at 6 000 taels; four years subsequently, this sum was raised to 10 000 taels, and in 1594, this latter amount, was almost tripled, and the collection fixed at 29 000 odd taels. This system of a fixed return, gave rise, however, to an immense amount of embezzlement; for the collector, after paying the amount required annually, into the treasury, instead of reporting any surplus there may have been, to the higher authorities, retained it as his own perquisite. With an extensive and flourishing trade, this was a very considerable amount, and in all probability, the sum which the collection might by law attain, was but a small portion of the actual total receipts. For, in spite of the fact that this sum was, on one occasion, increased to three times what it had previously been, the enormous fortunes amassed by the collectors, proved such a public scandal, (which culminated during the holding of Ying-so 縮贏) that the authorities found themselves compelled to insist upon the literal execution of a law, passed to regulate whereby the Superintendent was to be changed annually; and it was decided that, in future, a sub-prefect should be elected from some one district within the province, annually, to fill the post.

Control Transferred to Nai-chien

It seems probable that when the proposal made by Liu-jao-hui to apply this revenue to the maintenance of the troops, was acceded to, the sum collected by the Hai-têng Custom House, alone, was devoted to meet the expenses of the troops under the orders of its superintendent, the Commandant of the Coast guard. For mention is made in the local records, that some time subsequently, when the military treasury of Chüan-chou became exhausted, a proposal was made by the Intendant of the circuit of Chang-chou-fu, and Chuan-chou-fu, to establish an officer meanway between the two places at Chung-tso-so 中左所, as Amoy was then called, whose duty it would be to determine whether the vessel came from the Eastern sea, i.e. Japan or from the Western, i.e. Manila, or one of the many islands in the Malayan archipelago, which maintained tradal relations with this port. In the former case the duties were to be received by the Chüan-chou treasury; in the latter by that of Chang-chou. But this was, of course, found to be impracticable, so matters remained in *statu quo* until 1600, when

律条款，用于规范饷官的任命，即规定督饷官每年都要换人；并且决定每年从本省的某个地方选出一位佐官，来填补这个职位。

关税的征收移交给内监

或许是刘尧诲提出的用船税维持军饷的建议被采纳了，海澄一地的饷馆所征收的关税，被用来支付海防官下属军队的开销。当地文献中提到，后来泉州军饷匮乏，泉州府和漳州府的巡海道建议在两地中间的中左所（即当时厦门的称呼）任命一个官员，其职责是管理来自东洋，如日本，或来自西洋，如马尼拉或者马来群岛等地与厦门港之间有贸易往来的船只。东洋船只的税收到泉州财库，西洋船只的税则收到漳州财库。然而，此建议太不可行，因此只能维持现状，直到1600年，明朝万历皇帝对全国范围内执行公务的方式进行了一次大范围审查，之后被官方延续。在整个明朝，尤其是明朝后期，宦官身居高位，广聚钱财。一个名叫高寀的宦官被皇帝派往福建，担任海陆两方面的税监。此人颇有能耐，他揭露了很多近来发生的让税收体制蒙羞的滥用职权情况。他提出并施行一些激进的改革，但是由于他心里想的更多的是扩大自己的权势，而非致力于为国效力或改善民生，滥用职权的行为仍像以前那样继续蔓延；唯一的区别是，太监取代了当地官员，在征税时中饱私囊。而实际的主要的改变是，从福建省征收的土产品和海产品，要交由专门侍奉皇室生活的内务府，而对外贸易关税的征收，则转由皇宫中管理宦官的部门内监来负责。高寀即刻将自己人安插到福建全省。

控制权移交给当地官员

但是，这种体系并没有维持很久。14年之后高寀失势，他所倡导的改革也随之崩塌，在现在看来，其改革的实际后果只不过是扩大了宦官的权力。内监被剥夺了管理税收的权力，税收数额也削减到了之前的三分之一，而且征税的权力移交给了每年从当地任命的一位普通官员。不过，他必须将所有重要的事项报告给他的上级即知府，由后者决断。这种情况一直持续到崇祯末年，崇祯皇帝是明朝最后一个皇帝

a general enquiry and examination was instituted by the Emperor Wan-li, throughout the empire, into the manner of conducting public business, as then followed by the officials. One of the eunuchs attached to the palace, a body who throughout this dynasty, and especially during the later reigns, enjoyed posts of vast influence and great emolument, named Kao-ts'ai 高寀, was commissioned by Imperial decree to inspect the Superintendencies of Customs, both Inland and Maritime. A man of considerable ability, he laid bare a number of the abuses, which had of late disgraced the system. He proposed, and carried, some radical changes, but as he had the aggrandisement of his own order more at heart, than any patriotic desire to serve his government, or ameliorate the condition of the people, the abuses continued in much the same state as previously, the only difference in result, being, that the eunuchs, instead of the local officials, enriched themselves at the expense of the revenue. The principal changes effected were, reversion of the collection upon all the natural produce of the province, and of the sea, to the Nai-wu-fu, a metropolitan office charged with the direction of all matters of the Imperial household; and the transference of the control of the revenue derived from foreign, or oversea, trade, to the Nai-chien, or bureau charged with the control of the eunuchs belonging to the Imperial Palace. This officer lost no time in despatching members of his own class, to take up the appointments throughout the province.

Control Given to the Local Authorities

The system, however, did not enjoy a long life. Fourteen years after, Kao-t'sai fell into disgrace, and with him collapsed the supposed reform, whose real end, it was now seen, had been little else than to extend the power of the eunuchs. The Nai-chien was deprived of its control of the revenue, which was simultaneously reduced to one third its previous amount, and entrusted to an officer, to be appointed yearly, from among the ordinary local authorities. All matters of particular importance, however, he had to refer to his superior, the prefect, for decision. So matters continued till near the close of Chung-chën's reign, the last emperor of the Ming dynasty, when Chêng-chih-lung commenced his harassing descents upon this portion of the empire, as has been detailed above, seized upon the revenues, and in short caused an entire cessation of commerce.

First Establishment of Custom House at Amoy

When in the 22nd year of Kang-hsi, 1683, "Formosa" was incorporated with the fifteen provinces, and the Imperial authority firmly established on the mainland, the local magistrate, through the medium of the Board of Works, pointed out to his Majesty, the advantages the people were deprived of, by the maintenance of the old prohibitions against oversea trade; and prayed that the province of Fuhkien might be opened to this trade, as, three years earlier, had been done with that of Shantung. In consequence of these reports, the prohibition was withdrawn, and the sea opened up to the coastlanders, for both fishing and commercial purposes. This necessitated the establishment of another port, for, during the troublous times that were just finished, the alluvial deposits brought down by the river Lung, had so shoaled its bed as to render its navigation by vessels of such a size, as had previously frequented it, impossible. Amoy, situated just at the mouth of the river, and possessing admirable harbour accomodation, was, notwithstanding its political insignificance, its pauci-

了。当时，郑芝龙开始在闽南一带呼风唤雨，正如上文所言，他攫取了这里的征税权，简而言之，这导致了商业贸易的全面中断。⑮

厦门首次设立海关

1683年，即康熙二十二年，清朝统一台湾，政权逐渐稳固，福建当地官员通过工部向皇帝请奏，称海禁剥夺了老百姓的利益；请求开放福建省的对外贸易，就像三年前开放山东的对外贸易那样。奏章被批准了，禁海令被废止，海洋再次向沿海地区的人们开放，人们可以从事渔业和商业活动了。这就需要建另一个港口，因为在海氛时期，淤泥的沉淀导致九龙江的河床升高，致使之前能通过的船只现在却无法通过。厦门刚好位于九龙江口，拥有得天独厚的口岸条件，尽管它在政治上无足轻重，且缺乏（实际上可以说是极度缺乏）商业资源。但是选址仍确定在这里，同年厦门设立了海关。⑯

闽南人一向具有探险精神，同时为了逃避饥荒和海盗肆虐带来的灾难，当地很多人移民到马尼拉和马来群岛，结果带来这个地方的贸易大繁荣。的确，在这么短的时间内，贸易兴盛、规模庞大，是非常了不起的，它展现了在适当推动和关照下，从海外贸易中获利之丰。但是贸易繁荣36年[17]之后，当局中的反对派再次用他们惯常的卑劣手段进行破坏，以走私大米到马尼拉和巴达维亚违反了贸易规定为由，使贸易陷入停顿。

设立现行关税体系

接下来的几年，因生计被剥夺，加上庄稼歉收以及其他困境，当地人被迫入海为盗来度过饥荒。人们意识到这样一个现实，缓解贫困的唯一方法，就是给这些闲散赤贫的流民找一份工作，而废除禁海令，能为本地物产找到一条可以盈利的销路，大量人员得以受雇于海运业，而且刺激本地制造业和海外移民，从而实现上述目标。1727年，福建巡抚高其倬上奏朝廷，请求将对外贸易合法化。他的请求基于两个理由：第一，百姓的财富会大量增加，而来自对外贸易的税收也可以充盈省财库；第二，为了解决粮食常年短缺问题，可以从国外

ty, in fact, almost absolute want of commercial resources, the spot fixed upon, and a Custom House was opened there the same year.

The same spirit of adventurous daring, which had always distinguished the inhabitants of this portion of the empire, coupled with the necessity of seeking an escape from the calamities caused by famine, and the ravages of buccaneers, induced considerable emigration to Manila, and the islands of the Malayan archipelago. A large and flourishing trade arose in consequence, indeed, the dimensions it attained, in so short a space of time, are quite remarkable, and shew how lucrative it might have been, had it been properly fostered and looked after. But after flourishing and increasing for thirty-six years, official opposition again interfered with its usual baleful influence, and put a stop to it, on the ground that cargoes of rice were, in violation of the trade regulations, being smuggled away to Manila, and Batavia.

Institution of Present System

During the next few years, deprived of their means of gaining a livelihood, and harassed by failure of crops and other distresses, the people were forced to resort to brigandage and robbery to escape starvation. Recognising the fact that the only means of alleviating the distress, was to find some new occupation for the idle and destitute; and that the removal of the oversea trade prohibitions, by finding a profitable outlet for native produce, by the employment of large numbers on the shipping, &c., and by the stimulus it would afford to local manufacture and emigration, would be most calculated to attain this end,

Kao-chï-cho, governor of the province in 1727, prayed his Majesty to legalise this branch of commerce. His request was based upon two reasons, first, that the wealth of the people would be greatly increased, and the provincial treasury filled with revenue derived from it; and, secondly, because rice, to compensate the constant failure of crops, might be obtained from abroad. His prayer was granted, and from this date sprung up a flourishing and lucrative trade with the South, which has not, except by such indirect means as excessive taxation, and extortionate fees, been since interfered with.

The collection of the Revenue, was, as has been stated, entrusted to the local officials subsequent to 1614, and it would appear, continued to be so (if indeed the collection was attempted at all, during this unsettled period; it certainly was *not* during the latter portion,) at the time of the reduction of "Formosa", and the establishment of a Custom House at Amoy in 1683. The following year, however, in Fuhkien and Shantung, the two provinces, in which oversea trade had been legalised, two Superintendents of Customs, one Manchou, and one Chinese, were appointed to control the collection; but in 1729, after the prohibition, issued in 1719, had been rescinded at the instance of the governor, it was entrusted to him.

This arrangement continued up till 1788, when the General commanding the Tartar garrison of Foochow, was appointed Superintendent of Customs for the whole province, and deputies, appointed by him, had control of the subordinate posts. This is the system, which obtains at the present time.

Early Trade Relations with European Nations

To the Portuguese belong the honor of being the pioneers

进口大米。皇帝准其所奏，从那时开始，闽南与南洋的贸易开始繁荣起来，除了过高的税费和敲诈勒索等间接手段，贸易再没有受到其他干扰。

如上所述，1614年之后，征税的工作就交给了本地官员。情况似乎会持续下去（在这动荡时期，如果真的有收税就好了；后期肯定是没收过），直到1683年统一台湾，厦门建立了海关。第二年，福建和山东两省对外贸易合法化，朝廷派了两位海关监督来控制征税，一位是满人，另一位是汉人。但1729年，在废除了1719年颁布的禁海令后，根据福建巡抚的提议，关税重归巡抚管理。

这种情况一直持续到1788年，福州将军被任命为整个福建的海关监督。他委派代表管理下级部门。该体系一直延续至今。

与欧洲国家的早期贸易

葡萄牙人是与中国贸易的先锋。1516年，拉斐尔·佩雷斯特雷洛来到广州。第二年，一个由8艘船组成的船队，在费尔南多·佩雷斯·德·安德拉德的指挥下，到达中国沿海。他们的贸易迅速扩张。他们最先在泉州、厦门和宁波进行交易。这些早期贸易商看起来更像是周游各地的绅士和冒险家，而不是稳重的商人和放债人。他们好像更精通刀剑，而非和平地经商。他们在与中国人相处方面很不谨慎。他们诡计多端、出尔反尔、野蛮好斗，在沿海立足之后，就开始建立堡垒，随后而来的通常是试图收税或者敲诈勒索，他们的所作所为在中国人脑海中播撒下不信任外国人及其动机的种子。如今，这种动机有时也昭然若揭了。西班牙人、荷兰人和英国人步葡萄牙人的后尘。

16—17世纪，这些葡萄牙人、西班牙人、荷兰人和英国人等所干的勾当，在亚洲人心里留下了不良印象，他们也将怀疑、不信任、蔑视和仇恨转移到美国人身上。1838年《中国丛报》第7卷第77页的一篇关于美国对亚洲“大马”地区命运的影响的文章提到了这一点：

历史表明，日本孝德天皇（年号大化）、嵯峨天皇（年号弘仁）及其继

of foreign trade in China. In 1516 Raphael Perestrello, came to Canton; and in the following year, a fleet of eight ships, under the command of Fernão Peres de Andrade, arrived on the coast. Their trade spread rapidly, and at an early period they traded at the neighbouring port of Chinchew, here, and at Ningpo, ... The character of these early traders appears to have partaken more of the gentleman rover, or adventurer, than of the steady merchant and scrivener; and they seem to have been far more conversant with the sword, than with the peaceful ways of commerce. There was a want of prudence in their bearing towards the Chinese. They were intriguing, arbitrary, and aggressive; having gained a footing on shore, they proceeded to erect Forts, then usually followed an attempt to levy taxes, or other exactions, and otherwise they so conducted themselves, as to sow in the Chinese mind, that distrust of foreigners and their motives, which occasionally makes itself manifest at the present day. The Spanish, Dutch, and English, who followed them pursued much the same course.

Speaking of the transfer to the American people of a full share of all the suspicion, distrust, contempt, and hatred, which had been excited in the Asiatic mind by the acts of the Portuguese, Spanish, Dutch, English, &c., committed chiefly in the 16th, and 17th, centuries, the writer of an article on American influence on the destinies of Ultra Malayan Asia, in the *Chinese Repository*, 1838, Vol. 7, p. 77, says:

"It is a matter of history that Taiko, Gongin, and their successors on the Japanese throne, the sovereigns who gave its present shape to the foreign policy of that nation, were fully aware of the extent of European aggression on the soil of eastern Asia. Wherever the enterprising Japanese of those centuries, and their Chinese contemporaries, wandered, from India to Acapulco, they gathered and brought home one concurring story of European designs and conduct, varying only in the illustrations of their fraud, cruelty, and highhanded usurpations. The veil of many years is now drawn between us and those days, and the actors and their deeds are generally forgotten. But we have only to look into such records as still remain, only to look on the map, in fact, to see how true it is that scarce a spot on the then known world of the eastern Asia, entirely escaped European aggression. The weaker portions were seized on by right of discovery and conquest, sanctioned by the highest ecclesiastical authority; and where the native states were too powerful to be assailed, each trader sought to gain the same selfish ends by blackening, vilifying, and plundering, his rival of other nations. There was no restriction laid on one which had not been recommended by another. The Spanish denounced the Dutch, as the revolted subjects of his sovereign; and the Dutch told, in secret, of Cortes, Pizarro and Alva. No European people wanted an accuser while a subject of another European state was by; and had it pleased these pagan monarchs to pass sentence accordingly, none would have lacked an executioner. Such was the character of the times when Europe first came into contact with eastern Asia. Such were the impressions then made and ever since transmitted; engraven in literature, interwoven with tradition, identified with education, entering into every conception of the term, rising involuntarily at every mention of the name, European. Such is

任者们——他们制定了这个国家的现行外交政策——充分认识到欧洲对东亚的侵略。几个世纪以来，野心勃勃的日本人以及与他们同时代的中国人，从印度到阿卡普尔科⑱，无论走到哪里，都收集并带回一个关于欧洲人企图和行为的共同故事，差别只是如何描述他们的欺诈、残忍和横暴的篡夺行为。随着时间流逝，过去的历史已逐渐模糊，历史上的人及其行为被尽数遗忘。我们只能查看遗留的历史文献，事实上，只能通过查看地图来了解；真相便是当时东亚知名的地方，几乎都没能逃过欧洲的侵略。弱国被强国以发现和征服之名加以侵占，而这却得到了教会最高权威的认可；那些强大得难以攻占的国家，其贸易对手则通过抵制、诽谤、掠夺的手段，达到同样自私的目的。没什么可以约束一方对另一方实施的不良行为。西班牙人斥责荷兰人，说他们是西班牙君主的叛臣贼子；而荷兰人则揭露了科尔特斯、皮泽洛和阿尔瓦公爵⑲的真面目。没有一个欧洲人想遭到邻近的另外一个欧洲国家的人民的控诉；但如果这能取悦他们的君主并使其据此对其他人定罪的话，相信是不会缺少刽子手的。这就是当欧洲初次接触东亚的那个时代的特点，也是欧洲人当时给人留下的以及此后流传开来的印象，被刻进文字里，与传统相互交织，受到教育的认同，形成“欧洲”一词所有的含义，在人们提及这一词语时便不由自主地想起。这导致了一种可悲的结果，即东方人将这一历史传统观念也套用在了美国人头上；据此，美国人被赶出日本的港口，在中国港口也遭到限制。

给事中关于开海贸易的有趣奏章

这些带有偏见的高压手段带来的直接后果就是，外国人被赶出中国大陆。他们转而去往台湾等地，在中国的水域从事非法贸易。当地官员和商人很早就充分意识到对外贸易的价值，这可从上文以及下文给事中傅元初的奏章中看出。这是一份充

the sad entail, which is, as the Easterns suppose a part of the lawful patrimony of the Americans; under such ideas of descent they are driven from the harbours of Japan, and restricted in those of China."

Interesting Memorial by Minister on This Subject

The immediate result of these injudicious and high handed measures, here, was that foreigners were driven from the mainland; on which they resorted to "Formosa", Lum-pu-co, and to illicit trade on the China sea. That the value of foreign trade was fully appreciated by the local authorities, and the native traders, even at a very early date, may be gathered from what precedes, and from the following memorial to the Throne, from the censor Ki-shih-chung, which is such a liberal and statesmanlike paper, that I may be pardoned for inserting an abridged translation of it here.

"In the third month of the 12th year of Chung-chen 崇禎, of the Ming dynasty （1640） the Minister or Censor, Ki-shih-chung （給事中） a Foo-yuan-choo 傅元初, memoralises the Throne for the removal of the prohibition against oversea trade, and to make an additional port of entry at Amoy, so as to legalise the traffic in the province of Fuhkien. He represents that funds must be raised for mobilizing and provisioning the army, and that already, for this purpose, agriculture is taxed to its utmost by levies in kind. He therefore recommends that what might be argued in the abstract as either detrimental, or beneficial, is not to be considered at so critical a period as the present; and that some modification in practice must be tried. With the merits of a case such as the extension of maritime trade in Fuhkien, he being a native of that Province, is well prepared to speak, and knows that he has a precedent for his action, in the memorials of the Minister Ho-Keao-yuan, who several times, urged this measure, but was always met with Imperial commands to the effect that such innovations could not be sanctioned. The information he has been able to gather of the history of this sea border traffic, is shortly to this effect.

"In 1573, the annual oversea revenue of the district of Yue-keang, the harbour of Hai-têng, amounted to Tls. 20 000, being quite sufficient to maintain during a series of years its quota for local garrisons; no additional troops being required to take the field during that period of tranquility, yet no surplus funds were laid by to meet subsequent demands for the repulse of pirates, who, later on, infested the neighbourhood, carrying pillage into all surrounding districts. About the same time western buccaneers made their appearance, causing general consternation by piracy and robbing junks. The local officials then memoralised the Throne, on this state of affairs, which led to trade being stopped, and this source of revenue had to be abandoned. Writers of books have indulged in

满开明思想并且体现政治才能的奏章，我在此插入该奏章删减版的译文：[20]

明崇祯十二年（1640[21]）三月，给事中傅元初上奏朝廷，意在废除海禁，在厦门增设口岸，从而把福建的交通纳入法规管辖之下。并且必须筹集资金，以调动和供养军队，为达此目的，已最大限度地征收农业税了。因此，在此关键时刻，不必抽象地去争论利害关系，而是在具体做法上必须做出一些改变。关于发展福建对外贸易的好处，作为土生土长的福建人，他最有发言权。他知道，这样做是有先例的：何乔远[22]曾数次建议采取该措施，然而屡屡为朝廷所阻，未能实施；而他收集到的关于海疆交通史的信息很快就起了作用。

1573年，海澄县之月港对外贸易的关税达到白银两万两，足够维持本地守军多年的开销。在那段和平时期，不需要额外的军队来开疆拓土，但是也没有多余的银两来支付驱除海盗的开销，这些海盗后来骚扰邻近地区，并大肆劫掠。大约在此时，出现了西方来的海盗，当地官员为此上奏朝廷，于是皇帝下旨停止贸易，放弃征税。文人雅士沉迷于运用文学手法描写福建农民，称他们靠海而生，将大海视为牧场，因为他们将海产品作为食物来源。尽管海获数量不稳定，平常时期的供应或许是充足的，而在稀缺之时，百姓贫困潦倒、生活无着，是令人非常沮丧的。为了生计，老百姓铤而走险，入海为盗，啸集亡命。强行实施海禁的直接后果，便是沿海地区劫掠频发。每当官府颁布禁海令，百姓的生计就被切断，他们要么饿死，要么铤而走险。一个又一个村子被毁掉，百姓流离失所，无助的男男女女被残忍地杀害，年轻人被抓走，所有金银细软均被无情地搜刮殆尽。郑芝龙[23]自从归顺之后，屡立战功，局面便平顺了一些，黎民百姓得以重操旧业。然而，鉴于快速致富的强大吸引力，他们趋之若鹜；他们与外国人进

the literary conceit of describing the Fuhkien peasantry, as a seafaring race, who look upon the broad sea as their pasture lands, owing to their depending mainly on its products for their sustenance. Such resources in ordinary times, although precarious in their nature, might suffice, but in times of scarcity, it is distressing to witness the signs of extreme poverty amongst the people, who for relief are tempted to join gangs of desperadoes, and, utterly regardless of life, engage in piracy. These marauding forays along the coast, seem to be the immediate consequence of enforcing the prohibition against trade, for each time it is proclaimed, the people, whose ordinary sources of employment are thus cut off, and who would, otherwise, starve, are driven to resort to these desperate courses, and whole villages are destroyed by them, unresisting and helpless men and women, are cruelly murdered, the youth of both sexes carried off into captivity, and all the portable wealth of the place made away with in a remorseless manner. Since the return to allegiance of the piratical chief, Koxinga, the country has become somewhat tranquilised by the frequent defeats the rebels have sustained at his hands, and the people have had leisure to resume their ordinary occupations; yet such is the attraction of the chances of acquiring rapid gain, that they are entrapped, like silly geese, into breach of the laws by resorting to clandestine traffic with foreigners, which is either carried on at some distance from the coast, or by lurking about the 'Formosa' coast, and visiting the dens established there by foreigners, since the ports on the mainland have been closed to the latter. This they are the more readily enabled to do, as the distance from 'Formosa' to the principal towns of Chang-chou, and Chüan-chou, (in the Amoy district) is but a voyage of a couple of days and nights. The responsible Imperial Officers for preventing this, who reside in the south of 'Formosa', at Tai-wan-foo, content themselves with announcing the prohibition, and forbidding access to their port, but wink at the Portuguese, and Frankish establishments at Keelung, and Tamsui in the north of the Island. Thus foreign trade may have been prohibited in name, but it still exists in point of fact, owing to the connivance of petty officials, and the eagerness for gain on the part of the native traders. These facts which are well known, being the common topic of conversation in his native place, although attended at present with results much to be regretted, admit of a remedy by pursuing a different course. (The memorialist's plan is to legalise and foster, the maritime and junk trades, the character of which he proceeds to describe, as follows:) The character of the trade carried on with foreign vessels, and junks, from distant countries, may be thus classified: Besides the traffickers from the western seas, and the Japanese, there are also the Siamese, and Peguese, who bring products much needed, and consumed, by China; such as sapanwood, pepper, ivory, and rhinoceros horns, whereas the Franks and Spanish, whose

行的地下贸易违反了律令，要么在距离海岸较远的地方进行，要么潜伏在台湾岛海岸线附近，到访外国人在台湾的贼窝，因为大陆的港口已经对外国人关闭了。后者是更为常见的选择，因为台湾距离漳州和泉州（所属的厦门）两地只有几天的时间。为了杜绝此类事件的发生，驻扎在台湾岛南部的台湾府相关官员宣布禁令，禁止百姓进入港口，却对在台湾岛北部的基隆和淡水的葡萄牙人和西班牙人睁一只眼闭一只眼。由于这些小官员的纵容，以及当地商人获利心切，对外贸易虽名义上被禁止了，但事实上却依然存在。这些大家都心照不宣的事实，成了当地人茶余饭后的谈资，尽管其为当下带来了很多令人追悔莫及的后果，但人们只能采取其他手段来进行弥补。（上书者的计划是使海上帆船贸易合法化，并加以推动，其接下来描述海上贸易的性质。）与来自遥远国度的外国轮船、帆船进行的贸易，可进行如下分类：除了来自西方海域的商人，还有日本人，以及暹罗人、柬埔寨人，他们带来了中国人急需的物产，例如苏木、胡椒、象牙、犀角；而主要属地拥有银矿的葡萄牙人和西班牙人，则带来了制作精巧的硬币。与这些不同国家的人进行贸易时，国人一般情况下是用自己的物产交换上述物产，但是从西班牙人和葡萄牙人那里，他们收到的只有银圆。这两国人很乐意换取中国的丝织品，因为他们的国家不养蚕，他们很想买到生丝，用于织造最精美的布匹，做成华美的衣服来装饰自己。对他们来说，这种交易利润颇为丰厚；因为著名的湖州丝绸，即便在这儿也是按重量计价，以银两出售的；而在他们国家，价格要加倍。所有人对江西的陶瓷，以及福建的果脯和精美小吃都有很大的需求。这里成了我们国人做买卖盈利的好地方，因为我们有别人艳羡不已的物产，很容易成交；有了这些物产，我们只要花费一丁点儿的如西班牙人和葡萄牙人等的精力和聪明劲儿，就能很容易地走出国门与人竞争。百姓不被允许参与其中，但是高额利润诱使他们通

（chief） possessions are silver mines, bring coins very dexterously cast. Our people when trading with these different foreigners; in the one case, barter their goods in exchange for those above mentioned, whilst from the Spaniards and others, they receive nothing but silver dollars. These foreigners are well pleased to obtain our Chinese Silks, in exchange, and as in their countries they do not rear the silk-worm, they are glad to get the raw silk, with which they are able to weave the most exquisite fabrics, wherewith to adorn the person with rich garments. It is a profitable venture for them, as the celebrated silk of Hoo Chow, even here sold for its weight in silver, is, in their countries, worth double that sum. There is likewise much demand, from all comers, for the porcelain of Keangse, and for the preserved fruits, and delicacies, produced in Fuhkien. Now here is a fine field for profitable commerce for our own people, for we possess those much coveted articles, which are readily handled, and with such we might easily go abroad and successfully compete with them, had we but a fiftieth part of the energy and cleverness of these Franks. The people are prevented from having a share in these good things, and yet have every temptation thrust in their way to misbehave, and involve themselves in all the consequences of being engaged in illicit trade. As to the remedy above alluded to, there is not wanting a precedent, （the reverse of the course now pursued,） for the Imperial sanction was given permitting external trade, shortly after the commencement of the Ming dynasty, when the people of both the Eastern and Western, seas, on being summoned to send tribute, brought it to the Capital, and gave constant evidence of their loyal and respectful feelings, without leading to any rioting or disreputable results. In fact, nothing occurred to disturb the even course of the trade thus sanctioned, even during the disastrous times when all the countries to the west, and the states of Eastern Europe, were suffering disruption, from the Tartar hords under Tamerlane. (The period when Moscow was sacked and burnt, and Bajazet, the Ottoman Emperor, was captured in 1402, appears to be the time to which the Memorialist alludes, for in his next paragraph he makes a significant allusion to troops being sent to guard the frontiers, against an expected invasion of China, for which Timour, in his capital at Samarcand, had been making immense preparations, and was actually on his way for its conquest, when he was fatally attacked by fever.)

"In these times, amicable tradal communications, were uninterruptedly maintained with neighbouring states, and China incurred no embroilment with them, although she had to move armies of observation to guard her frontiers, against threatened invasion, (by the common enemy.) Subsequently, on serious complications arising in "Formosa", and on the neighbouring coast, the Ming dynasty became so apprehensive for the safety of those portions of the em-

过旁门左道来进行不法贸易。至于以上所谓的弥补，其实是没有先例的（和眼下追寻的方向背道而驰），因为自明朝建立之后不久，皇上下了谕旨，允许对外贸易，东西大洋的各色人等都来到都城进贡，随时献上忠诚和尊重，从而避免了任何可能的骚乱或者不体面的结果。事实上，当朝惠准的平顺的贸易进程没有遇到任何妨碍，即使所有西方国家以及东欧各国在帖木儿率领的突厥铁蹄下分崩离析。（这一时期莫斯科被洗劫焚毁，奥斯曼帝国的皇帝巴耶塞特一世1402年被俘虏，傅元初所指的应该是该时期，因为在下一段中，他给出了一个重要的指涉：派遣军队守卫边疆，抵抗即将到来的对中国的入侵。因为，帖木儿在他的首都撒马尔罕做了大量准备，事实上他正在来入侵的路上，然而却被致命的热病打败了。）

这一时期，中国依然不间断地维系着与邻国的友好贸易往来。中国与邻国没有纠纷，虽然不得不派军队守卫边疆，抵御可能的进攻（来自那位共同的敌人）。后来，台湾出现了严重的问题；明朝人非常担心其邻近的沿海地区的安全，于是禁止所有人靠近海岸线。禁海令未废除之时，对外贸易全由奸民把持着，并被沿海的海盗垄断。因此，每年无端损失的关税收入多达两万多两白银，给合法商人造成了巨大损失。国家的损失惨重，利益却被作奸犯科的海盗搜刮去，真是可悲可叹；但是，一群官员对这些不法贸易睁一只眼闭一只眼，幸灾乐祸地分享所获得的赃款，或者参与其中，因此这些事情对他们来说也没有那么可气了。同时，他们装聋作哑，无视银圆叮叮当当的声音。当前形势下的获利者，是一些卑劣的不法商人，他们攫取了利益；还有就是那些腐败官员，他们滥用职权为自己谋取了巨大的私利，这些都是关闭贸易所带来的恶果。然而，若对外通商，除了继续保持对军器、硫黄和硝石的禁售之外，福建商人被允许与所有外来者做生意，

pire, that they prohibited all access to the coast, and the prohibition not having been since rescinded, the trade has been at the mercy of reckless people, and has become the monopoly of the freebooters of the Coast, involving a needless sacrifice of derivable revenue, to the extent of, at least, Tls. 20 000, annually; and to the great detriment of the legitimate trader. The mere loss to the state is severe enough, and that the benefit should be absorbed by the law breaking freebooter, is deplorable; but these circumstances are not so irritating, as to have to witness the acts of a horde of conniving officials, and petty officers, gloating over their share of the spoils obtained by winking at the trade, and professing, meanwhile, to ignore the tinkling of the dollars, which proclaims its existence to all others less deaf than themselves. Those who under the existing state of things are benefited, are the base illegal traders, who absorb the gains; also the corrupt officials, who, usurping authority, extort a full share for themselves; and such are the consequent evils of keeping the trade closed. Whereas were foreign trade thrown open, with the exception of a prohibition against trading in munitions of war, sulphur and saltpetre; and the traders of Fuhkien, allowed to deal with all comers, and were other traders from Che-keang, and the northern provinces, encouraged to bring their silks, &c., and the porcelain dealers from Keangsi, allowed to resort here, the sum named would not only suffice for the troops, but many estimate that there would be produced Tls. 50 000 to Tls. 60 000 instead, which would admit of a surplus, beyond the provincial requirements, being remitted to Peking. The poor people on the coast would accumulate funds, to enable them, in times of scarcity, to buy food, instead of being, as now, so poor that they are driven to piracy. A third benefit would arise, in breaking up the opportunities afforded these minor officials, of employing their perquisites in investments for storing contraband, of which pirates, and others, stand in need, and who are enticed and prepared to pay any prices for such articles. To meet those changes, should it be permitted to again open the port to trade, all that would appear to be necessary, would be to issue a special Junk clearance on proceeding to sea, or else to reestablish Yue cheang, 月港, the port of Hai-ting, 海澄, as the port of entry; or to allow it to be fixed at Amoy in the Tung-ngan district. On leaving port, the junk's clearance or pass would suffice; on returning from abroad, the vessels would have to put into Canton, or Macao, to guard against their running their cargoes elsewhere on the coast. It would be necessary to entrust the prefects of Chang-chou-foo and Chüan-chou-foo, together with the sub-prefect of Amoy, as Maritime Superintendent, with the control of the trade. The Intendant of these prefectures, should be made the responsible head, reporting to the Lieutenant Governor the annual amount of collection;

鼓励来自浙江和北方省份的客商带来丝织品等商品，鼓励来自江西的陶瓷商人在这里进行交易，所产生的税收不仅能满足军队的开销，很多人估计可达五六万两白银。除了上交省里的税金，肯定会有结余，可以上交朝廷。沿海地区的贫民也会有所积累，以便在困难时期有钱买食物，而不是像现在这样入海为盗。再者，还能剥夺这些小官员利用手中特权去资助海盗和其他人从事走私行当的机会。海盗迫切需要这样的支持，走私带来的利益诱使他们愿意为此付出任何代价。为了顺应这些变化，应再次允许开埠通商，所需要做的，只是为入海的船只开一张特别许可证，或者将海澄县的月港作为进关的港口，或者在同安县之厦门设立进关的港口。离港的时候，只需出示船只许可证或通行证即可。从国外返回的船只必须驶入广州或者澳门，以防其将货物卸载到别的口岸。因此，很有必要委任漳州和泉州的知府，连同厦门同知，共同担任海防官，从而把控贸易。这三个地方的管理者应该被任命为负责人，每年向巡抚汇报关税总额的情况；所有盈余税金，即超过两万两的部分，需通过他送往北京，封上凭条，上交国库，用于国家开支。傅元初还提及一位本地官员㉔（并有心要为他谋个职位），后者在镇压海盗和保护帆船贸易方面有令人称道的成绩。他接着指出，根据当地方志的记载，早年间市舶司设置在泉州府，为海上来的帆船提供停泊之处，眼下在广东水域香山县之澳门仍保留有一处。除其本人外，许多人也认为广东和福建两省不必区分，所有福建人对此的看法颇为类似。他恭敬地请求皇帝降旨于福建巡抚和按察使，调查全面禁止海上贸易是否可行；若不可行，开放贸易是否真的毫无益处？巡抚和按察使应咨询泉州府和漳州府最开明的商人何种法规最好，以使贸易恰如其分地合法化，并阻止无视法规者的不法交易；同时，亦可为军队筹集兵饷。

and all surplus sums, beyond Tls. 20 000, should be transmitted by him to Peking, under voucher cover to the Board of Revenue, to devote to Imperial purposes. The memorialist here makes mention （with a view to obtaining an appointment for him） of an official of his district, who has rendered meritorious services in the suppression of piracy and protection of the junk trade, and then proceeds to say that in the old times, as recorded in the local topographies of the districts, there was a government anchorage at Chüan-chou-foo for junks arriving from sea, and that there is still one in existence in the Canton waters, at Macao, in the Heang-shan district, and that, in the opinion of many others besides himself, there need be no distinction between the provinces of Canton, and Fuhkien, for all Fuhkien people, feel alike on the subject; and he respectfully solicits, that orders be given to the Fohkien Governort and Provincial Judge, to investigate, whether, or not, it be really practical to entirely suppress maritime trade; and if not, whether there would not arise beneficial results from throwing that trade open, and that they should consult with the most enlightened amongst the traders of Chuan-chou-foo and Chang-chou-foo as to what the best regulations would be for properly legalising the trade, so as to terminate the illicit traffic carried on by the lawless; and, at the same time, husband the resources for maintaining the troops."

East India Company's Trade Relations with Amoy District

There are records that, in 1651, the Dutch were trading here, and that they lent assistance to the government in attacking Koxinga at Quemoy, and Amoy. About 1664, the East India Company opened a trade at Amoy, and at "Formosa", with Koxinga's son, "but this rude chieftain had little other idea of traffic than as a means of helping himself to every curious commodity the ships brought, and laying heavy imposts on their cargoes." A treaty was entered into with him by which freedom to go unattended where they pleased, access to the King, liberty to trade with whom they pleased, and to choose their own clerks, was conceded. It was also agreed "that what goods the King buys shall pay no custom; that rice imported pay no custom, that all goods imported, pay three per cent, *after sale*; and all goods exported, be custom free." In 1678, a factory was ordered to be established; and trade was continued for several years, apparently with considerable profit, though the Manchus continually increased the restrictions under which it laboured. The investments here, and at Zelandia, were $ 30 000 in bullion, and $ 20 000 in goods; the returns were chiefly silk goods, tutenague, rhubarb, &c. In 1681, the Company withdrew their facto-

东印度公司与厦门地区的贸易

据文献记载，1651年，荷兰人曾在厦门从事贸易，还帮助清政府攻打驻扎在金门和厦门的国姓爷。大约1664年，东印度公司在厦门和台湾与国姓爷的儿子郑经开展贸易。“但是这位粗鲁的首领对海上交通知之甚少，只知道借此觊觎船上运来的奇货，并对货物征收高额税收。”荷兰人与他签订协议，约定荷兰人可以自由出入，可以面见王爷郑经，可以和任何人做生意，并自由挑选自己的伙计。双方同意，“王爷所购商品无须上税；进口大米不交税；所有进口货物，售后纳税3%；出口货物免税”。[25]1678年，荷兰东印度公司设立了一个商馆。贸易持续了几年，获益较为显著，尽管清政府持续加强限制措施，商馆仍小心谨慎地运行着。东印度公司在厦门和热兰遮城投资达三万元的黄金，还有价值两万元的货物，换来的基本上是丝织品、白铜、大黄等商品。1681年，东印度公司撤掉了他们的商馆；两年之后，即康熙二十二年，靖海侯施琅[26]奏请圣上，重新设立海关。次年，闽海关建立，对外国和本国船只征收关税。1685年，随着“狄莱特”号的到来，东印度公司恢复了与厦门的贸易。1689年，公司在厦门的货主们被监禁。不久之后，一个货主又被关押在荷兰人自己的商馆中，重金贿赂之后他们才被释放。大约1702年，朝廷才准许享有特权的个别商人在厦门和广州开展对外贸易。然而，非法的横征暴敛和敲诈勒索严重地破坏了正常贸易。1725年，雍正皇帝颁布了第一部税则，以规范的方式，责令所有海关官员遵照执行。但海关税则被无视，“对货主征收高额税费，随心所欲，态度傲慢，敲诈勒索，作风拖沓”等积习难改。关于这些不恰当的行为，有一篇题为《中华访客》的文章写道：“倘若这些滥用职权的行为能够通过合适的方式转呈皇帝，毫无疑问，这种现象会得到纠正。厦门颁布的法令证明，当朝非常提倡对外贸易，任何有助于清除对外贸易障碍的诉讼，他们都会审理。难点就在于找到向朝廷禀报的途径，从而举报这些小官员的所作所为，可这些人却又是传达申诉的正常渠道。”1701年，东印度公

ry; and two years later, in the 22nd year of Kang-hi, the Marquis Hi-lang memorialized the Throne, to re-establish a Custom house. In the following year a Custom house for the collection of duties on foreign vessels, and on native junks, was established. In 1685 the Company's trade was again renewed by the arrival of the ship Delight. In 1689 the Supercargoes at Amoy were put in confinement, and not long after, one was chained in his own factory; heavy bribes were paid for their release. About 1702, both at Amoy, and Canton, the foreign trade was granted by the Government, as a monopoly, to a single privileged merchant. But it became so hampered with illegal exactions and extortions, that, in 1725, the Emperor Yung-ching published the first Tariff of duties, in the shape of a code, which was enjoined on the officers of all the Custom houses. The Tariff was not regarded, and "heavy duties, arbitrary, and haughty conduct towards the supercargoes, extortions and ruinous delays" were persisted in. Speaking of these improprieties "A visitor to China" writes: "Had a proper representation of these abuses been conveyed to the Emperor, there can be little doubt that redress would have been obtained. The Edict published at Amoy proved that the cabinet of that time was well disposed towards the promoting of foreign trade, and to the removal of any obstacles to its prosecution that were brought under their cognizance. The difficulty was to find means of communicating with the Court on the subject of wrongs committed by the very parties, who were the regular channels for the transmission of petitions." In 1701, the Company's investment at Amoy, amounted to £34 400 only; but trade was continued here, long after the greater part of it had been transferred to Canton, as, in 1723, Captain Hamilton loaded here. The extortions prevailing, together with the dangers of the "Formosa" Channel, probably induced the Company to withdraw. By 1720 the duties at Canton had risen to four per cent on all goods exported, and on imports, to about 16 per cent, besides a heavy measurement duty on ships, a present of Tls. 1 950 to the Collector of Customs, and a large fee from purveyors of provisions to ships; and, in 1728, an additional duty of 10 per cent was added on all exports, and it was not until 1736, that this impost was removed. These charges also obtained here. In 1725, the Hsia-mên-chih, speaks of the Spaniards as trading here, and paying tribute. The tribute paying is also ascribed to England, Holland, &c. In the collected statistics of the Ta-tsing dynasty, it is also stated that in the 58th year of Kien-lung (about 1793) Great Britain, first brought tribute, 英吉利國乾隆五十八年遣部臣入貢.

Spain appears to have been especially favoured by China, for when the commerce of Great Britain was restricted to Canton, she enjoyed the privileges of trade at Macao, and of access to this Port and Canton. She does not appear to have fully profited by the privileges she then, and subsequently, enjoyed; nor from the geographical positions

司在厦门的投资总额只有34 400英镑；但是，与厦门的贸易仍然在进行，虽然大部分的贸易都转移到了广州，正如汉密尔顿[27]船长1723年曾经载货到了那里。或许，敲诈勒索的盛行，加上台湾海峡的风险，使东印度公司撤掉了商馆。截至1720年，广州所有出口货物的关税都已经上涨到4%，进口货物的关税上涨到约16%；在高额的船税外，还要送给海关税员1 950两白银，给到船上的承办人一大笔小费。1728年，所有出口货物又增加了10%的附加税，这项税直到1736年才被废除。这种征税方式在厦门也同样存在。《厦门志》记载，1725年西班牙人在厦门做生意，并且向朝廷进贡。英国和荷兰等国也来进贡。清朝的数据资料表明，乾隆五十八年（1793年）英国第一次派官员来华进贡。

西班牙好像特别受中国的青睐。当英国在华的商业贸易被局限于广州之际，西班牙却在澳门享有贸易特权，被允许进入澳门和广州。西班牙似乎并没有从它当时以及此后享受的特权中获利太多，也没能充分利用它在美丽富饶的菲律宾群岛优越的地理位置。带着中国众多人口需求的商品，西班牙船只从菲律宾群岛出发，距离中国大陆只要四到五天的轻松航程；印度和马来群岛分别位于其西面和南面，太平洋上的群岛和新大陆上新兴的帝国㉘位于其东方。西班牙拥有的这些贸易上的区位优势，少有对手能与之媲美。1734年，一艘名为“格拉夫顿”号的英国船只驶往厦门，但是在此受到的敲诈勒索比在广州还严重；除了正常关税外，还要额外缴纳20%给海关，于是它驶离厦门。1744年，英国船只“哈德威克”号收到消息说3艘西班牙船停泊在澳门附近准备拦截它，于是便转向驶往厦门，但是当地官员命令它无条件地卸下武器弹药，并停靠在内港。船被扣留了15天，当发现无法进行交易并且被人一再勒索时，它被迫在空载的情况下，逆着季风驶向印度。德庇时在《中国人：中华帝国及其居民概述》第55～56页中提到广州时写道：“尽管商船货主多次提出申诉，被敲诈的次数还是增加了。行商想尽了办法，最终获得了成功，防止欧洲人与当地官员取得联系。官员们认为，通过这

of her fertile and beautiful insular possessions in the Philippines. With the wants of the teeming population of China within four or five days easy sail, India and the Malayan archipelago on the west and south, and the islands of the Pacific, and the rising Empire of the New World on the east, Spain possessed advantages for trade, with which few rivals should have been able to cope. In 1734, one English ship, the Grafton, was sent to Amoy, but the extortions were found to be greater than at Canton; as, in addition to the regular duties, there was an extra charge of 20 per cent for the Haikwan; she therefore withdrew. In 1744, the Hardwicke, East Indiaman, having received intelligence that three Spanish ships were lying off Macao to intercept her, sailed away for Amoy, she was compelled by the Mandarins to deliver into their charge her arms and ammunition, and to anchor in the inner harbour, without conditions, where she remained fifteen days, when finding no disposition to trade, and that she was being subjected to intolerable exactions, she was obliged to proceed to India without a cargo, and against the monsoon. Sir John Davis, writes of Canton, at this time, p. 55-56: "The extortions increased in spite of all representations on the part of the supercargoes. The Hong Merchants used every endeavour, and at length succeeded, in preventing the access of Europeans to the officers of government, finding that by that means, they could exercise their impositions on both, with the greater success and impunity. To the foreigners, they alleged that the Mandarins were the authors of all exactions on trade; to the Mandarins, that the foreigners were of so barbarous and fierce a temper, as to be incapable of listening to reason. The grievances suffered by our trade led to a remonstrance, in which the principal points were the delay in unloading ships; the plunder of goods; the injurious proclamations annually put up by the Government, accusing foreigners of horrible crimes, with the intent to expose them to the contempt of the populace; the extortions under false pretences of the inferior officials; and the difficulty of access to the mandarins." He adds: "It is to be apprehended that the want of union among the Europeans, had the usual effect of frustrating their attempts at redress."

It was, in those days, the practice on the arrival of a ship here, to despatch a boat to demand her name, nation, and business, an exact account of the number of her crew, and guns, her cargo, and the time she intended to stay. This being complied with, her arms, and munitions, were handed into the care of the authorities, a payment of about $1 700 for Port charges demanded, and a permit to remain in the harbour issued. The Mandarins appear to have adjudicated on matters concerning the internal economy of foreign ships, as in the case of the Success, in 1720, the Hai-fang-ting entertained a complaint from the sailors against her Captain, and directed the distribution of prize money as under:

Captain's share...... £ 1 466.10.10.

种方式，可以更容易地向双方提出要求，而且可逃避惩罚。对于外国人来说，这些清朝官员是贸易中所有苛捐杂税的始作俑者；而在官员眼中，这帮外国人野蛮无礼，脾气暴躁，听不进去道理。贸易过程中的不满引起了货主的抗议，抗议的要点是：卸船时拖拖拉拉；抢夺货物；政府每年颁布带有偏见的布告，指责外国人犯了可怕的罪行，意在使百姓蔑视他们；下层官员的敲诈勒索；难以接近地方官员。”他补充道：“要明白，欧洲人之间缺乏团结，这通常会导致他们在试图纠错时不是那么顺利。”

在那时，当一艘船抵港后，官方通常派一艘小船去询问并登记船名、国籍、所从事的生意、船员的具体人数，以及装载的枪炮、货物的情况，和船的预计停留时间。这些完成之后，船上的武器弹药必须交给官方保管。另需缴纳1 700元作为港口管理费，换取停靠港口的许可证。涉及外国商船的船员之间的经济纠纷，中国官员会参与裁决。以1720年的船只“成功”号为例，海防厅接到船员们状告船长的控诉，指导其奖金的分配如下：船长，1 466.101

英镑；副船长，733.55英镑；大副、二副和船医，488.168英镑；普通水手，97.154英镑。

但是，勒令船长分配奖金之前，“为了货主的利益，一半的货物被拿来作保，其中有现金、精制金银和珠宝，价值在6 000～7 000英镑之间。这批货立刻被运到一艘名为‘天使女王’号的葡萄牙商船上，船长是唐·弗朗西斯科·拉·维诺。不幸的是，这艘船于1722年6月6日在里约热内卢被烧毁，扣除打捞费用，货主们得到的不足1 800英镑”。一艘来自马德拉斯的“安”号英国货船，被船上主要货物的买家们狠狠地压榨（据说买家是官府推荐的），只得到大约价值1 500两的货物，很快就要破产了。“安”号的船长并没有大肆声张他遭到的不公，在拿到出港许可证和枪炮之后，马上枪上膛、炮上架，清理好船，准备战斗。他们劫持了一艘日本帆船，其装载的货物是“安”号的两倍，并将这艘船驶离海湾。大约有二三十艘满载船员的小船在后面穷追不舍，“安”号顽强的船长用船尾炮射击，打得它们节节败退。这件事情传到了皇帝

Second Captain's share......733. 5. 5.

Captain of Marines, Lieutenants of the ship, and Surgeon......488.16. 8.

Foremast-man......97.15. 4.

But before compelling the Captain to this distribution of shares, "he ordered one half the cargo to be secured, for the benefit of the owners; which, in ready money, wrought silver, gold, and jewels, amounted to between £ 6 000 and £7 000 sterling. This he caused to be immediately put on board a Portuguese East Indiaman, called the *Queen of Angels*, Don Francisco La Vero commander. This ship was unfortunately, burnt at Rio de Janeiro on June 6th, 1722, so that of these effects the owners received no more, the charges of salvage deducted, than £1 800." A British ship from Madras, *the Ann*, having been severely squeezed by the purchasers of the major part of her cargo, (who, it is stated, were recommended by officials,) becoming bankrupt, shortly after obtaining about Tls. 1 500 worth of goods; her Captain did not trumpet forth his wrongs, but on receiving his port clearance and his guns, loaded the latter, cleared ships, beat to quarters, and seized a Japanese Junk, worth twice the value of his cargo, and bore off with her into the bay. Some twenty or thirty boats, crowded with men, went in pursuit; but the stout Captain fired into them with his stern gun and put them to flight. This affair coming to the ears of the Emperor, the officials were ordered to be punished, and their property confiscated, after satisfaction had been made to the Japanese owners of the Junk. This well merited severity induced, for a time, more care in their dealings with British ships.

Amoy Reopened by *Treaty of Nanking*

It is unnecessary to particularise details further, and it will be sufficient to state that trade continued, with various checks and stoppages, until the issue of the Imperial edict ordering the East India Company's agents to withdraw, as all foreign trade was, in future, to be restricted to Canton. This edict was obeyed, and the port was closed against foreigners until legally reopened by the 2nd article of the Treaty signed at Nanking, the 29th August 1842.

Of the events which led to this Treaty, and subsequent Treaties with Great Britain, America, France, etc., etc., it is not necessary here to allude. It will be sufficient to take a brief glance at the progress of trade since the establishment of the Foreign Inspectorate of Customs.

Trade under the Foreign Inspectorate

Although the Treaties with Great Britain and France were signed at Tientsin in June 1858, and ratified at Peking in October 1860, it was not until the

那里，这些官员们受到了惩罚，财产充公，还要赔偿日本船主的损失。这种理所应当的严厉处置，使一段时间内中国人与英国商船打交道时小心多了。

《南京条约》签订，厦门再开埠

没有必要再列举更多的细节了，我们已经充分说明了即便伴随着各种审查和扣留，贸易依然在进行，直到皇帝降旨令东印度公司撤掉商馆，将未来的对外贸易局限于广州。遵照这条法令，厦门港不再对外国人开放，直到根据1842年8月29日签署的《南京条约》的第二款，厦门港才重新开放。

至于导致《南京条约》的签订，以及之后与英国、美国、法国等国签订种种条约的事件，在此不一一赘述。这里只粗略地回顾海关税务司建立以来的贸易历程，从而一斑窥豹。

海关税务司管辖下的贸易

尽管清朝与英法两国在1858年6月签订了《天津条约》，并于1860年10月在北京正式批准，但直到1862年4月1日，在海关税务司的监督之下，才首次在厦门开放海关。

之后的9个月里，所进行的贸易包括：394艘船、129 677吨货物进港；364艘船出港、119 412吨货物出港。进口贸易额为5 042 307元，按照当时的汇率，折合1 177 242英镑。出口贸易额为2 226 251元，折合522 199英镑。进口金银的金额达405 170元，出口额达到909 612元。收缴的关税、土货半税、吨税合计306 210两，折合102 070英镑[29]。进口的各种纺织品为布匹70 593件，毛织品5 866件，原棉15 468担，棉纱5 721担。进口金属18 953担；鸦片共2 047箱，或2 384担，其中273担用于再出口。

当时，再出口贸易额没有从进口贸易额中扣除，这部分是519 829元，折合121 933英镑。这些商品主要包括布匹、毛织品、原棉、金属、鸦片，以及当地的杂货。出口商品主要是：红糖39 921担，白糖8 898担，冰糖46 781担，茶叶5 329 283磅，其中英国只购买345 886磅，美国则买走3 318 752磅，以及纸15 963担，陶瓷6 956担，等等。以上只是粗略地列举了最重要的数据和商品种类，

1st April 1862, that the Customs was first opened at Amoy under the Foreign Inspectorate.

During the following nine months, a trade was carried on represented by 394 vessels, 129 677 tons entered, and 364 vessels, 119 412 tons, cleared, conveying merchandize, which represented an import trade valued at $ 5 042 307, or, at the then rate of exchange, £1 177 242, and an export trade valued at $ 2 226 251, or £522 199. The import of Treasure amounted to $ 405 170; and its export, to $ 909 612. The total amount of duties, coast trade duties, and tonnage dues, collected, was Tls. 306 210 or £102 070. The importation of Cotton piece goods of all descriptions, was 70 593 pieces; of Woollens, 5 866 pieces; of Raw Cotton, 15 468 peculs; of Cotton Yarn 5 721 peculs, and of Metals 18 953 peculs; that of Opium amounted to 2 047 chests, or 2 384 peculs, of which 273 peculs were re-exported.

The re-export trade, the value of which was not at that time deducted from the gross total of the import trade, was $ 519 829, or £121 933. It consisted chiefly of Cotton piece goods, Woollens, Raw Cotton, Metals, Opium, and native Sundries. The principal staples exported, were black Sugar 39 921 peculs, white Sugar 8 898 peculs, Sugar Candy 46 781 peculs, Tea 5 329 283 pounds, of which Great Britain, only took, direct, 345 886 pounds, against 3 318 752 pounds taken by the United States. Paper 15 963 peculs, Chinaware 6 956 peculs, &c., &c. The most important statistics, and articles of commerce are thus briefly enumerated, as no report on the trade of the port, was made for the nine months in question.

The following tables will show more readily than words at length the values of Imports, Exports,

因为这9个月的港口贸易情况没有相关报告。

下面的表格比文字更直观和详尽地体现了进口、出口和再出口的贸易额，以及自厦门海关开始运作至1871年11月31日，所征收税费的总额。

进口、出口、再出口的贸易额

时间	进口		出口		再出口	
	元	英镑	元	英镑	元	英镑
1862年4月1日到12月31日	5 042 307	1 177 242	2 226 251	522 199	519 829	121 933
1863年	8 430 991	2 048 036	4 092 574	994 129	382 447	92 369
1864年	9 419 625	2 276 409	3 773 811	912 004	774 877	187 261
1865年	12 974 724	2 919 313	2 699 286	607 339	1 225 636	275 768
1866年	12 004 531	2 701 019	3 989 843	897 714	1 251 288	281 539
1867年	9 814 144	2 208 182	3 597 057	809 337	1 019 092	229 295
1868年	7 421 750	1 669 894	3 226 078	725 867	1 017 357	228 846
1869年	9 136 900	2 055 802	4 147 893	933 275	1 168 244	626 854
1870年	8 513 009	1 915 616	3 410 710	767 486	1 673 938	376 673
1871年	8 511 074	1 844 066	4 583 576	993 108	1 713 883	371 341

征收的税费

时间	进口税		出口税		土货半税		吨税		总额	
	海关两	英镑	海关两	英镑	海关两	英镑	海关两	英镑	海关两	英镑
1862年4月1日至12月31日	126 793	42 264	150 169	50 056	13 787	4 595	15 461	5 153	306 210	102 068
1863年	184 121	61 373	237 984	79 328	29 201	9 734	19 686	6 562	470 992	156 997

续表

时间	进口税		出口税		土货半税		吨税		总额	
	海关两	英镑	海关两	英镑	海关两	英镑	海关两	英镑	海关两	英镑
1864年	219 502	73 167	206 514	68 838	26 693	8 898	22 200	7 400	474 909	158 303
1865年	245 000	81 667	167 318	55 773	27 898	9 299	31 762	10 587	471 978	157 326
1866年	252 250	84 083	224 204	74 735	34 996	11 665	21 698	7 233	533 149	177 716
1867年	243 781	81 260	212 829	70 943	25 857	8 619	20 860	6 953	503 327	167 775
1868年	235 671	78 557	158 597	52 866	17 214	5 738	14 562	4 854	426 044	142 015
1869年	230 342	76 781	283 090	94 363	23 785	7 928	19 187	6 393	556 404	185 468
1870年	229 653	76 551	229 450	76 483	18 683	6 228	20 889	6 963	498 675	166 225
1871年	223 007	73 336	262 933	87 644	20 870	6 957	17 450	2 816	524 260	174 753

根据对以上统计数据的分析，从1863年（1862年只记录了9个月，不完整，故省略）到1871年间每年的进口贸易额的进展并不能令人满意。虽然扣除再出口贸易额，净值从1863年的8 048 544元上升到1865年的11 749 088元，再到1866年的10 753 273元[30]，到1871年，进口贸易额又降到8 511 074元。

不计算再出口贸易额的话，1863年出口贸易额达到4 092 574元，1865年下降到2 699 285元[31]。之后，一直在350万到450万元之间浮动。1871年出口贸易额达

and Re-exports, together with the amounts of Duties collected, since the opening of the Custom House, under Foreign Inspectorate, to the 31st December 1871.

An examination of the preceding statistics of the annual value of the Import trade, since 1863 (1862 being a broken year of nine months is omitted) to 1871, does not afford so satisfactory a view of its progress, as could be desired. Although it rose from $ 8 048 544 net, that is deducting re-exports, in 1863, to $ 11 749 088 net in 1865, and to $ 10 753 273 net in 1866, it has gradually decreased to $ 8 511 074 in 1871.

The value of the Export trade, exclusive of Re-exports, reached $ 4 092 574 in 1863, from which date it fell to $ 2 699 285 in 1865, and since has fluctuated at between three and a half, and four and a half, millions of dollars. Its value in 1871 was $ 4 583 576.

It is in the value of the Re-export trade that developed between this port and "Formosa", principally that the most significant increase is apparent, it having risen from $ 382 447 in 1863, to $ 1 713 883 the largest value it has yet attained, in 1871.

The dues and duties collected, amounted to Haikwan Tls. 470 992, or £156 997, in 1863, and remained at near that amount until 1866, when the collection reached Haikwan Tls. 533 149, or £177 716. In the next two years it had fallen to Haikwan Tls. 426 144, or £142 015; from which it rose to Haikwan Tls. 556 404, or £185 488, the highest amount it ever attained, in 1869. In the following year, it had fallen to Haikwan Tls. 498 675, or £166 225; and in 1871 it again rose, and reached Haikwan Tls. 524 260, or, £174 753. During nine years the variation between the lowest amount collected, that of 1863, and the highest, that of 1869, is only Haikwan Tls. 85 412, or £28 471.

Having made these few remarks on the value of trade, and on the duties collected since the opening of this Custom House, I shall confine my observations to a brief retrospect of the trade of 1871, selecting where necessary the two previous years to illustrate its increase or decrease.

The value of this trade in foreign goods, (exclusive of Re-exports,) during 1871, amounted to $4 587 611. That of foreign Re-ex-

4 583 576元。

厦门港和台湾之间的再出口贸易额增长最为明显，从1863年的382 447元，到1871年达到峰值1 713 883元。

1863年海关征收的税费，达470 992海关两，折合156 997英镑。此后一直保持相近的数额，直到1866年，税费收入达到533 149海关两，折合177 716英镑。之后的两年，降为426 144海关两[32]，折合142 015英镑。1869年达到峰值，即556 404海关两，折合185 488英镑[33]。次年，降到498 675海关两，折合166 225英镑。1871年，再次提高到524 260海关两，折合174 753英镑。9年间，税费在1863年的最低值和1869年的最高值之间，只相差85 412海关两，折合28 471英镑。

就厦门海关设立以来的贸易额和关税略作评论后，笔者将自己的观察限于对1871年贸易情况的简要回顾，并就此前两年的有关数据，谈一下贸易额的增减。

1871年，外国货物的贸易额（扣除再出口贸易额）达到4 587 611元，外国货物再出口贸易额1 278 850元。土产的进口贸易额（扣除再出口贸易额）达到2 209 580元，土产再出口贸易额435 033元。以当地最重要的贸易商品棉纱为例，1869年进口10 235担，1870年增加了一半，达到15 724担，到了1871年增加到17 940担。（棉纱进口在3年之内几乎翻了一倍。也许值得一提的是，在海关税务司设立之前，众所周知，棉纱的贸易额是每年18 000担。）各种布匹贸易的增长情况也很类似。1869年，进口布匹107 914匹，1870年增加了63%[34]，达171 016匹，目前到了195 160匹，3年之内的增幅超过80%。

前面的数据也许会令对厦门对外贸易有所期待者失望，但是这些是根据1871年实际的消费量而得到的数据，以销售额显示为准。与1870年相比，它在如下方面有所增长：棉纱，增长20%；衣料，增长10%；T字布，增长45%。

以下进口商品的增长比例，比上述的多得多；但是还有未售的大宗商品需要被计入1872年，成为其销售额的一部分。

原棉。过去3年，从印度进口的原棉数量翻了两番。1870年达到19 195担，约是

ports to $1 278 850. The value of the import trade in native produce, (exclusive of Re-exports,) amounted to $2 209 580. That of native Re-exports to $435 033. To take, first, the important articles of commerce here, Yarn, the import was in 1869, peculs 10 235, in 1870 it increased one half, or to peculs 15 724, and in 1871 it reached peculs 17 940. (Thus nearly doubling its import in three years. It may be worthy of remark that previous to the establishment of the Foreign Custom House, the trade in Yarn has been known to amount to 18 000 peculs per annum.) A similar increase is perceptible in Cotton Piece Goods of all descriptions. The aggregate import was in 1869, pieces 107 914; in 1870 it increased sixty three per cent, or to pieces 171 016, and it now amounts to pieces 195 160, an increase of over eighty per cent in three years.

The preceding figures will probably be contrary to the expectations of those interested in the foreign trade at Amoy, but they are carried out by the actual consumption in 1871, as shewn by sales, which when compared with 1870, give an increase in:

Yarn············of 20 per cent.
Shirtings·········10············
T-Cloths·········15············

The importation, as will be seen, shews a much greater percentage than the above; but large stocks of unsold goods yet remain to be carried into, and form a portion of, the consumption of the year 1872.

Raw Cotton.—During the last

three years, the importation of this article from India, has quadrupled itself. In 1870 it amounted to peculs 19 195, or about double that of 1869; and in 1871, it reached peculs 38 313.

Of this quantity peculs 630, only, were re-exported to Chinese ports. Speaking in round numbers, the consumption may be said to have increased from 7 300 bales in 1869, to 14 600 bales in 1871. The cause of this is found in the comparatively low price of Indian Cotton, as compared with that of Chinese Cotton.

The importation of Chinese Cotton, peculs 24 872, from Shanghai, Ningpo, and Hongkong, also shews an increase, although a small one, over the importation of 1869, and 1870, namely peculs 20 191, and peculs 20 631. The entire quantity imported during the past year, went into consumption here, none being Re-exported.

Woollen Manufactures.—Consisting principally of Camlets, Lastings, and Woollen and Cotton fabrics, show also an increased importation as compared with 1869; and 1870; the two years being nearly on a par, namely 5 532 pieces imported net, and 1 708 pieces re-exported. The past year's Import was 6 113 pieces, of which 3 016 pieces were Re-exported. The consumption of the port however shews a decrease.

Opium—The Imports, and Re-exports, during the past three years, stand thus:

	1869	1870	1871
Imports··· peculs	5 709	4 995	4 808

1869年的两倍；到1871年，达到38 313担。

这些原棉中，只有630担再输出到中国其他港口。按整数计算，原棉的消费量据说从1869年的7 300包增加到1871年的14 600包。其原因是跟中国棉相比，印度棉相对便宜。

上海、宁波和香港所输入的中国棉达到24 872担，虽然增幅较小，同样有所增加。这是和1869年的20 191担，以及1870年的20 631担相比。去年输入的原棉全部进入了厦门的消费市场，没有再输出。

毛织品。主要包括羽纱、斜纹布、羊毛织品和棉织品，与1869年、1870年相比，进口量有所增加。这两年基本持平，净进口5 532件，再出口1 708件。去年进口6 113件，其中的3 016件再出口。厦门港的消费量有所下降。

鸦片。过去3年鸦片的进口和再出口数据如下：

鸦片的进口、再出口数据

单位：担

类别	1869年	1870年	1871年
进口	5 709	4 995	4 808
再出口	1 388	1 869	1 751

上面的数据显然表明，鸦片贸易量略有减少。过去3年，进口量减去再出口到台湾的量，港口每年的实际消费量大概在3 721担和3 057担[35]之间。从1866年到1871年的6年间，进口量在每年66 081担左右，最大进口量是1866年的546 669担，最小进口量正是1871年。1868年，再出口量减少到1 091担，而1870年则达到1 896担[36]。去年的大半年中，尤其是后半年，在厦门出售的鸦片的价格低于香港等量鸦片的价格，而厦门的鸦片正是来自香港；因此，厦门的大量鸦片未卖出去，而是囤积起来，留到1872年出售（或许该年度的鸦片进口量会压缩），以期价格上涨。但是，直到3月底或4月初，才出现价格上涨的迹象。

对贸易的总体评价

在关于厦门1870年贸易情况的报告中，笔者已经充分说明了对鸦片、棉织品收取的厘金的情况，如果只是随意地引用肯定会令人生厌，且没有必要。但是，回顾厦门的贸易情况却是合适的。需要说明的是，鸦片贸易在厦门已经合法化，且对

Re-exports········1 388 1 869 1 751

From the above figures, it is apparent that there is a small decrease in this branch of commerce. Deducting the re-export to "Formosa" from the quantities imported during the last three years, the actual quantity required for annual consumption at the port, would seem to be between 3 721 and 3 057 peculs. During six years, namely from 1866 to 1871, the quantities imported only varied peculs 66 081, the largest import peculs 546 669, was in 1866, and the smallest in the year under review. The Re-export dwindled to peculs 1 091 in 1868, and attained to peculs 1 896 in 1870. The prices for Opium offered here, during most of last year, but more especially the latter part, have been below the equivalent of those at Hongkong, whence Amoy is supplied; consequently a very large stock remains unsold, and will be carried into the year 1872, (probably lessening that year's importation of the drug) to be held for a rise in price; which however is unlikely to occur until the end of March, or beginning of April.

General Remarks on Trade

In my report on the trade of Amoy during 1870, I wrote so fully on the action of the Le-kin taxes, upon Opium, and Cotton Manufactures, that any but a casual reference to it, must be irksome and unnecessary. It is, however, proper when reviewing commerce here, that it should be stated that, as trade in Opium has been legalised, and a fixed uniform tariff rate put upon its importation, it would be well if the same principle were applied in Le-kin taxation. The entire removal of the Le-kin impost cannot be, and is not, expected by reasonable persons. Most of the wishes that I have heard expressed, would be met by the issue of a fixed uniform and just tariff, by the Imperial government, instead of leaving the provincial authorities to impose what tax they please, limited, it would appear, not by necessity, or by any system of valuation, but by the temper of the people they govern, the highest tax being inflicted that they are likely to bear, without risk of disturbance. Thus at Swatow, where the people are turbulent and aggressive, Opium is taxed to the extent of only Tls. 14.7.6.0 per chest, against Tls. 90.2.6.6, the amount imposed here, where the people are peaceful, and order loving. An uniform Le-kin tariff on the great staples of European import, and export, would, I feel convinced, be as beneficial to the Imperial Exchequer, as it would be to foreign trade.

The grain supplies imported, consisting of foreign rice, peculs 50 498, native rice, peculs 69 254 (of which peculs 3 936 only were re-exported) and native wheat peculs 36 242, are in the aggregate, much the same as in 1870. But a very considerable deficit, nearly 90 per cent, is apparent in the receipts of foreign rice.

This is, however, more than balanced by an increase, of nearly 130 per cent, in Native grain. The prices of these cereals during the latter part of the year, have been slightly above the usual average, though not to the extent antici-

鸦片进口采用固定税率，厘金的收取若能运用同样的原则就太好了。完全废除厘金是不可能的，理性的人对此也不指望。我所听到的大多数人的愿望，是当朝政府能够颁布一套固定、统一且公正的税则，而不是让地方官员随心所欲地制定关税征收标准，后者不是基于需要或任何评价体系，而是基于被统治者的性情，从而在避免招致骚乱的前提下，征收最高额度的关税。鉴于此，在汕头，当地人不守规矩、野蛮好斗，每箱鸦片只征税14.76两；相反，厦门人性格温顺，遵守秩序，每箱鸦片征税90.266两。和欧洲贸易的大多数商品若按照固定的税率征收厘金，不管是进口还是出口，笔者确信这对清朝的国库和对贸易本身都是有利的。

粮食。进口外国大米50 498担，输入本土大米69 254担（其中只有3 936担用于再出口），本土小麦36 242担，总量与1870年持平。但外国大米进口明显减少，跌幅将近90%。

这是因为本土粮食增加了130%，打破了平衡。下半年，这些粮食的价格比平常的平均价格略高，虽然没有达到某些中国人的预期，他们预计粮食短缺，价格高涨，就像他们今年的判断一样。豆类的进口量为228 437担，豆饼159 442担，一起作为肥料使用，跟1870年的进口量差不多。但是豆类的进口量增加了55%，刚好抵消了豆饼几乎等额的减少量。豆类在北方相对比较便宜。

金属。金属是进口贸易中不太重要的一类产品。1871年，进口6 273担洋铁，而1870年进口8 367担，1869年进口5 454担。进口铅5 688担，水银431担，与前两年的进口量几乎持平。进口铁制品2 879担，与1869年相比增加了90%。值得注意的是，这种产品的贸易在厦门已经被垄断。因此，外国进口商发现只要垄断存在，要处理他们的存货就特别困难，铁制品贸易的增长就很有限。铁制品进口数量的增长，并没有带来消费量的提高，而仅仅是停留在进口层面。

海运。1871年，进厦门港船只566艘，载货215 651吨；出港570艘，载货219 038吨。这些数据表明，与1870年相比，增加了9艘船进港，多了19艘船出港，尽管入

pated by Chinese, who predicted scarcity and high prices, as they now do for the present year. Beans and Peas, peculs 228 437, and Beancake, peculs 159 442, aggregated, have been used as manure to about the same extent as in 1870; but the importation of Peas shews an increase of about 55 per cent, replacing a decrease of nearly the same amount in Beancake. The former having ruled relatively cheaper in the North.

Metals are an unimportant branch of this trade. In 1871, peculs 6 273 of iron were imported, against peculs 8 367 in 1870, and peculs 5 454 in 1869. Lead reached peculs 5 688, Quicksilver peculs 431, or nearly the same as the two preceding years. Nail rod iron, peculs 2 879, shews an increase of ninety per cent, as compared with the importation of 1869. It should be observed that there exists a monopoly, here, of the Trade in this article. Foreign importers find the utmost difficulty in disposing of their stocks for that reason, and this branch of trade cannot reach its limit of expansion so long as the monopoly is maintained. The increase above alluded to in Nail rod iron, does not extend to consumption, but merely to importation.

Shipping.—566 vessels, representing an aggregate tonnage of 215 651 tons, entered; and 570 vessels, representing 219 038 tons, cleared in 1871. These figures shew an increase of 9 vessels and 19 vessels cleared, as compared with 1870, although in regard to tonnage there is a slight decrease both in vessels entered and cleared. The statistics in 1869, are so nearly the same that comparison is superfluous. The number of steamers visiting the port has greatly increased, and leads to the inference that were permission obtained to work the rich Coal mines of this Empire, they would soon entirely supersede sailing vessels. The supply of shipping up to about the middle of November was very large, and poor freights only, were procurable; but this supply falling off here, as appears to have been the case at other ports, at the same time, very high rates of freights obtained in December, with every prospect of their rising still higher during, at least, the early part of 1872. The Charters made were 162, against 171 in 1870. Had there been more vessels here in December, they would have been eagerly chartered.

Export Trade—The total value of the trade in native produce exported, and removed coastwise, during 1871, amounted to \$ 4 583 576. That of native Re-exports, to \$ 1 713 883. Of the articles of which it is comprised, it will perhaps be sufficient to enumerate but two or three. Tea being the most important export, and the one in which foreign merchants are most interested. I have prepared a return of the quantities exported since the opening of the Amoy Custom House up to the present date.

The figures in the return, include the quantities exported by

港和出港船的吨位略有下降。1869年的统计数据几乎一样，无须比较。进港的蒸汽船数量大幅度增加，这就引起了人们的猜测，即清政府如果允许开采煤矿，蒸汽船很快就会完全取代帆船。海运量一直到11月中旬都很大，只不过货运价格很低；不过，厦门港的海运量却有所下降，其他港口似乎也一样。然而到了12月，货运价格变得很高，而且至少到1872年初，货运价格可望涨到更高。今年发放了162张许可证，1870年是171张。如果有更多的船12月抵达厦门，对许可证的需求便是很迫切的。

出口贸易。1871年，当地土产的出口，加上输出到沿海其他口岸的产品，总额达4583576元。当地土产再出口的金额达1 713 883元。也许列举两三种出口商品就足够了。茶叶是最重要的出口商品，也是外国商人最感兴趣的。下面，将回顾一下厦门海关自设立至今的茶叶出口量。

这些数字，包括中国商人出口到海峡殖民地和各个其他口岸的，但是扣除了从台湾运往厦门，再转运到美国的淡水茶的数量。

厦门海关设立以来中国商人茶叶出口情况

单位：担

时间	出口至外国口岸	输出至中国口岸	总计
1862年	32 830.39	7 139.25	39 969.64
1863年	50 429.30	13 715.81	64 145.01
1864年	35 897.27	17 735.37	53 632.64
1865年	34 224.00	9 523.00	43 747.00
1866年	49 560.54	9 782.36	59 342.90
1867年	53 224.21	7 570.70	60 794.91
1868年	22 409.40	13 312.58	35 721.98
1869年	78 799.55	7 168.96	85 968.51
1870年	56 100.47	8 670.04	64 770.51
1871年	66 198.57	1 882.39	68 080.96
总计	479 673.60㊲	96 500.46	576 174.06

1868年出现巨大的贸易逆差，1869年逆差更有所增加，原因是1868年相当部分的作物直到次年才被运出去。

茶叶交易是如何进行的？为了向对茶叶贸易感兴趣的人介绍这一点，最好是以茶季出口量作为基础，而不是按照海关年来计算。即从一年的6月30日到次年的6月30日，在此期间所有的茶叶都将运出去（通常在1月底完成），茶叶销售季告一段落。这种计时方式的截止日期是12月31日，一直都是惯例。我在此插入另一份表格，只显示外国商人运到外国口岸的茶叶的数据，不包括中国商人运输到海峡殖民地等

Chinese to the Straits, and to sundry ports; but are exclusive of the Tamsui Teas sent here for convenience of shipment to the United States.

The great deficit in the export of 1868, and increase in that of 1869, arises from a very considerable portion of the 1868 crop not being shipped until 1869.

The progress of this trade will, however, be better conveyed to those interested in it, by basing my remarks on the quantities exported during the mercantile Tea season, i.e. from the 30th June to the 30th June, within which period the season is closed by the shipment of the entire crop, (generally completed before the end of January) than by basing them on the Customs year, ending the 31st December, which has hitherto been the practice. I therefore subjoin another

厦门海关设立以来外国商人茶叶出口情况

时间	重量（磅）
1862—1863年茶季	7 856 122
1863—1864年茶季	6 224 635
1864—1865年茶季	6 918 671
1865—1866年茶季	6 979 555
1866—1867年茶季	7 284 826
1867—1868年茶季	8 006 384
1868—1869年茶季	8 691 058
1869—1870年茶季	6 763 868
1870—1871年茶季	6 823 399*
1871—1872年茶季	8 171 494*

注：带“*”处数据分别包括遗失在太平市（Taeping）和孟加拉（原文为Cengala，疑为Bengala之误——译者注）的917795磅。

table containing the quantities exported by foreign merchants to foreign ports only, that is exclusive of the quantities exported to the Straits, &c., and removed coastwise, by Chinese.

The Teas in the preceding table are almost entirely composed of Oolongs, and Congous, the only other description ever in this being Orange Pekoe, which, when it comes at all, comes in too small quantities to be of consequence. During the last four seasons it has been altogether absent from the market.

Oolongs.—The export of

地和沿海其他口岸的茶叶。

上表里的茶叶几乎都是乌龙茶和工夫茶，厦门市场上仅存的其他茶叶是锡兰红茶，但即使偶尔出现，数量也太少，产生不了什么影响。在过去的4个茶季，这种茶几乎从市场上消失得无影无踪。

乌龙茶。在1869—1870年茶季，乌龙茶的出口量降到3 491 206磅，1870—1871年茶季回升到5 443 593磅。在刚结束的1871—1872年茶季，出口量达到7 766 534

磅，这是本港口迄今最大的一次出口量。历年对美国出口总量达7 393 258磅，而1870—1871年茶季对美出口量为5 073 484磅。

历年对英国出口的乌龙茶，总量达为380 109磅，其中1870—1871年茶季为176 665磅。值得一提的是，考虑到价格因素，比起福州茶，厦门的乌龙茶更受纽约市场的欢迎。

工夫茶。在1869—1870年茶季，工夫茶的出口量达到峰值，大约有50 000个半箱或2 109 232磅。之后，1870—1871年茶季出口量降到1 216 878磅，1871—1872年茶季为353 514磅。这也许是由于制茶人发现乌龙茶价高，且工夫茶所占市场有限，于是大部分人便倾向于将茶叶制作或乌龙茶。1871—1872年茶季的工夫茶质量上乘，297 916磅出口到美国，而只有55 598磅出口到英国；而在1869—1870年茶季，出口英国的乌龙茶达1 799 542磅，1870—1871年茶季为775 419磅。出口英国的数量下降，是因为这种平民工夫茶的质量较普通，导致工夫茶被逐出伦敦市场。而对于更高级的茶叶，美国买家比英国买家更大方。或许是因为工夫茶在本茶季供应不足，

this description of Tea, which had fallen in the season 1869-70 to 3 491 206 lbs. rose in 1870-71, to 5 443 593 lbs. and in the season just closed, 1871-72, it attained to 7 766 534 lbs. the largest export that has ever been made from this port. Of the entire quantity exported, the United States took 7 393 258 lbs. against 5 073 484 lbs. in season 1870-71.

The export to Great Britain was 176 665 lbs. against 380 109 lbs. in the season 1870-71. It is worthy of remark that Amoy Oolongs, price considered, are now prefered in the New York market, to Foochow teas.

Congou.—The export of this kind of tea reached its highest amount in the season 1869-70, when some 50 000 half-chests or 2 109 232 lbs. were shipped. Since then the export has fallen to 1 216 878 lbs. in 1870-71, and to 353 514 lbs. in 1871-72. This may, in some measure, be accounted for by the fact that the teamen finding high prices ruling for Oolongs, and but a limited market for Congous, have made most of their leaf into the former tea. This, 1871-72, season's Congous, were almost entirely of good quality, and 297 916 lbs. were exported to the United States, leaving the export to Great Britain at 55 598 lbs. against 1 799 542 lbs. in the 1869-70 season, and 775 419 lbs. in the season 1870-71. This decrease is attributable to the quality of the commoner Congous, which has caused their expulsion from the London market, while for the superior kinds, America is a mere liberal purchaser than England. Owing, perhaps, to a small supply during the season under review, no shipment has been made to the Colonies, which received, in 1870-71, 145 790 lbs. of this tea. In the coming season the export will probably recommence.

Amoy Teas, which, two or three years since, were unfavourably viewed on account of the large quantity of dust they then contained, are now steadily recovering their position in the American Market, (where, as has been shewn, most of them go) owing to a combination of the Hongs here in 1868, when they agreed not to purchase teas containing over 20 per cent of dust. This margin will in the season 1872-73, and in future, be still further reduced to 15 per cent. Before this combination was entered into, the teas contained sometimes as much as 60 per cent of dust, and the consequence was that Japan teas, which are singularly free from this defect, were gradually superseding them.

At the present time, Amoy teas have so far regained favour, that according to the last advices received, they appear to have been the only ones that have benefitted exporters.

Tamsui Teas, which are mostly shipped to New York via this port, have shown a remarkable expansion.

In season 1869-70 the export to New York was 370 238 lbs.

……1870-71……778 242

……1871-72……1 502 000

and next season it will, it is expected, be much larger. The reason these teas are becoming such favorites is, that they are, in the first

没运送去海峡殖民地，那里在1870—1871年茶季进口了145790磅的工夫茶。下一个茶季，工夫茶出口可能会重新开始。

厦门茶。两三年前，因为其中掺杂了大量的茶末，厦门茶给人的印象不好，如今正稳步恢复其在美国市场的地位（可见厦门茶多去了美国市场）。1868年，厦门的一些行商们联合起来，不再购买茶末超过20%的茶叶。他们要求在1872—1873年茶季及之后，把茶末减少到15%。在行商为此事合作之前，有时候茶末含量高达60%，导致厦门茶渐渐被几乎没有此问题的日本茶替代。

目前，采纳了行商们的建议后，厦门茶重新受到消费者的喜爱，它们似乎是唯一让出口商赚钱的茶叶。

淡水茶。淡水茶多半是通过厦门港运往纽约的，其出口增长得很明显。1869—1870年茶季向纽约出口370 238磅；1870—1871年茶季为778 242磅；1871—1872年茶季为1 502 000磅。预计在下个茶季，出口量将大幅增加。这种茶之所以如此受欢迎，首先是因为做工精良，且茶末含量特别少（5%～6%）；其次，这种茶含有一种天然的香味，也许是来自新茶树和茶树生长的处女地。普通等级的淡水茶，不用支付出口成本，主要是供当地人消费。

place, beautifully made and contain a very trifling proportion of dust (some 5 or 6 per cent); and secondly, they possess a very fine natural perfume, which probably results from the youth of the plants, and the almost virgin soil in which they are grown. The common grades of "Formosa" tea, do not pay the cost of exportation, and are chiefly used by the natives themselves.

厦门糖出口情况

单位：担

种类	1871年	1870年	1869年	1862年（仅9个月）
红糖	155 355	58 723	50 733	39 921
白糖	25 553	13 158	13 378	8 898
冰糖	83 519	61 416	60 438	46 781

上表中的数据非常理想，表明一年之内红糖的出口是之前的3倍，白糖几乎翻了一番，冰糖也增加了35%。从1862年厦门海关设立以来，这些增长非常显著。

纸出口24 300担，从1870年算起增加了3 000担；但是从1862年算起，只增加了9 000担。陶瓷出口30 312担，与1870年相比，减少了16 000担，不过与1862年相比，增加了24 000担。

厦门与台湾之间的贸易。以下数据显示的是厦门与台中、淡水、基隆之间的贸易状况。

These figures are very satisfactory, shewing that the export of Brown Sugar has trebbled itself, that of White Sugar nearly doubled itself, and that of Sugar Candy has increased about 35 per cent, in one year. The increase since the opening of this Custom House in 1862, is noteworthy.

The export of paper, peculs 24 300, has increased 3 000 peculs, since 1870; but the increase in its export since 1862, is only about 9 000 peculs. The export of Chinaware, peculs 30 312, shews a decrease of peculs 16 000 when compared with that of 1870, and an increase of peculs 24 000, when compared with the export of 1862.

Trade between Amoy and "Formosa".——The following fig-

厦门与台湾之间的贸易额

单位：元

种类	1871年	1870年
进口外国商品再运至台湾	1 127 438	1 242 946
厦门产品运至台湾	63 459	34 281
输入土产再运至台湾	14 854	19 350
总计	1 205 751	1 296 577

ures will show the valuable trade that has developed between the Amoy, and Takow, Tamsui, and Keelung, in "Formosa".

In 1869 the value of this trade was 1 031 375.

The nature and extent of this

1869年，贸易额是1 031 375元。

去年间，贸易的性质和规模可以参见以下3个表格。

1871年厦门进口外国商品再运至台湾一览表

种类		数量	贸易额	总额
棉织品	灰色衣料	50 500件	135 692元	167 122元
	白色衣料	2 296件	8 132元	
	染色衣料	100件	386元	
	染色印花衣料	246件	1 064元	
	T 字布	4 498件	8 982元	
	土耳其红布	1 890件	4 772元	
	美国斜纹布	570件	2 036元	
	英国斜纹布	1 460件	5 822元	
	印花棉布	100件	236元	
	以上合计	61 660件	—	
	棉纱	60担	2 241元	2 241元

续表

种类		数量	贸易额	总额
毛织品	英国羽纱	660件	10 485元	28 905元
	厚斜纹布	180件	2 828元	
	粗斜纹呢	1 719件	13 718元	
	条纹边薄呢	72件	1 874元	
	以上合计	2 631件	—	
鸦片	产自贝拿勒斯	1 058.40担	577 914元	905 274元
	产自巴特那	234.00担	134 901元	
	产自波斯	320.40担	184 257元	
	产自土耳其	14.16担	8 202元	
	以上合计	1 629.96担	—	
杂货	面粉	78担	348元	23 896元
	铅	1 976担	13 454元	
	窗玻璃	120箱	447元	
	其他	—	9 647元	
总计		—	—	1 127 438元

1871年厦门产品运至以及厦门输入土产再运至台湾一览表

种类	厦门产品运至台湾		厦门输入土产再运至台湾	
	数量	贸易额	数量	贸易额
砖	366 500件	2 133元	—	—
陶器	1 137件	1 310元	—	—
麻袋	237 780件	10 755元	—	—
铁器	1 518担	10 176元	—	—
药	8担	183元	—	—
南京棉布	225担	13 841元	—	—
1号纸	81担	1 176元	38担	573元
2号纸	156担	1 089元	—	—

续表

种类	厦门产品运至台湾		厦门输入土产再运至台湾	
	数量	贸易额	数量	贸易额
油纸	—	—	34担	1 185元
红糖	350担	1 022元	—	—
冰糖	97担	806元	—	—
茶垫	—	—	86 600件	3 402元
土烟	577担	10 647元	113担	3 279元
杂货	—	10 321元	—	6 415元
总计	—	63 459元	—	14 854元

trade during the past year, can be ascertained by an examination of the Tables numbered 1, 2 and 3 which follows.

The value of "Formosa" produce imported at Amoy for home consump-

厦门港进口的用于内销和再出口的台湾商品贸易额，1871年为515 775元[38]，1870年为290 207元，1869年为405 245元。

1871年厦门从台湾输入土产一览表

种类	数量	贸易额
樟脑	950担	13 134元
木炭	25 150担	12 407元
落花生	—	—
落花生饼	21 088担	33 109元
麻	497担	7 850元
大米	17 301担	31 898元
靛青子	100担	570元
胡麻子	1 637担	6 453元
胡麻子饼	570担	951元
乌龙茶	12 290担	403 314元
硬木板条	1 969件	1 626元
杂货	—	3 374元
樟木板	726件	1 189元
总计	—	515 775元

要注意的是，上表中贸易额为403314元的茶叶仅仅是为了方便运输而运到厦门，并在适当的时候再出口到美国。

在结束对去年贸易情况概述之际，请允许我对其运作方式说几句。多年来，外国人将信贷体系引进中国，使得二者之间的交易变得很不安全。信用的使用最终得到极大的提升，以至于取代了25%～35%的预收销货款，在许多情况下，信用被用来代替所有销货款，结果到了信用到期日，通常都没有任何款项还到账户上；用于清货的时间是两个月，通常会延长一倍，而且常常还会超过这个时限。与此同时，买家也不会支付逾期的利息。这个令人反感的体系近来受到了限制，所有外国商人商定，不允许赊欠超过20%的销货款，且把付款期限确定为两个月，违者将罚款1 000元。

这显然是最好的补救措施。当地经销商如果失去一定数量的信贷支持，就没有多少资金去做生意；如果没有信贷，贸易就会陷入停滞。

厦门港的金银贸易呈现出显著和有趣的特征。

tion, and re-exportation, amounted to $ 515 775, in 1871, to $ 290 207, in 1870, and to $ 405 245, in 1869.

It should be observed that of the above imports, tea to the value of $ 403314, was merely sent here for convenience of shipment, and was re-exported in due course to the United States.

In closing this sketch of trade during the past year I may be permitted to say a few words regarding its mode of conduct. For some years the system of credit extended to Chinese by foreigners, in their dealings with them, made commerce appear very unsafe. Credits became at last so extended that, in place of advances on sales being from 25 to 35 per cent, in many instances credit was given for the entire sale and in consequence when due date arrived, as a rule, hardly any payments to account had been made; and the time allowed for clearing the goods, two months, had generally to be doubled, and often to be allowed to exceed even that period; the purchaser, meanwhile, paying no interest on the overdue prompts. This objectionable system has of late received a check, by all the foreign merchants agreeing, and binding themselves under a penalty of $ 1 000, not to give credit beyond twenty per cent, and fixing the time for payment at two months' prompt.

This remedy was apparently the best that could be applied, the native dealers having too little capital to do business without a certain amount of credit; and without some credit being given the trade would

厦门港金银贸易情况

单位：元

时间	金银进口	金银出口
1870年	1 355 395	762 835
1871年	2 116 069	682 738
1862年（仅9个月）	405 170	909 612

have been at a standstill.

The Statistics of Treasure present an important and curious feature in the trade of the port.

This enormous increase in the import of Treasure during 1871, amounting to more than three quarters of a million of dollars, has been caused by foreigners pouring it into the port, for the purpose of meeting Bills of Exchange drawn from Manila, and the Straits. But no one knows what becomes of it. Notwithstanding the receipt of the large sum shewn above, it has been found that there is every day more and more difficulty in obtaining dollars from Chinese merchants. They will give in exchange, or do anything rather than pay up in coin, yet the amount sent to "Formosa" has fallen ten per cent. It seems evident, therefore, that the whole increase must have gone into the interior, or have been absorbed here; and unless there be some at present unknown outlet for it, the supposition remains that it is hoarded by the Chinese for purposes, and in a manner, of which foreigners know nothing.

It may here be remarked that the Chinese have, at last, begun to realize the advantage of using foreign Bills of Exchange in making their remittances to Hongkong, instead of adhering to their old custom of sending treasure.

金银进口在1871年大幅增长，增长金额超过75万元。这是由于为了兑换从马尼拉和海峡殖民地开的汇票，外国人将金银大笔运入厦门。但是，没人知道它变成了什么。尽管账面显示收到大笔款项，每天却越来越难以从中国商人那里收到银圆。他们采用商品抵换方式，或者想尽办法不用银圆来支付，但流入台湾的银圆也减少了10%。很明显，增加的款项一定是进入了内地，或者被当地市场吸收了；除非这些银圆有不明出路，否则不得不怀疑中国人将银圆囤积了起来，而外国人对其目的和方式却一无所知。

值得注意的是，现在中国人终于开始意识到使用外国汇票的好处了，汇钱到香港的时候，他们不再坚持邮寄金银的古老汇款习惯了。

【注 释】

① 德庇时（John Francis Davis,1795—1890），又译戴维斯、大卫斯、爹核士、德俾士等。英国人，中国通。18岁到广州，任职于英国东印度公司。1816年作为英使团随员到过北京。1833年成为英驻华商务监督。1844年就职第二任香港总督，兼任英驻华公使。——译者注

② 马拉巴尔海岸是印度西南部的一个沿海地区。所谓“远西”，与“近东”“中东”“远东”一样，都是欧洲中心主义的说法，有很大的随意性。——译者注

③ 泰国湾，旧称暹罗湾（Gulf of Siam）。——译者注

④ 婆罗洲是加里曼丹的旧称。——译者注

⑤ 元祐（1086—1094）是宋哲宗赵煦的第一个年号。北宋使用这个年号共9年。——译者注

⑥ 具体时间不详。《八闽通志》称是在1316年，而《泉州历官志》提到的时间范围是1298—1309年之间。——译者据原注整理

⑦ 据《元史·百官志》：“延祐元年，弛其禁，改立泉州、广庆、庆元三市舶提举司。每司提举二员，从五品；同提举二员，从六品；副提举二员，从七品；知事一员。”——译者注

⑧ 据《明史·职官志》：“市舶提举司。提举一人，从五品；副提举二人，从六品。其属，吏目一人，从九品。掌海外诸蕃朝贡市易之事。”——译者注

⑨ 成化年间应为1465—1487年，弘治年间应为1488—1506年。——译者注

⑩ 嘉靖二十六年应为1547年。——译者注

⑪ 明代称葡萄牙和西班牙为“佛郎机”。此处指葡萄牙。——译者注

⑫ 据《东西洋考》卷七“饷税考”:“隆庆六年，郡守罗青霄以所部雕耗，一切官府所需倚办，里三老良苦，于是议征商税以及贾舶。贾舶以防海大夫为政。”可见应为隆庆六年，即1572年。——译者注

⑬ 此处应有误。此事应发生在万历四十五年（1617）。——译者注

⑭ 据《东西洋考》卷七“饷税考”：“东西洋每引，税银三两；鸡笼、淡水，税银一两。其后加增东西洋，税银六两；鸡笼、淡水，二两。”——译者注

⑮ 实际上，郑芝龙大大发展了海外贸易，建立了一支强大的海商集团。这里所指的“中断”应为官方海外贸易的中断。——译者注

⑯ 1684年，清政府在厦门设立闽海关厦门衙署。——译者注

⑰ 据《厦门志·关赋略》：“（康熙）五十六年，因愚民私聚吕宋、噶喇吧，有盗米透漏诸弊，严禁通市南洋。”康熙五十六年即1717年，距1684年厦门设关间隔33年。——译者注

⑱ 阿卡普尔科，墨西哥南部港市。——译者注

⑲ 科尔特斯（Hernán Cortés，1485—1547），西班牙殖民者，建立西班牙在墨西哥的殖民地。皮泽洛（Francisco Pizarro，1475—1541），西班牙殖民者，开启了南美洲（尤其是秘鲁）的西班牙征服时期，是秘鲁首都利玛的建造者。阿尔瓦公爵（Fernando Álvarez de Toledo，1507—1582），西班牙贵族、军人和政治家，曾任西班牙所属的低地国家总督，镇压尼德兰革命。——译者注

⑳ 原文见傅元初《请开洋禁疏》。——译者注

㉑ 原文有误，应为1639年。——译者注

㉒ 何乔远（1558—1632），明代晋江人，杰出的方志史学家。为官多年，因性格刚直不阿，痛恨昏暗的官场，被弹劾，遂回归故里专心著书立说。在其十几部鸿著之中，《闽书》最富创见，影响深远。——译者注

㉓ 原文为“Koxinga”，即国姓爷郑成功，有误。——译者注

㉔ 即郑芝龙。——译者注

㉕ 见卫三畏《中国总论》第一卷。——原注

㉖ 施琅（1621—1696），福建省泉州府晋江县（今泉州市晋江市龙湖镇衙口村）人，祖籍河南固始，明末清初军事家。施琅早年是郑芝龙的部将，后两度降清，并被任命为同安总兵、福建水师提督。康熙二十二年（1683）六

月，施琅指挥清军水师先行在澎湖海战对郑军获得大胜。他上疏吁请清廷在台湾屯兵镇守、设府管理，力主保留台湾、守卫台湾。因功授靖海将军，封靖海侯。——译者注

㉗ 汉密尔顿（Alexander Hamilton），生卒年月不详。其为苏格兰船长和商人，曾入职东印度公司，于1688—1723年间在好望角与日本之间航行经商，写有日志《东印度新纪》（*A New Account of the East Indies*，1727）。据此书记载，其驶入广州时间应为1703年。——译者注

㉘ 指美国。——译者注

㉙ 据“征收的税费”表格，应为102 068英镑。——译者注

㉚ 据表格，应为10 753 243元。——译者注

㉛ 据表格，应为2 699 286元。——译者注

㉜ 据表格，应为426 044海关两。——译者注

㉝ 据表格，应为185 468英镑。——译者注

㉞ 据文中数据计算，应为58%。——译者注

㉟ 据上表，应为4 321担。——译者注

㊱ 据上表，应为1 869担。——译者注

㊲ 据表格，应为479 673.70。——译者注

㊳ 据下表数据统计，应为515 875元。——译者注

译后记
Afterword

通读完眼前的译稿，已是午夜时分。想起来，立项是2017年的事了。2017年2月，“*Amoy and the Surrounding Districts* 的翻译研究”有幸立项成为厦门市社科院重点项目。五年来，随着工作单位的变动，工作重心发生了不小的变化，我虽然坚持初心，一如既往地做着这个项目，但在思想认识和工作安排上，经常无奈地将此本该是当务之急的任务往后排，给似乎随时出现的紧急工作让路。一拖再拖之后，终于在2022年完成译稿。

我出生在淮河沿岸、皖豫交界，本科就读于安徽首府合肥，读研去了中国近现代史上一个风云激荡、群星闪耀的省份——湖南，多年来在长沙这座历史悠久、文化璀璨的城市工作和生活，读博则在气质前卫、在中国历史尤其是近现代史上不可替代的光荣之城广州。在长沙近三十年后，机缘巧合去了完美地融合了历史与现实、西方与本土元素的厦门。刚工作时，曾短暂地访问美国“中部崛起”、现代化和城市化过程中的标志性城市——芝加哥；后来两度赴美访学，分别去了新英格兰地区重镇、美国立国之都费城，以及美国在大西洋沿岸的东部开发多年之后，在西部的太平洋沿岸开辟的新战场——旧金山。后来曾工作访问过澳新和日韩等地。作为“宅男”，有幸在中外多个城市之间走动，不自觉地会将不同地区和城市相互比较。比如安徽、湖南、广东、福建，这些中国近现代史上分外耀眼的名字，它们一旦共同出现，便能勾勒出一幅幅大气磅礴、厚重生动的历史画卷。作为地处东南边陲、人口规模不大的城市，厦门的影响力却不容小觑。厦门是多元文化的复合体，内陆的中原文化与边疆的海洋文化、中华文明与西方文明，在这里实现了完美的融合。这是从空间的维度来看。而从时间的维度来看，作为鸦片战争后被迫开放的五个通商口岸之一，以及改革开放后的首批四个经济特区之一，厦门在中国历史上两个标志性的时间节点上，都发挥着不可替代的重要作用。

回到这个项目上，其进展之所以缓慢，难度大是主因。当初拿到该项目时，心里甚至有点庆幸，觉得这本书不算太厚，做起来应该不太困难吧。但知易行难，真正动起手来，才知道远非当初想象的那样。首先，原书的语言表达虽然不如理论著作那么晦涩、拒人千里，但原作者出身于西方受教育程度很高的群体，其文字表达的浓度和韧性使得翻译很具挑战性。其次，原书是对19世纪下半叶闽南社会的描写，翻译起来具有时间和空间的距离感的双重障碍，使所谓“设身处地”的要求显得有些苍白。

项目做到一半，才发现厦门文史学家何丙仲先生辑译的《近代西人眼中的鼓浪屿》一书。该书包含了西方有关人士所著11种关于鼓浪屿、厦门岛和其他闽南地区的文献资料，其中也有 *Amoy and the Surrounding Districts*（《厦门及周边地区》）。何先生的译本为我们提供了不少实际帮助，主要是在历史文献、人名地名的处理方面。我们认为，对于具有历史价值的外文文献，多种译本的存在是必要的；文学名著的重译已成常态，历史文献的重译也应被接受，因此我们便将该项目进行下去。

该项目是我与我在厦门大学任兼职教授和博导期间指导的博士生袁永丹共同完成的。几年来，她忙于学业之余，花了不少时间在这个项目上。承担该项目，对她而言是个难得的锻炼。永丹已经顺利毕业，入职我曾工作过的厦门理工学院，或许这是缘分使然，也是一种薪火相传吧。我在广西民大指导的翻译专业硕士生贲雨佳，基于该项目的部分内容，完成了其翻译实践报告的写作，是学以致用的典型，值得充分肯定。

该项目得以完成，当然要感谢许多人的帮助。感谢厦门市社科院和社科联的信任，并且容忍我的一再拖延。责编章木良女士以高超的专业水平、精益求精的态度和极大的耐心，保障了译稿的质量。非常怀念在厦门工作期间的同事和朋友许玉军、林祁、苏宗文、陈庆妃和郑亚捷几位学者，与他们的切磋琢磨是我在厦门几年间很愉快和温暖的记忆。入职广西民大以来，卞成林、谢尚果、张旭、覃修桂、杨令飞、李学宁和刘雪芹等教授，以及唐毅、王安民、龙靖遥、何云燕等博士，对我的工作和生活给予持续的关怀和支持，使我在一个陌生的城市和学校很快安顿下来，进入工作状态。我的博士生和硕士生一心向学，勤勉务实，和他们的交往是我一向看重的；在物质主义、实用主义大行其道的今天，能和一众同好时相往还，是极为奢侈和难得的。感谢我所指导的2021级和2022级翻译方向的硕士生，他们协助我完成对最后一稿清样的校对。最后，真诚地感谢我的太太和女儿，她们一如既往地理解并支持我的工作，她们是我工作的动力。

这些文字交出去了，但依然在并一直都在我的心中，与之前所有的写作和阅读的文字一样，是不会时时提起但始终温暖的所在。正是这些，构成了我们丰厚和柔软的精神世界。靠这样的情怀和担当，我们勇敢而坚韧地迎接生活中的种种艰难困苦，并战而胜之。

张跃军

2022年孟冬于相思湖畔